LEAF PLATE CORAL
Montipora capricornis

BIRDSNEST CORAL
Stylophora pistillata

LETTUCE CORAL
Agaricia agaricites

LETTUCE CORAL
Agaricia agaricites

STAGHORN CORAL
Acropora cervicornis

LEAF PLATE CORAL
Montipora capricornis

BIRDSNEST CORAL
Stylophora pistillata

STAGHORN CORAL
Acropora cervicornis

CAULIFLOWER CORAL
Pocillopora meandrina

CAULIFLOWER CORAL
Pocillopora meandrina

LETTUCE CORAL
Agaricia agaricites

LEAF PLATE CORAL
Montipora capricornis

STAGHORN CORAL
Acropora cervicornis

BRAIN CORAL
Colpophyllia natans

BIRDSNEST CORAL
Stylophora pistillata

LEAF PLATE CORAL
Montipora capricornis

BIRDSNEST CORAL
Stylophora pistillata

LETTUCE CORAL
Agaricia agaricites

LETTUCE CORAL
Agaricia agaricites

STAGHORN CORAL
Acropora cervicornis

LEAF PLATE CORAL
Montipora capricornis

BIRDSNEST CORAL
Stylophora pistillata

STAGHORN CORAL
Acropora cervicornis

CAULIFLOWER CORAL
Pocillopora meandrina

CAULIFLOWER CORAL
Pocillopora meandrina

LETTUCE CORAL
Agaricia agaricites

LEAF PLATE CORAL
Montipora capricornis

STAGHORN CORAL
Acropora cervicornis

BRAIN CORAL
Colpophyllia natans

BIRDSNEST CORAL
Stylophora pistillata

The Lost Continent

The Lost Continent

Coral Reef Conservation and Restoration
in the Age of Extinction

David Alexander Baker

imagine!

For Bailey

An Imagine Book
Published by Charlesbridge
9 Galen Street
Watertown, MA 02472
(617) 926-0329
www.imaginebooks.net

All photographs in the book are courtesy of the author, except for the following:
Photos on pages 10, 12, 26/27, 46/47, 62, and 70: courtesy of Justin Smith
Photos on pages 84/85, 122, 125, and 160: courtesy of Darryl Lai
Photos on pages 81 and 89: courtesy of Amy Eggers/Hawai'i Institute of Marine Biology (HIMB)

Library of Congress Cataloging-in-Publication Data
Names: Baker, David Alexander, 1971– author.
Title: The lost continent: coral reef conservation and restoration in the age of extinction /
  David Alexander Baker.
Description: [Watertown, MA]: Charlesbridge Publishing, 2022. | Includes bibliographical references.
  | Summary: "A celebration of the beauty of the world's endangered coral systems, a lament at their
  destruction, and a call to action to save what remains, as time is running out." —Provided by publisher.
Identifiers: LCCN 2021050497 (print) | LCCN 2021050498 (ebook) | ISBN 9781623545147 (hardcover) |
  ISBN 9781632892416 (ebook)
Subjects: LCSH: Coral reef conservation. | Coral reef restoration.
Classification: LCC QH75 .B2649 2022 (print) | LCC QH75 (ebook) | DDC 333.9—dc23/eng/20211117
LC record available at https://lccn.loc.gov/2021050497
LC ebook record available at https://lccn.loc.gov/2021050498

Display and text type set in Schnebel Sans Pro Condensed
Printed by 1010 Printing International Limited in Huizhou, Guangdong, China
Production supervision by Jennifer Most Delaney
Interior design by Nicole Turner
Art direction by Margaret Bauer

ISBN 978-1-62354-514-7

Printed in China
(hc) 10 9 8 7 6 5 4 3 2 1

Praise for *The Lost Continent*

"David Baker's *The Lost Continent* is at times desperate, at times hopeful, and always engaging, intelligent, and artful. Reading this book about the underwater world of coral and reefs is like attending a series of lectures by your favorite professor, the one who is concerned yet curious; amusing and informed; and whose narratives span the evocative past, the ever-changing present, and the slippery, tenuous future of the topic at hand."

Patricia Ann McNair
author of *Responsible Adults* and *And These Are the Good Times*

"David Baker brings a filmmaker's eye to this globe-trotting survey of Earth's coral habitats, and his skills yield a series of remarkably vivid close-ups of these evasive, crucial landscapes. The resulting book is an engaging, comprehensive presentation of one of our planet's most fascinating ecosystems."

Elena Passarello
author of *Animals Strike Curious Poses*

"*The Lost Continent* is encouraging in the deepest, strictest sense of the word: it'll stir up courage in the heavy hearts of those familiar with our ecological emergency."

Tim Jensen
author of *Ecologies of Guilt in Environmental Rhetorics*
and Director of Writing at Oregon State University

Opposite: Even struggling
corals provide structure and
habitat for these clownfish
and anemone.

Introduction:
The Tide

THE TIDAL SWING between elation and desperation that comes from documenting the struggle of the world's coral reef ecosystems—a flood of grim statistics followed by brief surges of beauty and hope —can take a toll on a person. In the past eight years I've heard more people utter the unlikely phrase "I cried into my dive mask" than I care to recount. But those words best describe the experience of people who study and work on the problems facing reef-building corals and the vast and magnificent habitats they construct in the clearwater deserts of our tropical seas.

It hasn't helped that I set up a feed delivering news to my in-box every morning, harvesting stories with the keywords "coral reef decline." The dire headline "Climate change could kill all of Earth's coral reefs by 2100" is followed by the more promising "How seaweed-munching crabs could help save coral reefs." The idea of silver bullets and unlikely saviors in the face of enormous odds is tantalizing. It is the plot of

ancient legends, blockbuster movies, and entire religions. It is an understandable temptation to imagine that salvation lies outside of ourselves. But in the case of saving coral reefs, it most certainly does not.

If you dig past the headlines into the social media fray or research listservs, you're likely to find inspiring tales and cranky critiques. A new discovery offers promise; it's not enough. One patch of reef shows surprising resilience; a drop in the bucket. A team of volunteers restores a swath of coral the size of a football field. Someone chimes in to remind us that the Great Barrier Reef (GBR), which has experienced mass die-offs due to unprecedented coral bleaching from global warming, is the size of seventy million football fields.

If you follow the plight of the world's corals, hope and despair engage in a sort of tug-of-war for the soul. Every time you submerge on a reef, beautiful or scruffy, you ask yourself what it looked like a generation ago, or even five years ago. The baseline is shifting below our feet, reefs are declining, and even when you come across rare beauty—that healthy stretch of reef completely encrusted with vibrant stony corals—you can't help but wonder if it is the last of its kind.

If we lose coral reef ecosystems, the rest of the biosphere will follow, and our planet will descend into a mass extinction far more rapidly than any of the five such events that preceded it in the long history of life on our planet. Reefs are among the first ecosystems to vanish wholesale during mass extinctions and the last to return after gaps lasting millions of years. It is more than likely that the next extinction will also include our own species. A vision of the boneyard that is a bleached coral reef is a glimpse into our own future.

But something else is also true. In the people who are working on the problems of coral reef decline, the depth of determination to make a difference is profound. Passion to save reefs burns even in those who have long ago read the writing on the wall and who believe with all their intellect that these ecosystems are already lost. Their hearts betray them as they show up day after day to devote all their energy to that lost cause of saving what remains. In such people—the cynics and optimists alike—the human spirit soars.

Once we become aware of the scale of the problem, we can change. I've seen it time and again, even in the most callused hearts. From small, individual choices to changing one's whole life, abandoning a career or launching an entire movement that inspires ranks of big-hearted believers: humans will change. The only question is if it can happen fast enough. Time, our ever-patient mistress, will ultimately answer that question for us.

For now, I know that a person can make the journey from indifference to commitment. A person

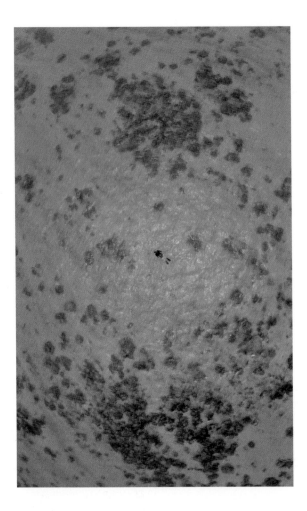

Page 10: Healthy corals growing in a variety of shapes provide ample habitat for fish and other reef life.

Above: Researcher Ryan McMinds inspects the shallow lagoon surrounding the island of Mo'orea in French Polynesia.

Page 13: These *Pocillopora meandrina* in Maui are hardy corals that inhabit shallow, wave-hammered stretches of reef.

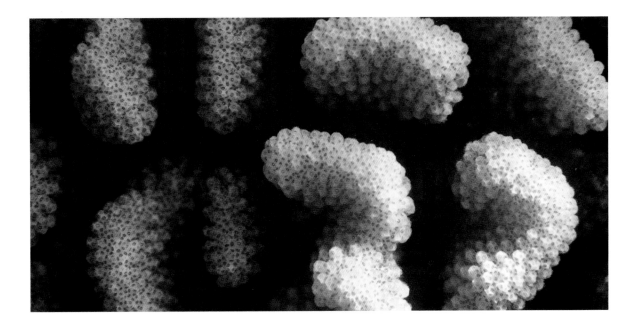

can learn to care. I know this because it happened to me. A chance assignment and a glimpse of a coral reef out an airplane window changed the trajectory of my life. This book charts the journey of my discovery of what corals are and what problems they face at this flickering instant in geological time when we can expect to lose most of them. But this book is about more than reefs. It is also an introduction to many of the amazing people and astonishing places that exist where corals do at this instant in history, persisting in a sort of desperate symbiosis on the edge of oblivion. This is a story of disease, Hail Marys, hidden wonders, wanton destruction, surprising adaptations, and ancient tales that takes us to some of the most spectacular corners of our planet. It's the story of eons of evolutionary wonder and excruciatingly slow geological upheaval that is suddenly slamming up against industrial Armageddon. Our species has our collective finger on a biological kill switch, and we have only a fraction of a second to make a decision.

It's enough to overload your senses and break your spirit. And as tempting as it is to turn away, to lose oneself in other work, other problems, I've continued to stare—even now and from thousands of miles away—at that marvelous and troubled world of disappearing tropical reefs.

The tide will continue to surge between hope and desperation. It is unlikely that seaweed-eating crabs will scuttle to our rescue. The savior is not outside but within. And there's a struggle ongoing, one that is seeded in the human heart and that can change the course of the future of our planet. In times of great distress, the human spirit soars. The tireless, flawed, curious, optimistic, and alternately despairing and hoping humans involved in this struggle—along with the myriad species they are trying to save—will always be, even if only in memory, wonders to behold.

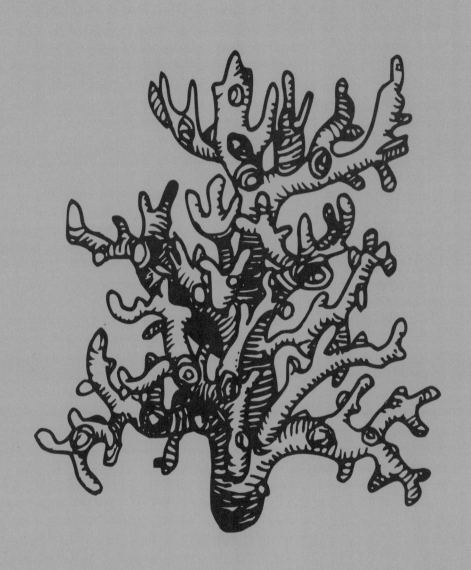

Part I

Discovering Corals

"*Hanau ka 'Uku-ko'ako'a, hanau kana, he 'Ako'ako'a, puka.*"
"Born was the coral polyp, born was the coral, which came forth."

The Kumulipo, Hawaiian creation chant

"We feel surprise when travelers tell us of the vast dimensions of the Pyramids and other great ruins, but how utterly insignificant are the greatest of these, when compared to these mountains of stone accumulated by the agency of various minute and tender animals!"

Charles Darwin, *Voyage of the* Beagle

1

An Island at the Edge of the World

Lizard Island, Australia

TWENTY MINUTES INTO THE FLIGHT the plane banked hard, and as my stomach dropped, I glanced out the window and saw a bejeweled splotch against the blue of the sea. It was a patch of brownish-green with a gold heart and concentric bands of turquoise and cerulean. No sooner had this formation slipped from view than another tracked across the plane's window. I pressed my camera to the porthole and did my best to capture it. These irregular shapes pulsed with auras of foaming waves. Even from thousands of feet in the air they seemed alive, like brilliant amoebas thrumming under a microscope.

As the plane leveled again and the paisley pattern stretched toward the horizon, it hit me. I was flying over the largest construction project on the planet: the Great Barrier Reef. My heart fluttered. If you're a filmmaker, a storyteller, or any sort of eager traveler, you will recognize that greedy rush of the new. For better or worse, ours is a pioneering species,

ever striving to spread ourselves to the ends of the earth—a trait we share with weeds.

I was flying to Lizard Island, an isolated outpost on the northern reaches of the reef, home to only a small research station, a hurricane-ravaged resort, and a bunch of lizards the size of house cats. I planned to film interviews for a video series I was producing for the National Science Foundation and Oregon State University on coral reef research. I hadn't expected to be so smitten by corals—especially not before the plane had even touched down and before I'd had the chance to pull on a mask and snorkel. I also didn't expect, during the course of this short tour, to meet all of the archetypes in the operatic struggle to save coral reefs.

If these ecosystems are operas, then the Great Barrier Reef is Wagnerian. Although built by tiny, simple life forms, the reef is so big you can see it from space. Tiny animals measured in millimeters

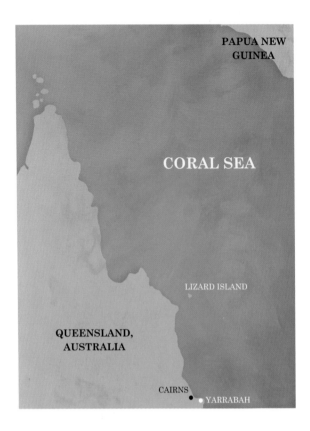

PAPUA NEW
GUINEA

CORAL SEA

LIZARD ISLAND

QUEENSLAND,
AUSTRALIA

CAIRNS
● ○ YARRABAH

Page 16: Researchers Ryan
McMinds and Katia Nicolet
enter the waters off Lizard
Island to sample corals.

are the architects of a submerged continent. It is by far the largest structure made by living things. China's Great Wall, the Pyramids of Giza, the US interstate highway system...these are all impressive feats of engineering, but they don't hold a candle to what these industrious marine polyps have created on the northeastern edge of *Terra Australis*.

Corals are also ancient. The oldest fossils date back 500 million years. Stony, reef-building corals like those we know today, called scleractinians, first appeared in the fossil record 240 million years ago but were likely around much longer. That means they've been around at least 800 times longer than our own species has existed and twice as long as the very first flowering plants.

Coral reefs are also infinitely mysterious. Researchers estimate that less than 10 percent of the life on coral reefs has been accurately described by science. New discoveries about what makes them tick are published daily.

And reefs are essential to ocean life—and even our own. They feed us, enchant us, prop up our economies, and protect us. This all hit me as I gazed out at the patches of reef scattered toward the horizon like jigsawed pieces of a cosmic puzzle.

But then a feeling of dread crept over me.

A statistic I had read stood in sharp relief: 40 percent of the world's reefs have been destroyed in the past half-century, mostly due to human activity. The Intergovernmental Panel on Climate Change has projected that if global warming races past the 1.5°C agreed to in the Paris Agreement, reef destruction could reach 99 percent.

I flirted with denial. Surely this was some miscalculation? The devastation scientists have been predicting for decades must be exaggerated.

My evidence for such denial?

The myriad reefs below us. Protected by the Great Barrier Reef Marine Park, a feat of human stewardship that covers an area larger than California, this wonder was in good hands, wasn't it? I saw proof out my plane window. To understand the situation, I needed guides. Below I caught sight of a cluster of rooftops perched on the edge of an island where it met the sea. That's where I would find them.

The plane's tires squawked as we hit the sun-cooked tarmac. I emerged blinking, the heat rising off the black surface, still reeling from the mix of wonder and dread I'd felt on the plane.

Despite its isolation, the island has a long human history. It was sacred to the Dingaal people, the traditional custodians who had voyaged there for millennia in canoes for religious rites or to catch fish, hunt dugongs, or gather shellfish. Captain James Cook stopped while charting the great southern continent. He'd become lost in the labyrinth of the reef and climbed to the island's highest point to search for a way out. That peak is called Cook's Look.

The island still provides an important perspective. Surrounded by endless reaches of reefs far from population centers and human pressures, it offers a baseline view of coral reef ecosystems. And just as it once attracted Dingaal people seeking enlighten-ment, it brings scientists by the thousands, empirical pilgrims striving to unlock the celestial forces that hold our world in balance.

As the airstrip's lone attendant helped us unload our cargo of camera and scientific gear, Anne Hoggett arrived in a truck to lend a hand. Here was the first of the archetypes I'd meet: the station manager. Anne had been codirector of Lizard Island Research Station, along with her husband, Lyle Vail, since 1990. She exuded a sort of windblown self-sufficiency, useful on this rugged rock in the middle of the heart of nowhere. It was clear that she feels at home, so why shouldn't I?

After a short drive along a sand track, sloshing around meter-long lizards that waggled into the brush, we creaked to a halt in front of the barracks that I was to call home. The building stood on stilts with a half-dozen unadorned, whitewashed rooms that opened on a wraparound veranda connecting the commercial kitchen and a shared shower that came complete with a dinner-plate-sized huntsman spider for a drain cover. It was spartan but comfortable.

I stowed my gear and explored the research station, a sprawling laboratory complex with covered breezeways and concrete paths connecting outbuild-ings to a central hub, along with collections of aqua-riums that were netted to discourage birds from snacking on the experiments. PVC pipes and tubes sprouted everywhere, circulating water from the sea, which lay just beyond the sandy edges of the station. Massive palms rustled in the breeze in a slow-motion dance.

Like a visiting scientist, I was shown my very own "bench space," a corner of a one-room labora-tory building with a stool, a table, and plenty of outlets where I could stow and charge my camera gear and laptop. The door to the lab was never locked or even closed; there was no one on the island to take it, and why shut out the comforting ocean breeze?

Despite the informal setting, where bathing suits were the most common attire, flip-flops were optional, and formal dress meant a tropical print shirt with at least half of the buttons fastened, these researchers and their students worked long days and nights gathering and processing the data that fuels the impressive research the station produces. Exper-iments were underway on everything from the abundance of sharks to the energy content of coral eggs and the effects of climate change on foramin-ifera, tiny creatures whose shells make up much of the world's seafloor sediment and sand. That year, 144 scientists from around the world would come to Lizard Island Research Station to conduct research. A hundred scientific papers would be published on research that covered everything from the latest genomic analysis to cobbled-together experiments like something out of a Terry Gilliam film.

The complex bustled with activity by sunburned people peering through microscopes, taking water measurements from aquariums, or tapping data into spreadsheets. As the light waned, I followed a pair of PVC pipes from the station across the nearby beach to the edge of the sea, where they drew water to feed the aquariums. I stood at the edge with waves licking my feet. The late afternoon sun slipped to the horizon and I saw patches of reef just below the surface. A tidy collection of yellow boats bobbed in the waves. The dread I'd felt earlier as I mulled dire statistics abated. Here, in this remote and peaceful spot, there was a hive of people abuzz in their searches for solutions. And the next morning I would meet a pair of them.

We assembled at the dive shed at the edge of the beach. Ryan McMinds was an affable, rusty-haired PhD student from Oregon. Katia Nicolet was a Swiss PhD student studying at James Cook University in Townsville, Australia. They were working on different projects and studying at different universities in different countries, but they'd come here to conduct experiments on corals, pairing up to help each other out. One never dives alone on the reef or anywhere— standard safety protocol.

I shot photos and video while they gathered gear, hauling tubs with wet suits, coolers, and heavy tanks out to one of the yellow launches. It was a lot of hard work so early in the morning. Ryan's day had started even earlier, preparing syringes and labeling sterile collection bags in the lab. He was gathering coral samples for something called the Global Coral Microbiome Project.

I was meeting another pair of archetypes in the coral saga: the graduate students. They represent how a lot of research actually happens in the field. The Global Coral Microbiome Project (GCMP) began, as most such projects do, when top scientists, mostly associated with universities, write a grant proposal to a funding agency like the National Science Foundation (NSF). The NSF funds a quarter of all academic research in the US to the tune of $8.5 billion in 2021. The top researchers, known as "principal investigators" or "PIs," pose the question, write an exhaustive proposal and pitch it to the NSF. Only a quarter of the proposals are funded.

While $8.5 billion sounds like a lot, when it's spread across 12,000 proposals and more than 300,000 researchers and students at 2,000 institutions, the funding gets thin fast. Grant-funded science operates much like a business with very small margins. And like many businesses, cheap and skilled labor is key. While PIs scramble for funding and manage labs running multiple projects, often while teaching classes too, bright graduate students like Ryan and Katia head into the field, working for tuition, room and board, and—if they're lucky—a small stipend. They're the inexpensive shock troops of the research enterprise. Also, they're young and can lift heavy things into boats.

Ryan shoved us off and climbed aboard while Katia ripped the motor cord and grabbed the tiller to thread us through the maze of the lagoon, reading the checkerboard map below the water. With her face in the wind, eyes scanning the water, she made sudden swerves and looped through the labyrinth with the skill of a seasoned mariner.

The aim of the Global Coral Microbiome Project was ambitious: to map the microbial communities

Lizard Island Research Station inhabits a pristine beachfront on a remote island in the northern Great Barrier Reef.

Researcher Ryan McMinds samples coral mucus with a syringe, delicate work in the surging shallows.

associated with corals to a level of detail—and in a breadth of geography and coral species—that had never been accomplished before. Like us, corals also have relationships with a host of microbial communities that live in their tissues, in the waters around them, and even inside their skeletons. "We have entire ecosystems of bacteria in our guts, on our skin, in our eyes—everywhere over our bodies," Ryan told me. "These bacteria aren't all bad. And they're doing good things for us."

As in humans, when these good microbial relationships turn sour, corals will get stressed, become diseased, and often die. By understanding the microbial underpinnings of the pressures facing corals, the researchers hope to find ways to better manage and protect them.

The first step in figuring all of this out is collecting samples for laboratory study, and Katia eased up on the throttle as we approached our first location. Ryan tossed the anchor in a patch of sand and then the researchers began to wriggle into wet suits. The wind kicked up a chop, and brooding clouds massed. We put up a red-and-white-striped diving pennant, and it snapped in the breeze.

Katia and Ryan began a Kafkaesque transformation. A science diver out of water is an ungainly creature in fins, mask, tanks and a vest bristling with hoses and buckles, reels of measuring tape, clipboards, cameras, lights, and mesh bags of sampling supplies. In the end, a loaded-up science diver looks like a cross between a penguin and a festooned Christmas tree. Accomplishing this transformation in a bobbing boat on a windy channel is no small feat. Once their preparation was finished, they sat on opposite gunwales with their backs to the sea, pressing their masks to their faces. I readied my camera to capture that moment of free fall—the instant when they abandon the terrestrial world for the marine.

"For science!" Ryan said, jabbing his finger in the air, and then they rolled backward into the froth. They disappeared, resurfaced, and then bobbed in the churn, adjusting their kits. Then they exchanged thumbs-down signals, slipping below the waves in a flurry of bubbles.

Katia would later describe that moment of transformation for me using a comparison I would come to hear often. "When you get into the water it's a completely different world. It's almost like a different planet."

I was not yet a diver, but I still wanted to experience this alien landscape. So I grabbed my underwater camera and pulled on a mask and a pair of fins. I splashed into the water and bobbed on the surface, chained to the world of air and sky by a snorkel clenched in my teeth. I peered down into the coral-walled canyon below me where Katia and Ryan were already at work measuring water visibility and taking temperature readings, writing results onto clipboards. I saw immediately how these awkward creatures of the surface world were now transformed into graceful beings, slipping like shadows through the water with the elegance of manatees. I envied their serene mobility, their gentle drifting and puffed clouds of bubbles.

I tracked them from above as they finned toward a tall gray shelf of corals. As we approached the wall, the corals transformed. Water absorbs light and color, so it's only when you draw close that you begin to see their detail and multihued brilliance, not to mention the clouds of fish and creatures that swarm like a living halo around them.

We approached the escarpment and the scientists drifted onto the top of the mesa bristling with colonies of coral that reached within a meter of the surface. There were massing corals—boulders shaped and grooved like huge brains the size of Volkswagens. There were endless thickets of antlered corals reaching toward the surface with living fingers. There were fanning plates of corals, columns and pipes, thickets, domes, and spirals. There were pinks and blues and oranges and reds and browns and golds. There were huge, blue-lipped clams the size of sofas encrusted onto the reef structure like fat jewels.

And everywhere: swarms of fish of all shapes and colors.

Then there were smaller critters: crabs, snails, feather-duster worms, flatworms, sea slugs, urchins, and anemones waving in the surge like prairie grass. Sharks drifted at the edges of my vision. Three turtles glided past like hang-gliding manhole covers.

I had snorkeled in the past and spotted a few straggler corals on degraded tourist reefs in Florida and Mexico, but I'd never experienced anything like this. I was suddenly immersed in the shimmering landscape I'd spotted from the plane the day before, and it was vast, electric with life, and—it seemed to me—emphatically healthy.

I bobbed above them snapping photos while Ryan scouted an area, circling like a shark. Once he found a colony to his liking, he positioned himself in the wave surge so that he could work without bumping other corals. He fished out a clear plastic collection bag and a packet with a clean syringe from his kit. Katia, hovering just over his shoulder, snapped a reference photo. Ryan pulled on surgical gloves and unwrapped a syringe. The pair clustered around the colony like medical staff in an operating room. Ryan scraped the side of the coral, distressing the individual polyps so that they produced a mucus, and then he sucked this coral snot into the syringe, the goo rich with tiny microbes.

Ryan pulled out a hammer and small chisel. He chipped off a piece of the coral, the hammer blows echoing unnaturally through the water. I found this distressing, but Ryan would later assure me that a healthy colony would regrow the missing fragment

in no time. He dropped the chunk into the marked bag. Then they moved on to the next colony.

After the first dive, we crawled back into the boat. Ryan and Katia dragged in their gear and tanks, stowed the samples in a cooler and then we were off to the next location to repeat the process.

It was past midday when we returned to the station where the unloading process mirrored the early morning work. Ryan blasted the coral samples with air from a compressor to separate the animal tissue from their skeletons. Then it was off to the lab, where the mucus samples, the coral tissue, and ground-up bits of skeleton would be separated and stored in tubes of buffer solution so that the microbes in each could be studied separately.

Around sunset, scientists emerged from their labs and aquarium rows, the straggling boats arriving to unload. Some brought microwaved dinners out to a picnic table and others carried meat for the grill. There were researchers from Switzerland, Germany, France, and Brazil. A few nursed bottles of beer, alcohol a precious and expensive commodity that arrived only by bimonthly barge. They chatted and exchanged ideas, some of which might make their way into new proposals.

At dinner, Katia explained her project. She was monitoring impacts of disease on corals. She had five different plots of ten meters square that she'd been watching, recording the progress of different diseases, trying to learn what helped them spread.

There were cheers, whistles, and a few clinked bottles as the last lip of sun slipped below the horizon and the researchers dispersed back to their tasks. Their day wasn't over. The time difference between here and his home base in Oregon meant that Ryan had email to attend to and data to log into spreadsheets. I needed to back up my footage and photos and charge batteries.

Later, I shuffled back out onto the dark beach. I set up a camera to take time-lapse photos, one image every sixty seconds. I'd let it run all night long. In the morning, I'd retrieve it and stitch together the photos to make a video of a field of stars and the Southern Cross whirling overhead while moonlight flickered on the water.

I turned back and walked toward the station, noticing a different constellation. Light flickered in the lab windows where scientists were still at work. I thought of the opulence of the coral I'd just seen magnified by the endless ribbons of reef I spied from the plane, and then the young doctoral students I'd met who were so smart and committed. Everyone here was pouring every ounce of available intellect and imagination into making a difference in the future for coral reefs. There were research stations just like this one all over the world, pinpricks of hope in the dark, uncertain veil of the future.

On the morning of April 5, 2014, a few months before my visit, Anne Hoggett had received a call from the Bureau of Meteorology office in Brisbane. She was ordered to evacuate Lizard Island Research Station. A low-pressure system had developed over the Solomon Islands a thousand miles to the east and then exploded in intensity as it moved west. It was now registering as a category-5 cyclone. And it was heading right for the island.

Anne and her husband had weathered a number of storms in the three decades they'd lived and worked here, and they'd always stuck to their post. But this storm was different.

Anne wasn't rattled. Thirty years living on a remote outpost had left her sanguine in the face of raw nature. It took them two days to evacuate the researchers and close up the station. Anne and Lyle were the last to leave. They spent a full day bolting doors, beaching and tying down boats, locking shutters, and securing the aquariums. Some experiments were abandoned, their survival at the mercy of the storm. Others had to be scrapped entirely: hours, weeks, months of painstaking fieldwork was lost. Anne and Lyle released some captive fish back into the wild.

The eye of the storm passed within three miles of the island and the wind speed reached 140 miles per hour. The codirectors waited out the worst of it in the city of Cairns on the mainland. "It took them three days with chain saws to clear the track to the airstrip. And we were closed for two months," Anne said.

The station buildings suffered minimal damage. Nobody was hurt. Their hurricane plan had worked. But while the laboratories survived intact, it wasn't until Anne put on dive gear that she saw the full extent of the wreckage caused by Cyclone Ita. Some of the reefs had been completely stripped of corals. Massive corals as big as a living room had been tipped over on their sides. I asked Anne if she attributed the damage from Ita to climate change.

"The IPPC [Intergovernmental Panel on Climate Change] report certainly suggests that there will be changes in the pattern of big storms, to become, perhaps, not more frequent but more intense. And I guess that's what we saw this time," she said. But then she paused and laughed. She's a scientist, after all, and was reluctant to jump to conclusions without proper data. "But we're talking about a sample size of one, so that's not very good."

Cyclones and hurricanes are ancient enemies of coral reefs, capable of turning them to rubble and scouring them of their live coral. But corals have evolved to deal with these disruptions. Coral reefs grow slowly and steadily, locked in a constant struggle with the forces of erosion, fighting to keep their polyps in the shallow, sunlit waters just below the surface where they thrive. This continuous building counteracts a host of natural pressures,

A reef wall with a variety of
species and growth forms
near Orpheus Island, Australia.

from slowly subsiding continents and rising sea levels to battering waves and smothering flows of sediment swept out from mainland during floods. A healthy reef can rebuild after damage from cyclones like Ita.

But if storms become more intense, and reefs are weakened from other pressures, they might not bounce back. Opportunistic, fast-growing algae can muscle out the corals, forever shifting a reef of stony corals into a slime-covered mess.

Until recent decades, the Great Barrier Reef and other coral ecosystems around the world have been able to hold their own in this constant erosive struggle. Waves and sediment, even rampant out-breaks of harmful coral-eating starfish have deci-mated stretches of the GBR, and it's recovered. Reef-building corals, the kind scientists call *scleractinian*, have evolved brilliantly to meet these natural pressures, and a tropical cyclone like Ita should only be a minor setback for the Great Barrier Reef writ large.

While supercharged climate storms are an increasing threat to that balance, there are other human activities that have been joining the natural forces of erosion to stack the deck against reefs. Overfishing, sediment runoff, pollution, intensified diseases, unscrupulous tourism, dynamiting, harvest-ing corals for souvenirs or construction—the list of insults is long and the Great Barrier Reef has experi-enced most of them. All of these pressures, working in concert against reefs around the world, had led to mass destruction that fueled the 40 percent loss figure that had haunted me.

But I had also seen so much bounty here: the maze of reefs through which Katia steered us, the endless sunken escarpments and canyons I'd snork-eled. To me, the reefs around Lizard Island looked healthy. But Anne told me that coral cover was down by about 50 percent from twenty-five years ago.

I had just discovered coral reefs. But I would never see what Anne and Lyle had seen.

I boarded the plane back to Cairns a few days later, leaving Lizard Island Research Station with a stew of contrasting emotions. I felt the thrill of finding a new frontier, but at the same time I was burdened with the knowledge that this frontier was fading. I admired the hopeful idealism of the young scientists. I was heartened by Anne's steady stewardship. But I also knew that Lizard Island Research Station was only one location, a single scene in the epic saga of corals and humans. To really understand what was happening on the Great Barrier Reef, and around the world, I would have to meet the full cast of characters.

My head in the clouds and with thought swirling amid questions of the salvation, science, and business of corals, I made a left out of the one-way street onto a busy avenue in the tourist town of Cairns.

I carefully drove to the harbor, parking near a pier bustling with tourists streaming toward a flotilla of sailboats, catamarans, and glass-bottomed boats. There are few nice beaches in Cairns, which sits at a muddy estuary. What draws visitors is the sunken landscape that lies offshore. The flocks of tourists that strolled the boardwalk hailed from around the world. And they were all here to see corals.

I met Col McKenzie at a cafe overlooking the docks. We shook hands. He didn't waste a smile. He has the plainspoken demeanor and righteous, no-bullshit delivery of a union organizer. If I were to have an agitator fighting on my behalf, I'd want it to be someone like McKenzie.

He was the executive director of the Association of Marine Park Tourism Operators, and there was plenty of economic muscle in his corner. "Our association carries about 90 percent of the tourists to the Great Barrier Reef," he told me. He said that tourism employed 63,000 people and funded a $5.8

billion economy, serving as the largest employer in the region. His job was to protect the interests of this industry, which meant protecting corals.

Col wasn't always a marine steward. He told me how, as a younger man, he'd often go spearfishing, and he'd easily skewer a half-dozen large coral trout within a hundred meters of the boat. But then a day came when he was spending hours in the water without seeing a single fish.

"While I'm ashamed to say I was part of the problem, I'm now going to be part of the solution," he said.

We watched tourists march past. All of those visitors were bound to have an impact on the corals. I asked if tourism compounded the problem. "The Australian government has an obligation to showcase a part of the world heritage area," he said, brushing off the notion that tourism might cause harm. "We showcase the reef, and people come away from it saying, 'Wow, this is worth saving.'"

He also pointed out the acts of stewardship that tourism operators performed. Each operator had a mooring they were required to use, so they managed those sites carefully. They remove damaging crown of thorns starfish. McKenzie said that these managed areas protected the coral diversity and helped to reseed surrounding areas after devastating events like Cyclone Ita.

But pressures on the reef were mounting. A massive mining conglomerate had been granted permits to dump 100 million tons of dredge spoil in the lagoon. While McKenzie's organization had earned recent wins in reducing agricultural and grazing runoff from rivers, and the government had spent hundreds of millions of dollars in protecting riparian areas and installing filters to keep sediment off the reef, this mining operation would undo all of that work in less than a year. Not to mention the problem of climate change.

I left the port with the same mixed feelings as when I departed Lizard Island. I was heartened that the goals of this powerful industry aligned with those of the scientists I'd met. Col valued research, but his overall outlook seemed bleak. I knew I needed more perspective, and nearby there were people who knew and understood the Great Barrier Reef better than anyone.

Though the Yarrabah Aboriginal Shire lies only fifteen miles as the crow flies from the bustle and mud of Cairns, it took some effort to get there. I followed the highway out of town and then cut onto a side road through stretches of flat, sweltering cane fields until the track began to weave through the Murray Prior Range, rugged coastal hills that surround the small community like a rampart. As my diminutive rental car whined and buzzed up the steep, potholed grade, I pulled to the shoulder near a ridgetop break in the trees and looked down on a village of colorful houses that edged a pristine horseshoe of golden beach.

I eagerly descended the other side of the range, but as I emerged from the forested hills, the town that had looked so cozy from above was shabby and weather-worn up close. Kids wandered, bored and shoeless. People sat on porches, warily watching me pass. Scruffy dogs trotted in my wake, dragging bellies swollen by generations of litters. Horses grazed untethered on the roadside. I passed an empty, sunbaked park. A weedy mission schoolyard stood next to a cemetery studded with wooden crosses. There was a single store. Men sat in plastic chairs outside. They watched me, not saying a word as I slipped inside to pluck a mango soda from nearly barren shelves.

The most prominent feature of the village was the beach that edged Mission Bay, and the most prominent feature on the bay was the rusted brown skeleton of an abandoned ship sunk into the sand.

The tide was out and the sand flats glistened like wet concrete.

As I walked the town while waiting for my appointment, I saw no other visitors even though this coast and beach, edged by the green escarpment of the range and with views of the islands dotting the reef beyond Mission Bay, was achingly beautiful. The road leading here was in poor repair. I'd read unemployment was staggering and opportunities few. But when it came to natural beauty, it was far richer than Cairns.

The population of Yarrabah is made up of Aboriginal and Torres Strait Islander peoples, those who can trace their roots on the reef back at least 40,000 years. But the most recent history of these people is the all too familiar story of indigenous subjugation, cultural cleansing, forced relocation, and disenfranchisement. The town is a former Anglican mission. Working and living conditions were poor enough that residents staged a general strike in the 1950s, which was brutally repressed. It was only in the 1980s that they achieved a level of self-government and some control over traditional lands, finally gaining a mandate to reconnect with their heritage.

I had come to speak with the mayor about the economic and cultural connections to the reef. After all, they'd been living on it longer than anyone, canoeing out to the islands and patch reefs for thousands of years, some of their stories recalling the last great ice age, when much of the reef was dry land. Traditional owners have the oldest stories on the planet. Their songs recall changing geology and balance with the natural resources. Many of the stories, full of ecological wisdom, are cautionary tales: a fisher or hunter takes a fish or animal in the wrong season and is punished by the gods, for example.

But when Europeans arrived, everything changed. Land was partitioned and transformed. Aboriginal people were massacred during the "killing times" for transgressions that included stealing and eating the sheep that had displaced native species. They were deemed unfit to raise their own children, and boys and girls were spirited away to mission schools to have religion beaten into them. Sharing ancestral stories and language was criminal behavior.

Environmental devastation proceeded on a parallel path with the destruction of Aboriginal society. Australia leads the world in mammalian extinction. And now, the Great Barrier Reef was facing decline. The natural world, which had long been the beating heart of Aboriginal life, was being obliterated.

But despite all this, the stories and culture survive. Corals still grow. Indigenous people are slowly carving out some autonomy, reclaiming a toehold on their culture and influence after centuries of oppression. I thought there must be some hope in this.

The council building was the most modern structure in town, though it still had a sort of drab, municipal quality. It was as empty and listless as the rest of the town in the blistering noon sun. There I met Errol Neal, mayor and head of the council, in a side conference room. He had a weary demeanor and a cautious, soft-spoken delivery that contrasted with his football jersey and the bright reds, yellows, and blues you see in Aboriginal flags and standards.

With a population of 2,500, Yarrabah was the largest Aboriginal community in Queensland. Economic development was the biggest issue: 80 percent unemployment, and 65 percent of that in those aged 16 to 30. This despite its proximity to the tourist engine that drove the regional economy. The town was planning to develop a deep-water port through a partnership with a Chinese cruise company. It would employ 250 locals, some of them working as cultural tour guides. The concept included a golf course, which gave me a momentary cringe. But then, why not? I thought of paved-over and industrialized Cairns.

Thickets of healthy *Porites cylindrica* near Lizard Island.

But the mayor saw the reef as more than just a ticket out of poverty for his people. Aboriginal and Torres Strait Islander peoples are also the custodians of the land. He saw the plan as a way of looking out for his community and looking after the country for future generations.

I know that stories can be a sensitive topic. In traditional cultures, stories have special currency. Only certain people were empowered to tell stories in Aboriginal societies. In other Pacific cultures, the more stories were told, the more they lost their power. Reluctance to share stories is understandable when they are your only cultural capital and everything else has been taken.

"Our stories protect the land, look after the land, not only for today but for tomorrow. We want it there for the next generation to come. We want it there for another forty thousand years. It's a very fragile planet we're living on today. It's endangered itself. We're going to be an endangered species." He laughed dryly and shook his head.

I asked him what gave him hope.

"There's always hope in Aboriginal belief," he said. "We believe in our creator. We're believing that... those who be greedy and selfish...will be called upon and punished."

It was retribution that gave him hope. That didn't comfort me. Maybe it was part of the 40,000-year view. If your people had witnessed ice ages come and go, and if your cultural memory strayed beyond human time into the geologic, then perhaps it's easier to look far into the future where the relatively recent environmental affronts are rectified after the perpetrators are dealt with through divine punishment.

I asked a final question about climate change and coral bleaching, that phenomenon still rare on the Great Barrier Reef at the time but on the rise. He looked at me with a sly smile. "In the old stories, they say—when the Mother gets mad at us—then the seas will begin to boil."

And with that perfect metaphor for global warming, I clicked off my camera. It seemed like he knew what the weather was about to deliver.

A year after I spoke with Mayor Neal, researcher Terry Hughes led an assessment of the worst mass bleaching event on the Great Barrier Reef in fifteen years. Hughes is director of the Australian Research Council's Center for Excellence on Coral Reef Sciences. He spent 75 hours flying 9,000 kilometers over the Great Barrier Reef to assess the damage. It was "something I hoped I'd never have to do," he said in a 2016 lecture. Out of the plane window, he saw vast swaths of bone-white corals. He'd assessed prior mass bleaching events in 1998 and 2002, "but this time around, the severity of the bleaching was off the scale," he said.

Corals are sessile animals. They can't move. And they live at their thermal threshold. When the water gets too warm, the coral polyps get stressed and expel helpful algae and microbes that live inside of them, robbing them of nutrition. When this happens, they're likely to starve to death. When it occurs across wide swaths of reef, the entire ecosystem collapses. But this time around, the water was so warm for so long that this was something beyond coral starvation: "These corals didn't starve to death...they actually cooked," Hughes said. I recalled what Errol Neal had said about boiling seas. The age of the angry Mother had arrived. And she was just getting started.

At the end of his 2016 lecture, Hughes reflected on the three mass bleaching events he'd experienced in his quarter century studying the Great Barrier Reef. "When will the fourth event be?" he wondered. "More than likely in the next warm El Niño period, which might be five years from now."

But Hughes was wrong. Mass bleaching wouldn't wait another five years. It hit the GBR again in 2017. The unthinkable had arrived: back-to-back bleaching. "If the world continues its business-as-usual greenhouse emissions for several more decades, it will almost certainly spell the end of the Great Barrier Reef as we now know it," Hughes wrote in 2017.

He didn't give in to despair. He channeled it into righteous anger. He relentlessly harangued the Australian government for its lackluster response and flat-out denial of climate change, using all the tools at his disposal: media appearances, scientific papers, and even social media.

Dread was tempered when 2018 and 2019 passed without a major bleaching event. Maybe 2016–17 had been an anomaly. Maybe the Great Barrier Reef would get a chance to heal. But then came 2020. Globally, it was the hottest year ever recorded. The Great Barrier Reef again experienced a record-shattering mass bleaching event. "It's been a shitty, exhausting day on the #GreatBarrierReef," Hughes posted on Twitter in March of that year, along with a clip of yet another aerial survey of the devastation. "I feel like an art lover wandering through the Louvre...as it burns to the ground."

All of this devastation has happened since my first visit to Lizard Island Research Station in 2014. The 40 percent total global destruction figure that had haunted me then has crept steadily upward to 50 or even 60 percent according to some estimates. A recent UN report offers the terrifying projection that 100 percent of the world's reefs are expected to bleach by the end of the century.

But that's looking ahead. Let's go back to 2014. Let's gather all the hope we can muster. We'll need it for the end of our journey.

My first visit to Lizard Island and the Queensland coast offered me some of that hope. I'd met a cast of characters in the saga of saving reefs. The archetypes included the pragmatic station manager, the idealistic graduate students, the bulldog tourism advocate, and the cultural custodian. All of them had the same goal: to see the Great Barrier Reef survive for future generations.

And I'd also witnessed how vibrant a remote reef could look to an untrained eye. It may not have been as spectacular as what Anne Hoggett first saw thirty years ago, but it was still a wonder and worth fighting for.

Throughout the rest of this book we'll ride the tidal surges of hope and devastation. We'll learn about corals in the Red Sea that are thriving in warmer conditions that cook corals in other parts of the world. We'll trail a merciless killer known as stony coral tissue loss disease (SCTLD) that's decimating Florida reefs. We'll relearn the forgotten wisdom of the original Hawaiians. We'll visit Polynesia, Colombia, Belize, and the deserts of the American Southwest looking for clues to coral survival.

And along the way we'll learn the story of stony corals. It's a 240-million-year-old song of wonderment, evolution, and destruction. It's a bleak, beautiful, and heartbreaking tale of geological upheaval, human greed, ingenious evolution, grit, and determination.

In 2014, I didn't know where this coral journey would take me or how many continents, islands, and field stations I'd visit. I didn't know if the search would lead me to hope or despair. But I was fairly certain about one thing—if I was to commit to this adventure, I would have to learn how to dive.

2

Of Humans and Corals

Thuwal, Saudi Arabia

AHMED CRANKED THE THROTTLE of the Boston Whaler and we surged up one side of a swell, plunging into the trough on the other with the belly tickle of a carnival ride. Ahead of us, huge waves slammed against a wall that rose from the depths to just below the surface, heaving froth over the ragged barrier. We approached too quickly to drop anchor. Shaking his head, Ahmed wheeled the boat around to make another run.

I was nervous. It was clear that, once in position, we wouldn't have much time to wrestle ourselves into dive gear and descend. As a newly minted diver, I'd learned that most accidents happen at the surface: divers inhale water, slam into boats, or are tossed by waves onto sharp corals. This seemed a situation where all these things could happen. Not how I'd envisioned my first dive on a tropical reef.

Ahmed wheeled us around and positioned the boat so that we could surf the swells toward the reef wall. Reading the water, he reversed thrust, and his deckhand, Rodrigo, hurled the anchor overboard, aiming for a pale patch of sand in a turbulent sea studded with coral crags. The anchor caught and the line snapped taut, holding us just beyond the break. We scrambled into action.

We were four divers: two filmmakers and a pair of scientists performing an ungainly ballet as we pulled on wet suits and strapped together cumbersome gear while the boat rose and fell on the swells.

"Very dangerous here," Ahmed said, hurrying us. The surface was crashing chaos. This would be my first dive from a boat and my first without an instructor present. I didn't want to rush. But every swell caused us to tug on the anchor. If it gave, we'd all hurtle against the reef. As we bucked on the waves, we tugged on our wet suits and hefted scuba tanks while screwing together the steampunk architecture that would somehow allow us to breathe underwater.

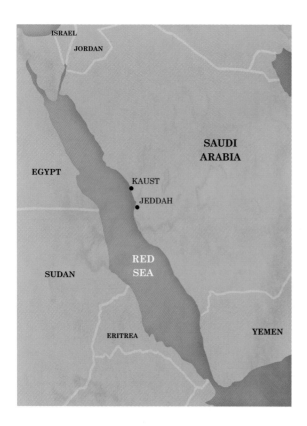

Page 34: Fishing boats ply the coral-rich waters of the city of Al Lith on the Red Sea coast of Saudi Arabia.

I was soon sitting on the gunwale, pressing my mask to my face, certain I was forgetting something required to keep me alive below the surface. But there was no time to waste. I sucked a deep breath from my regulator and back-rolled off the edge.

The world inverted in a churn of foam and suddenly I was bobbing in the water alongside the boat as Ahmed handed down my camera rig. I grabbed it with difficulty, buckling it to my vest to keep it from slipping into oblivion. I spun in the froth, searching for my filmmaking partner, Justin Smith, another neophyte. We exchanged a quick "thumbs down," ignored each other's wide-eyed panic, and dumped air from our vests to sink below the surge.

The world suddenly changed. The chaos of the surface disappeared, and now we were floating above the vista of Shib Nazar, fully visible now in remark-able clarity below the veil of waves. Rising from the deep was the great wall causing so much trouble above. The reef was an escarpment running as far as we could see in both directions. It was cut with rills and canyons and outcrops. It was darkly mottled in color, studded with hints of fantastic shapes and billowing with shoals of fish. We drifted in awe.

In such moments, metaphor fails us. We use words like alien, surreal, and fantasy. Cathedrals. Mountains. We call them the "rain forests of the sea." I often invoke Dr. Seuss. It's a three-dimensional world of water and aragonite rock, pulsing with layer upon layer of life, the surge of wave energy, so chaotic on the surface, rocking us now in great pendular swings along with entire schools of fish in the gentle arms of the sea.

I forgot about the worries of the surface world, the scheduling, the last-minute visa clearance, the security inspections of our camera gear at the airport in a country where journalism and photogra-phy are suspect. I forgot the disorienting immersion into the baffling rules of Saudi society. I forgot about the physics of the scuba apparatus keeping me alive under enormous pressure. I forgot about the camera in my hands and the complicated rules for how light works under the water. Instead, I stared at this masterpiece called Shib Nazar, a *War and Peace* of stony corals, this ecosystem in its most Dickensian expression. Had I not held a scuba regulator clenched in my teeth, I would have dropped my jaw in wonderment at this living wall rising from depths to kiss the surface.

Justin caught my attention. It was time to get to work. We exchanged the "okay" gesture and I shook myself from the rapture. He pointed up. Our scientific duo, whom we were supposed to be filming, were about to roll out of the boat, which still hove up and down on the waves above. We pressed "record" and were now, suddenly, underwater cinematographers.

I'm not sure if it's normal, when learning to dive, to dream of drowning. Many divers are driven by passion or curiosity for the process itself. Perhaps their dive adventure began on a tropical vacation, learning the basics within view of the cabana bar. For me, diving was a means to an end. I needed to get close to corals in order to film them. And with the grim fatalism of the last-chance tourist, I also wanted to witness a miracle that the world was losing. So, I took a crash course in diving. In Oregon. In the winter.

Working on grant-funded science films is a bit like playing the lottery. You write a letter of support for a researcher to include with her proposal and then you forget about it. Maybe it'll come through but probably it won't. If it does, you'll hear back in a year or two. If you do eventually secure funding, you'll have only a short window to plan, do background research, and pack, and then you're off to some field station or research site to figure out how to turn science into stories.

That's what happened with the Saudi trip. Rebecca Vega Thurber, a coral microbiologist and coleader of the Global Coral Microbiome Project, told Justin and me that a new round of funding had come through and that we'd be traveling to Saudi Arabia in a few months to film her team's work. "Oh," she said, as if it were an afterthought, "if you want to film underwater, the university requires you to be science certified."

As a marine neophyte with only a limited grasp of how to work a snorkel, the idea of attaining the status of "scientific diver" in three months seemed daunting, if not impossible. I thought back to my last biology course a pair of decades earlier—I doubted my ability to do science on land, let alone while trying to stay alive under the sea.

It began easily enough with an online course for a recreational dive program. I watched tedious videos every evening and took snap quizzes online. But the subject matter was heavy. From nitrogen narcosis to exploding lungs, decompression sickness or just plain old drowning—the list of what can go wrong is long and sobering. After all, we weren't born with gills. Diving seemed like an insult to the genius of evolution that had freed us from the sea more than 350 million years ago.

But a patient dive instructor named Chloe took us through the basics in the deep end of a swimming pool, and Justin and I gained a little confidence. Still, the idea we'd be traveling around the world in a couple months trailing a pair of expert divers to the depths of the Red Sea seemed absurd.

After another week we were ready to take our first open-water dives in the actual ocean. And here arose another problem. It was December. In the Pacific Northwest. The calmest seawater was six hours to the north in Puget Sound. But calm didn't mean it wasn't cold, so we drove up with rental wet suits and borrowed gear to take the plunge. We parked near the water, strapping the heavy tanks to our backs and marching across a bustling road to climb over rocks between a pier and the foul-smelling culvert of an outflowing stream. The ill-fitting rental wet suits did little to contain the icy waters, and I learned to dread the initial shock of cold water slipping down my spine.

I was beginning to wonder—was something wrong with Chloe? How could she enjoy this? But after following her into the water time and again, I began to see what drew her into the frigid depths. I watched her marvel over the sea life: tiny crabs, fat starfish, crusting barnacles, and spiny purple urchins. We swam through a forest of white anemones with translucent stalks and waving tentacles. I trailed her with restrained but rising wonder, still more focused on trying to keep my lips sealed on the scuba regulator despite my chattering teeth.

In that icy water, we removed and replaced our masks on the bottom of the sound. We descended to ninety feet. We used a compass to navigate through the murk to practice retrieving lost gear. We used float bags to lift concrete blocks from the sea floor. We worked on the difficult dance of buoyancy control to add or dump air and regulate our breathing so that we wouldn't sink rapidly to the bottom and squeeze our ears or shoot to the surface and blow up our lungs, a formula that seemed to change with every meter of depth.

But the claustrophobia faded and our worst fears never materialized. Every dive gave me confidence, and there were even moments of grace when I forgot the discomfort. I recall the glimpse of an octopus, its liquid shape slipping under a sunken rowboat. I remember an evening dive in Seattle, when a curious seal swam suddenly out of the darkness into the beams of our lights, as gregarious as a Labrador. Then we surfaced to see the Seattle skyline glittering across the black water.

For the last leg of the training gauntlet, we had to prove ourselves to our campus dive safety officer. And when he told us to show up at the pool at "oh-seven-hundred," we figured we were in trouble. Raised in a military family, Kevin Buch took seriously his job of keeping his science divers alive. He ran us through more advanced challenges, from assembling puzzles underwater while wearing thick dive gloves to hovering inside a PVC rectangle without bumping the sides to performing rescues on a bulky mannequin.

Under Kevin's austere gaze, our class of trainees lost flippers; gracelessly bounced on the bottom of chilly lakes, sending up clouds of silt that fouled the water; knocked crabs off of pier posts; and became hopelessly lost within three feet of our entry into a murky bay. I often surfaced from a blunder-filled dive to see Kevin bobbing in the water, shaking his head slowly like a disappointed father. Beneath his calm critiques, I always had the sense there was a simmering level of exasperation. But to this day, when I'm diving and I flirt with the idea of taking a shortcut or blasting through safety checks, I picture Kevin shaking his head in weary disappointment, and it redoubles my commitment to the rules.

After a three-month ordeal we were somehow in possession of a scientific diving certificate and cleared to film Red Sea reefs on the heels of experienced coral scientists. I won't say that I'd fallen in love with diving. That would come eventually. But I was thrilled to finally have the chance to see corals up close, these mysterious organisms that were fast becoming an obsession.

While some societies have lived alongside and observed corals for countless generations, it's only recently that we've been able to study them in their own habitats the way a terrestrial naturalist can.

Shoals of fish surround coral
formations on a reef near Al
Lith on the Red Sea.

Aristotle mentioned diving bells more than two thousand years ago, but these inverted cauldrons didn't have view ports, and quick sprints into the murk wouldn't have been long enough to study corals. Sponge divers and the famous Ama pearl divers in Japan likely opened their eyes in the ocean as they sought their prizes, but they wouldn't have been able to see anything very clearly because of the way our eyes work underwater. Scientists have long been hauling bits of coral to the surface for better observation. The scientists on James Cook's *Endeavor* voyages performed "coral fishing," using nets, drags, and trawls to rip off bits of reef and haul them to the surface for analysis, but that was the equivalent of studying a forest in the stacked timber at a sawmill.

Early scientists employed glass-bottomed buckets to get a subsurface glimpse of reefs. In 1867, Baron Eugen von Ransonnet-Villez published the first documented images of coral reefs viewed from underwater after sketching them while sitting in a diving bell fitted with a glass viewing port. A diving bell cost a small fortune, so it probably helped that he was a baron. Still, such viewing must have lacked intimacy, like gazing at an exhibit through the glass wall of an aquarium.

By the early 1900s, pioneering American marine biologists like Alfred Mayor and William Beebe used diving helmets. These were clumsy by today's standards. Helmets could weigh eighty pounds or more, and views out the small portal were limited. These cumbersome suits were also dangerous. Jacques Cousteau, while in the French navy, knew divers in patched suits and dented helmets who leapt into the water and shot down hundreds of feet. "The old fellows had crippled arms and legs from 'pressure strokes'—actually due to the bends. They considered themselves lucky to be alive," he wrote.

Cousteau pioneered a new technology that revolutionized coral observation. He paired the nimble dive mask, refined in the 1930s by Mediterranean spear fishermen, with the demand regulator—a device that allowed divers to breathe compressed air from a tank they carried with them. No diving bells. No lead-footed suits tethered by a hose to the surface. This technology empowered that most fundamental of scientific tools: observation. As oceanographer Sylvia Earle has written, "For marine scientists, scuba was a breakthrough comparable in some ways to the development of the first microscopes." Observing corals *in situ*, studying their behavior and seeing how they interact within the dynamics of their ecosystem, was revolutionary.

Scuba diving had the additional advantage of democratizing science for people for whom this world had been off-limits. Science had once been the province mainly of men with connections to wealth or sponsorship who took long, expensive voyages and gathered trunks' worth of samples to study. Like the baron with a diving bell. But scuba gear changed that. A new breed of adventurer was drawn to the sea. Certainly Sylvia Earle was one.

It wasn't long before scientists devised ways to look at corals even more closely, thanks to more revolutionary technology. In the 1950s in Discovery Bay, Jamaica, Thomas F. Goreau and Nora Goreau applied radioactive tracers to corals in the sea, unlocking keys to the relationship between corals and how their zooxanthellae helped them create skeletons. In the 1960s, the use of new carbon-14 labeling techniques allowed researchers like Len Muscatine at UCLA to figure out that the tiny plants living inside corals supplied carbon to their hosts, essentially feeding them. By the 2000s, metagenomics coupled with powerful bioinformatics computing provided another new tool set in coral research, offering researchers a window into the microbial communities that cohabit with corals. This is what allowed Rebecca Vega Thurber and the team on the

Global Coral Microbiome Project to study the vast diversity that exists in swarms of bacteria, viruses, protists, and other microscopic critters that make up the "consortia organism" that is a coral colony.

And we're not only looking at corals and their microbes more closely; we're also examining them from greater heights. A network of 170 satellites has been created to detect coral bleaching as it unfolds and to identify "grazing halos" around reefs, also called a Randall Zone, areas that herbivorous fish and invertebrates keep clear of vegetation. Such a perspective can help scientists make quick assessments about changes in coral health.

It has been an amazing time for coral science, as each new year brings another revolution in tools and techniques. But the closer we get to unlocking the secrets of corals and how important they are to us and all other life on this planet, the more rapidly they are being destroyed. Our species has overlapped stony corals for only a tiny fraction of their existence on the planet. During that time, coral reefs have provided us with much. But we haven't been generous in return.

The original Hawaiians prized corals. They tended reefs like gardens. They collected live corals from neighboring islands and brought them to their home reefs. Corals were used to reinforce walls of Hawaiian fish ponds like living cement. Some were used to make dyes, and the role of reefs as a nursery for fish was well understood. Hawaiian chants gave prominence to corals, which held the honor of being the very first animals mentioned in the litany of life in their most famous creation story, known as the Kumulipo.

While the first Hawaiians might have prized living corals, it's the calcium carbonate skeletons that have held the appreciation, and sometimes contempt, of much of the rest of the world. Captain

James Cook, when exploring the Great Barrier Reef for the first time, saw the endless system of reefs as a deadly labyrinth frustrating navigation. A wreck on coral shoals nearly ended his first voyage. Columbus's first voyage concluded with the *Santa Maria* ramming a reef off of today's Dominican Republic.

Perhaps in revenge, Columbus's son dismantled entire coral reefs to construct a fortress in 1503. Mexico's largest port of Veracruz, founded in 1519, was constructed from *piedra de mucor*, or coral rock. Entire cities on the Sudanese and Saudi coasts of the Red Sea were also *created* from coral skeletons. Temples throughout Polynesia are made of the stuff, and if you've ever driven the twisty road to Hana on Maui you may have seen an old church built with chunks of fringing reef.

The Second World War saw the use of crushed coral rock for air bases across the Pacific, with one engineer gushing that "coral might well be called the world's best natural material for runway construction." By the end of the war, the world's largest airfield, located on Tinian near Guam, was made of coral aragonite, the bones of countless colonies. It was from this runway that nuclear devastation was launched against the Japanese cities of Nagasaki and Hiroshima.

Coral use and misuse continues today, and when reefs stand in the way of progress, for resorts, ports, and shipping channels, they are often wantonly destroyed or, in some cases, "relocated," as if it's possible to move an entire functioning ecosystem. Unscrupulous or desperate fishermen blast reefs to rubble with dynamite. In the process of a single increased catch, the habitat is forever destroyed.

Coral reefs are mined for souvenirs to sell to tourists, for bits of living coral for the aquarium trade, or simply to be ground up for calcium and minerals to be plowed into fields. When an Australian sugarcane magnate proposed dredging the Great

A dive boat with a team of
researchers speeds out of
the harbor at the King
Abdullah University of
Science and Technology
in Thuwal, Saudi Arabia.

Barrier Reef for limestone, he galvanized the movement leading to the creation of the Great Barrier Reef Marine Park and eventually a World Heritage Site designation by the United Nations.

Thanks to such advocacy and a lot of ongoing research, we're only just beginning to relearn what the original Hawaiians already understood: that corals are far more valuable alive than dead.

The term "ecosystem services" is often used to describe the value of coral reefs. For some, the term is suspect. Why should economic value for humans trump the moral and ethical imperative to protect an ecosystem from extermination? But we're a selfish species, so it's useful to consider the services that living reefs provide us. Various studies estimate the economic output of coral reefs as ranging from hundreds of billions to trillions of dollars per year. At least half a billion people rely on coral reef ecosystems for their only source of daily protein.

Reefs also provide shoreline protection, creating barriers that shelter towns and resorts from damaging waves, storm surges, and hurricanes. Their biodiversity creates a chemical complexity that makes them ripe for the discovery of medicines. Every obliterated swath of reef could forever erase a potential cure to cancer or Alzheimer's. Coral skeletal material is also biocompatible with our own bones. It can be used for everything from replacement eyes to dental implants and reconstructive facial surgery.

And then there is tourism. Corals reefs are food for the soul, creating stunning landscapes that draw throngs of visitors, driving economic activity. In many parts of the world, tourism is the only game in town.

Despite the rocky relationship between humans and stony corals during the short time that we've coexisted on this planet, they continue to feed and support us. But do we repay their ecosystem services in kind by giving them the space and conditions they need to flourish?

Not at all.

There are the local pressures of overfishing, pollution, dynamiting, dredging, and outright removal. Then there is the global pressure of climate change, the slow, steady warming of the planet that hammers corals with increased disease, mass bleaching, and the most insidious byproduct of carbon emissions: an acidifying ocean. Research already shows reduced coral skeleton development. Fossil-fuel emissions are a global killer of corals, and coming on the heels of an array of local insults, it's the wicked knockout uppercut of a one-two combination.

Our journey from the diving bell to bioinformatics is a blip in geological time. Will recognition of the services reefs provide along with an expanding ability to look more closely into the world of corals summon enough awe and respect to stem the tide of destruction? Or will it simply be a flash of revelation before the coming darkness?

Returning from that first day of diving on Saudi Arabian reefs, I was bone weary. I'd found the process both wondrous and unsettling. I still didn't feel like I'd mastered the necessary skills. I struggled to recall everything I'd learned in my crash diving course. And as for the camerawork—I'd barely been able to keep the images in focus. Still, I felt like I'd crossed a sort of threshold. I'd tumbled over the side of the boat, dwelt among corals and been rocked in the gentle embrace of the sea. And I'd survived.

The water of the inner lagoon was more tranquil than the wave-hammered outer reefs like Shib Nazar. Late-afternoon sun lent a glow to the distant coast, where I could make out the shapes of refineries and minarets. Ahmed pointed to a small island as we passed. It sprouted a thicket of palms and was ringed in a sandy beach. A lavish Bedouin tent squatted in the middle and a long pier covered in red carpet jutted into the lagoon. "The king's," Ahmed said. He steered away so we didn't get too close.

King Abdullah was the reason we were here, albeit indirectly. We were motoring back to his eponymous King Abdullah University of Science and Technology, or KAUST. It loomed ahead of us now, a blocky collection of soaring black buildings that looked like a starship recently landed on the shore. It was surrounded by a village of austere structures: housing, restaurants, stores, and mosques. The complex bristled with scaffolding and construction cranes.

If the campus looked like an uninhabited construction project, that's because it largely was. Despite having star international faculty, labs stocked with the latest technology, and a university endowment second only to Harvard, KAUST was brand-new. Built for a cohort of more than twenty thousand students, only a thousand or so were enrolled at the time. Funded by the king's wealth, forty thousand architects and workers constructed buildings, laboratories, student apartments, faculty houses, a yacht club, resort-like recreation facilities, restaurants, a golf course, the nation's sole movie theater, and the "Beacon of Knowledge," a concrete tower of geometric shapes pointing to the heavens like a giant finger of coral. The new university could boast one of the world's fastest supercomputers. It was the first institution in Saudi Arabia to allow women and men to take classes together. The dark, blocky buildings of the main campus were cavernous, with catwalks and canyon-like breezeways reminding me of the Death Star from the *Star Wars* films. Large tracts of apartments and houses stood empty, awaiting more faculty and students.

The Mutwa, the notorious Saudi religious police, were forbidden from the campus grounds. There was no enforcement of the strict religious codes that require women to cover up or prevent them from driving. Like college towns in rural America, KAUST was an island of relatively progressive thought plunked down in a sea of cultural conservatism. This all helped to attract expatriate students and scholars, the top minds that could be lured from abroad with state-of-the-art facilities and generous funding.

It has long been a practice for Saudi students to study at foreign universities in hopes that they'll bring the knowledge and prestige back to their homeland. But some students don't return, leading to a brain drain. KAUST was trying to flip this model. Here was an island of cutting-edge academic modernity built entirely within the borders of a cloistered nation.

KAUST is a fascinating story, but what brought us here were the reefs. This magnificent campus was perched on the edge of a coral-studded sea. KAUST has its own "house reefs," which included Shib Nazar, where scientists can study within sight of their laboratory windows. Instead of threading the gauntlet of international travel to get to a remote place like Lizard Island to collect samples, it was merely the matter of a morning commute.

Our team included doctoral student Ryan McMinds and postdoctoral scholar Jesse Zaneveld, both from the Global Coral Microbiome Project, who were working with a team led by a scientist named Christian Voolstra, a molecular biologist who worked in the Red Sea Research Center at KAUST.

The little-explored reefs of the Saudi coastline form a connected system even longer than the Great Barrier Reef. The Red Sea is the northernmost tropical sea. It's a young sea, still growing into an ocean as Africa rips away from the Arabian Peninsula. It offers unique opportunities to learn how corals have adapted to conditions that exist nowhere else in the world. The Red Sea is a kind of future ocean scenario. It's a very warm and very saline ocean. Examining how organisms live under these conditions can help scientists like Chris Voolstra relate it to other oceans.

Red Sea corals thrive under conditions that would bleach or kill corals in other parts of the world, and by looking at their genetics, Voolstra's team hoped to uncover the secrets to how these corals adapted to such a harsh environment. Voolstra shared my awe at the size of Shib Nazar. He described the scale of the underwater structures as feeling like you are on top of a mountain. Also, the arid conditions of the Saudi coast mean there are few rivers and less runoff and sedimentation, so the clarity of the sea is spectacular.

Having these reefs at the doorstep of the university labs meant that Voolstra's team could collect samples and process them in the same day. Voolstra was doing with corals and genomics what Monet did with his water lilies and oil paints.

When Voolstra moved to Saudi Arabia, he did have concerns over the cultural differences, and he brought with him the stereotypes and expectation of danger most of us in the West carry. But on a dive during his interview process he saw large reef sharks in his first ten minutes—and he made his decision to stay.

Beyond the KAUST complex, Saudi society could be challenging, especially for visiting women. There was the prowling, red-bearded Mutwa policing women's attire; the dark, ghost-like shapes of women in abayas drifting through air-conditioned shopping malls; the prohibitions against alcohol; and the simmering regional intrigue and conflict. I'd met some female researchers who'd refused to go, unwilling to add another layer of difficulty to the already gendered barriers in science. But those who did go gained a new perspective on this strange and, at turns, fascinating and troubling nation. "This country, and KAUST within this country, can only be understood if you actually come here," Voolstra said.

The corals in the Red Sea
off the Saudi Arabian coast
survive in fairly diverse
conditions that kill corals
in other parts of the world.

Our visit to Saudi Arabia was punctuated by the muezzins' haunting calls to prayer echoing through the half-empty streets, when shops pulled down their shutters, restaurants closed, and the devout disappeared into mosques leaving their shoes behind on the steps. These moments gave us time to wander the streets or perch on steps, waiting for Allah's permission for the world to reopen. Justin and I had the chance to eavesdrop on the musings of the researchers. Even their casual conversations were punctuated with big words and bigger ideas, and it was like struggling to follow a Nobel lecture. Ryan's fascination with evolution stemmed from a visit to Galapagos and his readings of Darwin. Jesse had spent much of his youth growing up on a boat in the South Pacific, his mother rowing him to school across coral lagoons. They'd each visited a wide range of reefs around the world in their quest to map coral microbes. But both were stunned by the diversity of what they found here. I asked them what gave them hope. Jesse marveled that he could spend weeks studying an area a meter across on these reefs. Biodiversity equals ecosystem resilience. Ryan was impressed by the Red Sea corals' ability to survive in conditions that killed corals elsewhere in the world. I asked our host, Chris Voolstra, about hope. "As long as we live and there are coral reefs present, there is hope. And it's the next generation of researchers that gives you hope," he said.

One member of that next generation was Gaida Haidadi, a Saudi doctoral candidate whose grit and persistence had so impressed Voolstra that he offered her a lab position coveted by an international pool of candidates. When I met Gaida, I asked what she thought the key was to protecting the reefs that gilded the edge of her home country. She felt it was education. Like most Saudis, she hadn't even known about the existence of reefs. But when she saw them while snorkeling, they sparked her interest, both as a biologist and as someone who appreciated the beauty of nature.

She told me that she was now about to take a diving class. I thought of the ordeal I'd just endured to achieve science certification. I asked her if she was nervous.

"A little bit. But I think I can do it," she said with a confident shrug.

I thought of the other Saudi women I'd seen—or rather, hadn't seen—during this trip. In nearby Jeddah, I'd found it unsettling to see women in abayas in the shopping malls, only their eyes visible, most of them escorted by a male relative. I paused outside of a Victoria's Secret and watched one cloaked woman holding lingerie up against her shapeless black form and evaluating it in a mirror. How many of those women had ambitions like Gaida? And how many of those dreams were smothered in black linen?

But now there was no abaya in sight, no head scarf, just a born-and-bred Saudi woman scientist who looked and acted no different from the other graduate students from around the world, even though she'd never left Saudi Arabia. When I asked what worried her most, she summed up the challenge perfectly: "If nobody finds the solution to coral reef decline, coral reefs will be lost."

Before leaving Saudi Arabia, Justin and I joined the Voolstra lab on a research cruise from the south-central coast near Yemen. We disembarked from the town of Al Lith in the evening as small fishing boats bobbed in the sunset, nets flying over water and birds circling to poach the catch. We settled into our bunks for a restless night punctuated by the rocking of waves, the chug of the motor, and the smell of diesel exhaust.

Over the next few days we followed Ryan and Jesse through coral canyons as they collected samples while Voolstra and his students gathered data for their projects. We filmed and photographed corals that looked like the complex architecture of the oil refineries we passed on the highway or the minaret towers we'd seen outlined against desert sunsets.

Ryan and Jesse filled a "dry shipper," a round freezer cooled by dry ice, with their samples for the global genetic map they were painstakingly assembling. Chris Voolstra led the students on tours of sunken grottoes, and we watched their bubbles trail off into the blue as we filmed what we hoped would not be the last reefs in the world.

The night after our last dive, I found a student named Mohammad on the top deck of the boat, where he was leaning on the rail looking out at the dark sea. The orange ember of a cigarette glowed in the darkness. He was the only smoker on the boat, so I bummed a cigarette in solidarity, an old interviewer's trick for prompting candid conversation.

We gazed toward the south where there was talk of a coming war with Yemen. Beyond the railing in the other direction was the length of the Red Sea, with Sudan, the Levant, Jordan, Egypt, and Israel lying beyond the edge of the night. I wondered what it would take to bring all of these nations together in the cause of coral conservation.

I spoke with Mohammad about the brewing conflict, stereotypes, religion, politics: all of the taboo subjects that are the journalist's privilege. He was a modern graduate student. He was concerned about the health of the Red Sea and the fate of corals. He'd studied abroad. He talked in American slang and listened to hip-hop. But he was also a devout Sunni. He spoke disapprovingly of dissidents, who were branded as "witches." He would soon be married. He would not meet his wife alone until after the wedding, where all the guests, even the bride and groom, would be segregated by gender for the entirety of the ceremony.

Then he flipped the interview, and I was soon telling him how strange and fascinating I'd found Saudi culture. I told him what troubled me about it. I told him what I admired, especially the way families came together on grassy medians of wide boulevards in the evenings, the smell of turmeric and grilling meat, the laughter of children, groups of men and women talking, face coverings lowered as prohibitions relaxed in the cooling darkness. I spoke of my own shattered stereotypes.

"It's not all Fox News," he said with a smirk.

Saudi Arabia was an enigma. It was beautiful. It had troubles. I'd heard the stories. A faculty member's son deported for false accusations. A Filipino construction worker carted off to jail for drinking alcohol. A guest worker, his passport seized, forced into indentured servitude. A blogger flogged in public for criticizing clerics. All while KAUST administrators remained silent. I asked Mohammad about the conflict between Saudi Arabia and the Houthi rebels in Yemen. He looked to the stars with disgust.

"What is the meaning of Islam? All religions?" he asked. "It's peace!" He thought for a moment more. Then he held out his arm and made a chopping motion with his other hand. "We are all the same," he said. "If I am cut, I bleed. If someone else is cut, he bleeds. I can give my blood to them and they can take it and give it to anyone." He gestured across the sea. "To someone in Sudan...anywhere."

I considered our ability to share blood with people of other nationalities, genders, ethnicities—the artificial differences between tribes melting away. Then I thought of the potential of these resilient corals in the dark waters below us—how they could share their genetic material with other corals around the world to help them survive the coming storm of climate change. I thought of Gaida, who would soon be learning to dive and would explore these same reefs that, until a short time ago, neither of us had known existed.

I know it's not fair to rely on the youth to save us. We've left them a big enough mess as it is. But if these students were the future of Saudi Arabia, then maybe corals—and the rest of us—have a fighting chance.

3

Animal, Plant, Mineral

Santa Cruz del Islote, Colombia

THE *LANCHA* SLAMMED THE WAVES with the precision of a metronome. A pair of chops was followed by a deep drop into a trough, rattling the empty dive tanks at the bottom of the boat and turning my spine to jelly with each slap of the hull against the waves. A speck of an island appeared ahead and Pablo, our captain, mercifully pulled back on the throttle. The jarring waves softened to a cushion and the color of the water changed from blue to pale green as we slipped over sandy shallows.

We putted closer to the island and the outlines of colorful buildings materialized. "Island" didn't really seem like the right word; it looked more like a storybook village floating on a raft. A halo of fishing boats bobbed around the rim and colorful strings of laundry flapped like semaphores.

We circled and found a concrete pier bordering a tiny plaza. Pablo guided us close and Charlie, the first mate, tossed over the bumpers and cinched us tight. We climbed out of the boat and filtered into the plaza, blinking in surprise at finding a cozy village in the middle of this watery expanse. A quaint canyon of a street twisted away from the plaza. People peered out of houses. Children ran through puddles. An old woman lumbered past carrying two sacks of water. It was a movie set come to life. Old men sat clustered in the shade of a cabana next to piles of fishing nets; wizened, salty characters straight out of a Hemingway story. We'd come here in search of tales of corals and the sea. And it seemed we'd found the right place.

Along with the crew, we were two filmmakers and five scientists. Cameraman Darryl Lai and I were tagging along with Colombian researchers Mateo Lopez Victoria and Beto Rodriguez-Ramirez and their team. We'd been filming them as they took core samples of area coral colonies to study the impacts of sedimentation. The nearby Canal del Dique had been dumping runoff from the Magdalena River onto these reefs for five centuries, since first being dredged by

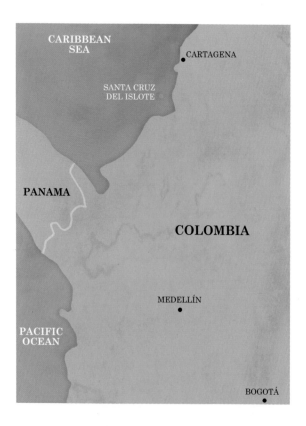

CARIBBEAN
SEA

CARTAGENA

SANTA CRUZ
DEL ISLOTE

PANAMA

COLOMBIA

MEDELLÍN

PACIFIC
OCEAN

BOGOTÁ

Page 50: Close-up of polyps of
Orbicella faveolata, a slow-
growing, mounding coral and
key reef-builder that is also
listed as endangered.

the Spaniards. Taken back to the lab, the vertical core samples—meter-long cylinders as thick as my forearm that had been drilled straight down through the heads of ancient corals the size of sofas—would reveal the colonies' growth rates, calcification rates, and skeletal densities. These data could provide a sort of road map to the history of stressors, much as the growth rings of trees might mark forest fires or drought.

The coring had been a difficult process to observe, like watching a painful lobotomy on the massive brain corals. But Mateo assured me that once they'd drilled the hole and capped it, the healthy colonies would heal over. The story the scientists would capture in those skeletal cores would provide valuable tissue to judge the health of the archipelago's entire reef system.

These scattered islands are tucked in the corner of the Caribbean along the Colombian coast and are officially part of the Rosario and San Bernardo Corals National Natural Park, 460 square miles of seascape comprised of reefs and sea grasses, clusters of mangroves, and a handful of low-slung islands mostly dotted with resorts, plus a few fishing communities.

While the scientists were gathering evidence of human impacts on the nearby reefs, we filmmakers sought data of a different sort. We wanted to hear the stories of the people who knew these waters best, their memories revealing, in layers, the history of this place like the rings of the core samples.

So after the scientific work was finished, the team brought us to Santa Cruz del Islote, which translates as "Little Island of the Holy Cross." Barely three acres in size, with every meter put to good use, it is part of a cluster of ten islands forty-five kilometers from Cartagena. Unlike the other islands in the grouping, though, Islote isn't natural. It was built on a reef of coral rubble as a stopover for fishermen, a breezy refuge from mosquitoes and malaria. Today it supports around a hundred houses and a thousand people, mostly descendants of the Afro-Colombia diaspora scattered along the nation's Caribbean coast, a people tracing their roots back to the *palenques*, escaped slaves who built self-reliant, independent communities on the area islands. For centuries they survived on fishing or cutting wood from the nearby mangrove stands to make charcoal, though now tourism was transforming the subsistence economy, bringing roughly 300,000 visitors to the archipelago every year.

There are few amenities on Islote. And there is no space for resorts. They do get visitors, and for a few thousand pesos, the equivalent of a dollar, you can take a tour guided by one of the locals. But there's not enough room to develop a sustainable tourist economy. This is a place whose survival is inextricably linked to the reef landscape around it.

Mateo slipped a few bills to one of the old-timers hovering in the shade for a docking fee and a tour, and the man cheerfully led us into the warren of houses. There was a store and a plaza with the island's namesake "holy cross," six feet tall and painted blue to match the church. Our guide showed us a recently added diesel generator that provided the only power, and also the tanks of fresh water filled weekly by the navy. For entertainment, there's a small cock-fighting ring and even an "Islote Sea World," where, for another buck, you can view concrete pens of barracuda and a massive nurse shark curled in its cramped bin like a big dog in an armchair. The proprietor prodded the lethargic animal into action with jabs from a broom handle despite Mateo's protestations.

On the surface, this place appeared to be a tropical idyll, free of the plagues of modern life, from traffic and crime to consumer culture and dreaded email. A parade of uniformed schoolchildren marched past. Neighbors leaned out windows to chat across laundry lines. Teenagers flirted while old men told

stories in the shade. It seemed in balance with the surrounding reefs, with its bobbing rim of fishing boats promising to bring in the daily catch of fish, octopus, and lobster, or to ferry some of the islanders to jobs at the nearby resorts. The houses were crisply painted and tidy, and so tightly clustered that doors spilled neighbors onto each other's laps.

But sitting a half-meter above the surrounding water, Islote seemed a prime candidate for obliteration by rising sea level. Many of the houses were reinforced by coral riprap. And with 80 percent of Caribbean reefs already decimated, what future would these people have as climate change, sedimentation, overfishing, and other insults continued to hammer the local reefs that fed and employed them?

I also saw young men missing limbs—the scarred stumps a sign of dynamite fishing employed out of desperation when fishing declined. One man who sat sullenly on a stool in the shade was missing *both* hands, arms ending in smoothed-over, misshapen lumps. What had compelled him to try dynamite fishing a second time?

We twisted through the streets that narrowed to corridors and then reemerged by the docks feeling as if we'd slipped back in time. The old fishermen in the shade of the cabana smiled at us and beckoned us over. They were ready with their stories.

As soon as we set up our camera, a young man strode out of the maze of houses, waving his hands. He was different from the rest of the villagers, without the singsong Caribbean music to his Spanish and lighter in complexion. He demanded to know who we were and what we were doing here. He told us that we weren't allowed to film.

I only understand a few phrases in Spanish, so I didn't grasp what he was telling us, but his manner set me on edge. He had the swagger of a bureaucrat and the air of a pedant. Mateo came over and the pair were soon locked in an intense conversation. Mateo stayed calm while the other man grew louder, clearly delivering a diatribe meant as much for the growing audience of townsfolk as for us.

As Mateo translated, it became clear. The man was the teacher at the island's one-room school. It seems that El Profesor had been elected, or possibly had appointed himself, spokesman of the town. Some journalists had recently breezed through and written stories that reflected poorly on the community. Add to that the constant parade of tourists marching through snapping photos while contributing little to the island's economy, it made them feel like a museum exhibit. This fellow was protective and concerned about exploitation. My attitude toward him softened, though only a little.

After more debate, as Mateo explained the work he and his team were doing to assess the health of the reefs and how we were making a science film about coral conservation, El Profesor relented. We were granted permission to interview the fishermen. But we would also be required to interview him. Evidently he was eager to air his grievances on camera. And there was one more condition: he wanted us to return the next morning to deliver a lecture about coral ecology to his students.

Having thus negotiated terms, Darryl set up the camera and El Profesor watched us carefully, scowling the whole time. We spoke first with a man called El Tiburón, or the Shark. He had a trimmed white beard and a habit of pursing his lips as if he were suppressing a smile. He told us that he had attended school through the fourth grade but had quit in order to fish alongside his father. He had fished for the rest of his working life. Now he lived in semiretirement and gave tours of the island. This career change to town historian and gadfly came about through necessity, as he'd seen large declines in fishing over his lifetime.

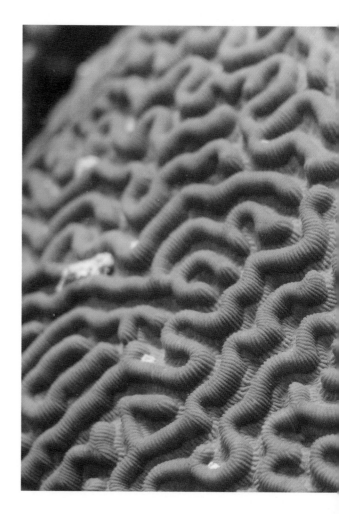

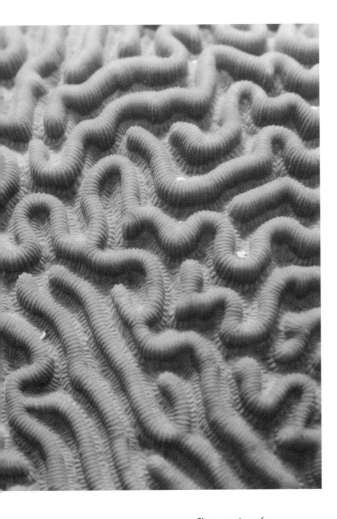

Close-up view of a
symmetrical brain coral or
Pseudodiploria strigosa,
another of the mounding
species that add mass to
Caribbean reefs.

He told us how he used to go out for four days
and bring back up to a hundred fifty kilos of lobster.
Now the fishermen went out for a month and barely
came back with fifty. He blamed the downturn on
what he called "viking" ships, the industrial fishing
fleets from Northern European countries that
prowled the Caribbean. Also, islanders from other
local communities had been coming here and
competing for a greatly depleted catch, leading
to conflict.

"There are aggressive fishers who do not speak
with dialogue, but with violence," he told us.

I asked him about the corals. He said reefs had
declined. In the past, people would collect corals for
construction or income. They would dry them out and
sell them to the tourists. Now some of the reefs were
gone. He also explained that the water coming from
the Magdalena River carried sediment that settled
on the reef and was killing the corals.

I thought of the research our scientists were
doing. They were merely confirming something these
fishermen already knew. I sought out other fishermen, who told me that between fifteen and twenty
years ago the corals had turned white and many of
them died. Those dates coincided with the late 1990s,
one of the worst periods for coral bleaching in the
Caribbean and around the world.

The biggest worry for these men was for the next
generation. With the fishing in decline, how would
they make a living? Though there was hope: some
youth had enlisted in conservation programs run by
local resorts to help sea turtles. The kids were
learning to protect coral. They were also lobbying
the government, which had always treated these
islands as an afterthought, for more support. They
wanted more access to electricity and help to
manage and enforce fishing regulations. But the
outlook was still grim.

We returned early the next morning, bleary-eyed, having spent the night in a workers' dorm at a nearby resort. It had been a fitful rest, with the pyrotechnics of a tropical thunderstorm electrifying the stifling air.

But El Profesor's class was sharp. The children sat to attention at their desks, wearing crisp blue shirts, striped ties, and navy shorts. It was early, but the heat was already rising. We filed into the tight classroom on the second floor of the cinder-block building, some of our team spilling into the hallway and down the stairs. The students sat with their notebooks open and pens at the ready.

Mateo drew a diagram, the outline of a coral colony, on the whiteboard. The students began sketching it into their copybooks. It was an interesting contrast: these sharp students hanging on the words of a man in Bermuda shorts, rash guard, and tie-dyed bandanna smelling of yesterday's seawater. But Mateo, a professor at a private university, had the command of an experienced teacher—even if he did look like a tourist. He sized them up and clapped his hands together and they straightened in their seats.

"Que es un coral?" he asked. *What is a coral?*

There was a moment of hesitation. He turned back to the board. He wrote the words *planta*, *animal*, *mineral*. He drew a question mark. The students scribbled in their notebooks.

"Que es un coral?" he asked again, more impatient this time.

Then one arm ratcheted hesitantly into the air, a girl in the front row.

In a quiet voice she answered. Mateo smiled and nodded at her answer. And for the benefit of the rest of us, he began to elaborate.

What *is* a coral? Is it a plant, an animal, or a rock?

Before Islote, I'd read the latest scientific papers along with the journals of naturalists and explorers.

I'd interviewed dozens of scientists. But I still wouldn't have felt confident raising my hand in that class. It's basic biology, but it's still not an easy answer. There are caveats. A solid case could be made for all three answers.

Let's start at the end: *mineral*. Reef-building corals are a lot like rocks. They are fixed in place. Their stony skeletons are what create the habitat. Like any rocky reef, they frustrate waves and smash holes in the hulls of ships. You find the remains of their ancestors embedded in mountaintop cliffs. You can find houses and fortresses constructed from them. But after careful observation, by hauling a coral to the surface and seeing the tiny polyps, the slimy layer of skin, or studying them over time to see that they grow—it becomes clear that these are no mere minerals.

Then what about plants?

Corals are certainly plant-like. They are sessile, meaning fixed in place and not able to swim or scuttle around. Their colonies branch and grow like shrubs. They often look like woody plants when we stare down at them through the water. They grow toward sunlight in thickets, competing for light like trees in a forest canopy, and they provide structure to fish and a range of creatures much in the way that a forest serves birds, insects, fungi, and other creatures. They start very small and can grow to great size. Up close they sport an array of brilliant colors like the most vibrant flower garden.

In fact, corals are so plant-like that most early scientists considered them to be plants. The French doctor and naturalist from Marseille Jean-André Peyssonnel thought otherwise and tried to set the record straight in the early eighteenth century. He worked up the courage to make this claim in a letter to the prestigious Académie des Sciences in Paris after a journey at sea where he observed Mediterranean corals "opening and closing their little pestles."

In his letter, he made the shocking suggestion that these creatures were actually a type of "un-insect"—an animal, not a plant.

The letter was read anonymously before the academy to protect the author's reputation from his absurd assertion. It was greeted with derisive laughter. It would take another couple of decades before the rest of the scientific world recognized that Peyssonnel had been right.

So despite their rock-like dispositions and their plant-like behavior, corals are most definitely animals. They're in the phylum Cnidaria, which includes other sessile animals like sea anemones but also medusae, or free-swimming creatures, like jellyfish. Corals are cousins to both, and they have both sessile and free-swimming stages to their lives. All Cnidarians share a construction of hollow, jelly-like bodies with a mouth at one end surrounded by tentacles, which they use to defend themselves, capture food, and sometimes fight with others of their kind.

Coral polyps are tiny. Their jellyfish cousins, by contrast, can grow to be enormous. The lion's mane jellyfish, which can reach lengths of a hundred feet or more, is one of the longest animals on the planet.

Being sessile makes breeding a challenge for corals. They can't swim around to find mates. As the marine biologist Kristen Marhaver has described it, "Most spawning coral species solve this puzzle by sending their sperm and eggs to meet at the water surface, cleverly turning a three-dimensional problem into a two-dimensional one." So they create an inverted flurry, synchronized by just the right temperature, lunar cycle, and time of day. On the surface, the gametes mingle and fertilize; cells begin to divide, forming blastocysts. Some corals are hermaphrodites, able to produce both eggs and sperm. Others are male or female. Some don't spawn but are brooders, with fertilization taking place inside of them rather than in the water. But they all produce larvae, which

are propelled by tiny hair-like cilia as the corals enter the all-too-brief free-swimming stage of their lives. Some get right to work finding a permanent home. But others ride the ocean currents for months before settling. And in this way, they can spread their genes around the world.

Unlike their jellyfish cousins, corals are homebodies at heart. Once their journey brings them to a promising spot—a rocky, solid surface on the seafloor, where the water is clear and the temperature is right, like Goldilocks finding her third and perfect bed and bowl of porridge—the larvae settle by attaching to that rocky substrate to live out their lives.

While it might sound dull to spend life fixed to a single spot on the bottom of the sea, this is only the beginning of an epic tale. Corals are ingenious little chemists. Once situated they get to work absorbing calcium from seawater. They can also absorb and manipulate carbon. They combine these elements to form calcium carbonates, making a material called aragonite and transporting this substance through their bodies to create a thin, crystallized layer, a sliver of aragonite rock, between the polyp's body and the hard substrate to which it clings. Through building a skeleton outside of its body, it grows the rock to which it is affixed, expanding its domain.

While corals may be homebodies, they are not loners. As they begin to expand their rocky home, one layer of aragonite at a time, they're building room for company. The polyp now performs a miracle, as it feeds and begins to thrive, gathering the strength to grow a friend: it clones itself, asexually, producing an exact genetic copy. A colony is born. Large colonies can have thousands of exact genetic clones of the original pioneer polyp.

So now the simple question—What *is* a coral?—has become more complicated. Yes, a coral is a single polyp. But a coral *colony* is a group of genetically identical copies, all made of the same code that was written when the original pair of gametes fused in a freewheeling, sea-born accident. And this colony builds itself a rocky skeleton outside of its body. So, technically speaking, isn't it a coral a rock as well?

Then what about all of that plant-like behavior? Why were the early scientists so sure that they were right when they scoffed at Peyssonnel? Perhaps one could argue, on a technicality, that corals are a sort of plant as well.

And this is where coral reefs really get interesting.

Corals act like trees in a forest, providing structure and making reefs some of the planet's most biodiverse hot spots. But it's more than just the physical shape that makes them seem quite plant-like. They not only *look* like trees, they also *act* like trees. They grow. Some species, like the staghorn corals, *Acropora cervicornis*, are brushy and weedy. They grow quickly. Other towering or bouldering corals grow slowly like ancient sequoias. Corals also engage in one of the most plant-like behaviors around: photosynthesis. All this growing into wild shapes—spreading out into squat boulders, twisting around their neighbors, fanning out into great plates like the positioning of satellite dishes—is done with one purpose in mind: to gather sunlight.

Now, a coral polyp is no more a plant than a jellyfish, an octopus, a shark, or even a person is. And it isn't born with a plant's magic trick—the ability to transform sunlight into food. But these clever little architects have devised a work-around. They employ *symbiosis*. They coax other living things to "do that work" for them. They have evolved to allow tiny single-celled plants, a type of algae called *zooxanthellae*, to live within the walls of their translucent bodies. These microscopic plants absorb light, filtered through the shallow water above and through the clear walls of their polyp patrons, and convert that sunlight into sugars, oxygen, and organic compounds, offering their bounty to their coral hosts.

In return for sharing their surplus, the zooxanthellae gain shelter and a commitment from their coral hosts to always put them in the best position to carry on their autotrophic work. The wild, ragged, twisting, snaking, spreading, growing landscape of a stony coral reef is one massive, dynamic, slow-motion competition to place algal partners in position to absorb light. Zooxanthellae also gain access to inorganic nutrients like carbon and nitrogen, much of it through the waste products of their coral hosts.

And there's something else zooxanthellae give to their translucent hosts: their color. When you look down through the water, live coral colonies have a brownish-greenish-grayish hue. This is a healthy look for corals. And the color comes from the zooxanthellae living in the coral tissue. Otherwise corals would appear bone-white, showing their aragonite skeletons through translucent skin.

If you jump into the water and swim in for a closer look, you'll see the reefs come to life with color. Water absorbs light, and when there is a lot of water between you and the coral, they look dull, dark, and rocklike. But the closer you get, the more their colors begin to bloom. Shine a light on them and amazing things happen: they take on a multi-hued palette that would put a box of crayons to shame. Under the right light, corals even fluoresce, glowing vibrant in the darkness, mimicking the Milky Way and northern lights.

So, plant, animal, or mineral? Which is it, really? Can a coral be seen as a combination of all three? And why stop there? When you factor in the vast microbial life associated with corals, their complexity grows even more magnificent.

Coral microbiologist Forest Rohwer and his colleagues were among the first to refer to a coral as a *holobiont*. *Holo* comes from the Greek for *universe*. *Biont* means to *live*. Each coral colony is a living universe. The coral holobiont contains ten times the bacteria found on human skin or healthy soil.

It takes a team to drill cores of skeletal material in the massive old colonies near Colombia's San Bernardo Archipelago.

A reef is a collection of these galaxies that houses three times the animal phyla of tropical rain forests. "Knowing that there are approximately a thousand coral species," Rohwer has written, "each with over a hundred bacterial species that are found exclusively in association with them, we realize that there may be as many as 100,000 different bacterial species that live with one coral or another."

So what is a coral? The girl in the classroom on Islote knew that they are, technically speaking, animals. But I know now that there are no wrong answers. Mineral? Plant? You can make a case. And then...how about an entire universe? Maybe this is the best answer: corals are miracles.

And what is more miraculous than the corals themselves? It's the worlds they create.

In the Islote classroom, scientists Mateo and Beto tag-teamed the lecture on coral biology. Even with my limited Spanish, I was enthralled by the clarity and simplicity of their talk. As the temperature climbed outside and the air in the little room grew thick, none of the students squirmed or yawned. I peeked at their notebooks and saw precise pencil copies of the scientists' sketches. I chalked up their attentiveness to the discipline of El Profesor, who stood in the corner with his arms folded and his trademark scowl.

Beto and Mateo expanded their lecture beyond the coral itself to the habitats that corals build. They sketched a globe and circled spots around the middle of the planet where stony corals are found, including the section of the Caribbean where Santa Cruz del Islote resides.

Reef-building corals have evolved to thrive in tropical seas, they explained. That ribbon of bathtub water that circles the world along the equator is so crystal clear because it's the marine version of a

desert. It lacks the soup of nutritious plankton found in more temperate waters toward the poles. But coral reefs transform this underwater Sahara into one of the most biodiverse habitats on the planet. Coral colonies build structures that become magnets for life. Though reefs can grow to be huge, they still only cover less than 0.2 percent of the earth's surface. Yet a quarter of all the world's marine species spend all or part of their life cycle on these reefs.

The most noticeable layer of life is the fish. Wrapped in the lurid brilliance of their colors and varying in size from tiny to massive, often traveling in dense schools of their kin, fish are the first indicators of the health and diversity of a reef system. There are massive whale sharks the size of railcars and tiny gobies no bigger than a thumbtack. There are resident fish that spend their entire lives on reefs and pelagic, or open-ocean, fish that only stop by to hunt or rear their offspring in sheltering corals. There are benthic, or bottom-dwelling, fish like rays and flatfish that hug the sandy floors of coral lagoons. The variety of fish is astonishing. There are fish that eat plants and algae, fish that eat corals, fish that eat waste material, and fish that eat each other. There are thousands of species of fish that spend part or all of their lives on coral reefs, and new species are routinely discovered.

Then there are the reef invertebrates. These animals range from the jellyfish cousins of corals to sponges, sea squirts, snails, sea stars, urchins, sea cucumbers, octopuses, cuttlefish, and crabs. There are flashy floral slugs called nudibranchs that look like candy but are actually advertising their toxicity through gaudy colors. There are club-clawed shrimp strong enough to smash glass and jellies so toxic that their stings could drop a linebacker in seconds. There are worms that burrow holes into coral rock and then reemerge in flowery bouquets to filter the water for plankton. There are giant clams the size of lounge chairs whose blue lips are colored by their own symbiotic partnerships with zooxanthellae, and at low tide when they just kiss the surface, they'll arbitrarily clamp their great jaws shut to send a spray of water into the air.

And then there are plants. There are sea grasses, mangroves, plankton, and the tiny, single-celled zooxanthellae. There are more than five hundred species of red, green, blue, and brown algae found on reefs. There are pink and purple algae that fuse rock and rubble together to create more substrate on which the corals can grow. There is dense, weedy macroalgae that seek any opportunity to choke out the coral colonies, and it's only the effort of helpful herbivorous fish and invertebrates that keeps them in check.

And there are other creatures: turtles, dugongs, manatees, sea snakes, whales, and dolphins. And there are birds: terns, noddies, gulls, pelicans, and more. From whale sharks down to the invisible microbes of the coral holobiont, it's estimated that more than a million species, most of them yet to be identified by science, inhabit the world's reefs. These layers of life are all built up from that single swimming coral polyp that decided to settle in one particular spot, either by chance or that random wisdom of nature, to create a world where once there was nothing.

As we left the schoolroom after Mateo and Beto's lecture, I considered one more species for which coral reefs had built a home—our own. Tiny Islote and the people who live there are as much a part of the surrounding reefs as the coral canyons that sheltered fish and lobster. The reef provided the coral rubble from which the island was built. Houses were rein-forced with coral rock. The reef fish fed islanders and provided their only vocation for hundreds of years. And even now that fishing was giving way to tourism as the primary source of income, corals were still vital.

Without reefs, little Santa Cruz del Islote, built through a combination of ingenuity, determination, andcorals, would never have existed. With rising seas and declining reefs, the long-term odds of survival for this little island seemed daunting.

At the start of our visit, I'd asked El Tiburón, the local historian and retired fisherman, what the island needed most to survive.

"The people need information. Train the people," El Tiburón said.

Through the exchange I'd witnessed between the sharply dressed students and the scruffy band of scientists, I felt the odds tipping, ever so slightly, in a hopeful direction.

4

What the Moon Was Called

Mo'orea, French Polynesia

EVERYONE ON THE ISLAND OF MO'OREA turned out for the festival. There were French government officials in slacks, American scientists in safari shorts and flip-flops, and an array of locals dressed in bright floral prints. The women wore flowers in their hair, and some of the men went shirtless, sporting tribal tattoos and palm skirts. A trio of musicians sang in Tahitian, the tune's sweet notes mournful despite the rhythm of drums and plucky ukuleles. Palms swayed overhead, and through them were glimpses of the jagged green fingers of island peaks and the sapphire of Cook's Bay across the road. And there was food: huge pans of baked plantains and breadfruit; pit-roasted pork belly that melted on your tongue like butter; and *po'e*, a pudding of fruit and bread baked in banana leaves.

Mo'orea is a bewitching volcanic island in French Polynesia rimmed with a turquoise halo of shallow lagoons formed by coral reefs. Draw a line between Australia and South America, and another straight

down from Hawai'i, and you'll come close to this tiny neighbor of Tahiti, a part of the Society Islands cluster of French Polynesia. The festival was celebrating the thirtieth anniversary of the Atitia Center and the adjoining Richard B. Gump South Pacific Research Station, a unique pair of facilities devoted to the region's two most abundant resources: the island's tropical biodiversity and its rich cultural heritage. The cross-cultural blend of partygoers reflected the center's dual mission of fusing science and tradition.

Our goal here was to make a connection and open a door into the local community. We wanted to film local fishing practices for a documentary. After more than a week on the island shadowing researchers, Justin Smith and I wanted to break out of our Western research station bubble and capture a local's perspective on the health and pressures facing these reefs. So I asked Hinano Teavai-Murphy, the center's director and our host, to suggest a good contact. She pointed us to a man wearing a fedora from a 1940s

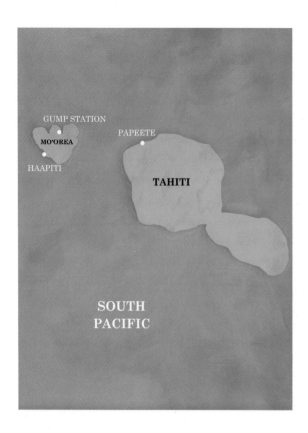

GUMP STATION

PAPEETE

MO'OREA

HAAPITI

TAHITI

SOUTH
PACIFIC

Page 62: Researcher Rebecca
Vega Thurber inspects coral
formations in the lagoons of
Mo'orea in French Polynesia.

gangster film and a wide grin more brilliant than his
flower-print shirt. Storytelling is about characters,
and it looked like we had found one.

"You come with me, we catch fish," Franck
Tapatuarai said, his eyes wide and his grin gleeful.
He seemed a willing ambassador of the often reticent
local fishing community. It made sense when we
learned that he was a local politician, deputy mayor
of a small island community. But he also seemed
passionate about traditional fishing practices. And
like fishers everywhere, he seemed eager to prove his
prowess. He held his hands apart to indicate the size
of the creatures he planned to ensnare the next day,
using the efficient techniques developed to a deadly
art by his ancestors.

Locals have good reasons to be wary of outsiders.
Throughout history, travelers who stepped on the
shores of Mo'orea have acted as colonizers, tourists,
polluters, and carbon emitters from consumptive
continents, in each case disrupting the balance of
"the traditional way of life that had developed over
centuries. Interest in local fishing practices often
comes with government-mandated regulations,
despite the fact that the Mo'oreans had figured out
how to sustainably manage their resources over the
course of a millennium. But far from being reticent,
Franck seemed eager to share traditional practices
with a couple of strangers.

Within moments of a handshake with Franck our
itinerary was set: "We meet tomorrow," he began.
"I show my presentation, you come to my house, we
eat, we go fishing, you sleep by me...not in the same
bed, but in my house...we wake up early and sell the
fish, then we eat again. Is good?"

"Yes," I nodded. "Is good."

After we parted, I wondered what had he meant
about showing us a presentation. Were we in for a
time-share pitch? I wasn't sure what we were getting
into, but I suspected it would be an adventure.

Justin and I had come to Mo'orea, as we had in Australia and Saudi Arabia, to film the work of Dr. Rebecca Vega Thurber of Oregon State University, codirector of the Global Coral Microbiome Project. Up to now, we'd followed her team. On this trip, we had the opportunity to see her, the lead scientist, in action.

We would learn that while Vega Thurber loved corals, it was the microscopic creatures that cohabit with them that she found most fascinating, and which, as she told us, she suspects hold the key to coral survival in light of the myriad pressures these animals face. As she explained it, there doesn't seem to be an evolutionary reason why some groups of corals do poorly and others do well. She believed that true understanding of how and why corals die lies in the holy trinity of microbiome investigation: the corals themselves, their symbiotic algae, and the bacteria and microbes they live with. Looking at all three can provide a holistic understanding of how organisms have evolved in their environment and how that evolution of the entire group contributes to its success or its failure under certain environmental conditions.

Studying corals' interaction with their microbes could lead to different treatments for disease or bleaching, the way a physician might attack an illness in a person with multiple therapies or medicines. Indeed, "coral doctor" is how Vega Thurber has described her work to her toddler son in an attempt to explain to him why she has to leave him behind for weeks and even months at a time.

When Vega Thurber told me that we are in a race against the clock to figure out what we can do to preserve these important habitats, she captured my feeling exactly. And the guilt she experienced over how often her work took her away from her son was also something I could relate to. More than once, as I packed my dive and camera gear to head somewhere

magical, my daughter has asked to come along. These requests became more poignant when I realized that many of the reefs I visited will likely be gone by the time she's my age, if not sooner. The baseline shifts below our very feet. And when Vega Thurber was diving, that internal conflict subsided and she realized that her ultimate aim was to be able to share beauty and value she found on coral reefs with the next generation.

"I'm here for a reason, and that reason is him," she told me.

Mo'orea draws tourists because it is beautiful, and it draws coral researchers because there is something special about its reefs. Pete Edmunds is an ecologist from England by way of California who also works out of the Gump Station. Having spent most of his career studying reefs in the Caribbean, where he observed a slow and steady decline over decades, he was amazed when he came to Mo'orea nearly twenty years ago and saw more coral there than he thought he'd ever see in his entire life. But after five years of working in these bountiful lagoons, the unthinkable happened. First, a crown of thorns starfish outbreak hit in 2009, and these spiny coral predators munched their way across the lagoon, devouring live coral polyps by the acre. Increases in pollution and runoff exacerbate plagues of the prickly, coral-hungry echinoderms, and the steady growth in the island's tourism industry certainly increased pollution.

Then in 2010 a hurricane battered the outer reef, breaking off coral heads and swirling them through the lagoon like a giant blender. Corals are used to rebuilding after devastation from hurricanes, but climate change is increasing the frequency and intensity of such storms beyond what occurs naturally. Edmunds feared that the steady decline he'd been watching for years had now reached this remote refuge. "In 2010 there was about as little coral cover as I'd ever seen anywhere in the world.

And I thought, 'That's it, it's the Caribbean all over again,'" he said.

But then something unexpected happened— Mo'orea's reefs rebounded, with one of the fastest year-on-year increases in coral cover anywhere in the world. I'd seen evidence of this recovery in our multiple dives with Vega Thurber while filming her sampling work. At one location, the reef was covered with perky little coral heads of uniform size, like a tidy midwestern soybean field. Hurricane be damned— this reef was rebuilding.

So there was a mystery about the corals and conditions in Mo'orea. What allowed these reefs to make such a strong and fast recovery? Vega Thurber was looking for clues in the coral microbiome. And Edmunds's search for ecological answers had him returning year after year. But the local Mo'oreans, who had been watching these reefs for countless generations, had some answers of their own.

On the other side of the island from the Gump Station, on a concrete block foundation, was the drab city hall of the village of Haapiti. Franck Tapatuarai led us inside, explaining that his father had served a term as mayor and proudly noting that he was on his second. He offered us seats in folding chairs in a large, plain municipal room where mismatched floral print curtains kept out the blazing sun.

On the city's laptop projector, Franck showed us a PowerPoint presentation. It wasn't the sales pitch I'd feared. Instead, it was part biography, part philosophy and fishing treatise, something he'd prepared for a pan-Polynesian conference of community leaders. It was detailed and personal. He narrated his way through the slides in weighted, reverent words. He explained that each of the thirty phases of the moon has a different Tahitian name—his father taught him all of them. *'Ore'ore-tåhi* is the moon when the fish

Katrina Munsterman, a graduate student from UC Santa Barbara, samples young corals recently recruited to a hurricane-damaged reef in Mo'orea.

disappear. *Rā'āu-tahi* is when fish run through the passageways of the reef, and it's also when ghosts of the risen dead walk. *Tāne* is another good moon to fish, and it's also a good night to make love or plant sweet potatoes. During each moon the fish behave differently, interacting with the tides surging in and out of the lagoon channel.

The names of the moon and associated fish behaviors are lessons handed down through the generations, and they applied only to the single stretch of reef Franck could see from his house. And now these lessons lived on a thumb drive. The level of detail in his presentation was granular, specific to this one place. At first I wondered why he was so determined to share it with us, but then I realized that he was translating his cultural knowledge into our language. Westerners—scientists especially—have a long tradition of ignoring local expertise. But Franck used the language of clip art, charts, and conference presentations to express his vast mountain of ancestral knowledge.

We emerged blinking from the drab building, armed with a new appreciation for the lunar cycle's role in fishing. Franck checked the moon on his cell phone and cross-referenced it with his grandfathers' lessons, which told him that the fish would be running for deep water at sunset. It was time to prepare.

We headed to a family property across the island's rim road from the ocean and followed Franck into the forest, where he stripped bark from young trees. He'd use the strips throughout the day like natural bungee cords to mend nets and tie them down while fishing, and also to string the catch together for sale along the roadside the next morning. "Nature can help you," he said, his English accented with a thick blend of French and Tahitian as he fashioned his fishing tools from the bush. "But you must love the nature. All the time."

He led us across the road to a palm tree leaning over the water. He told us that his grandfather had planted it. He hacked a few green coconuts from a low-hanging cluster with his machete and then notched holes in them with a pair of quick slices. He passed them to us and Justin and I tipped them back and drank deep. The coconut water was warm, like milk from a living animal, but also clear, substantial, and refreshing.

As the afternoon shadows lengthened, Franck's nephew and ten-year-old son, Houtu, joined us. We loaded Franck's small outboard and shoved it into the water. As we motored out to the reef, Houtu sat on the bow, his legs dangling over the front. Franck watched his son and smiled.

"When I was small, maybe two or three years old, I went with my father in his *va'a* to gather the fish," he said.

Va'a is the Tahitian word for boat, and I sensed a certain power in the emphasis. The Polynesian pronunciation gives the word weight from deep in your chest near the heart. A boat is not just transportation in Polynesia, it is identity. The word is derived from *wangka* in Proto-Austronesian languages and represents one of the most important innovations in ocean navigation: the outrigger canoe. The development of the dugout canoe allowed the ancestors of Polynesians to cross between mainland China and Taiwan as early as 6000 BC. With the addition of an external support, an outrigger, these early seafarers were able to travel to neighboring islands. They next added sails, and even greater distances became possible. The outrigger design eventually evolved into great double-hulled voyaging canoes that opened up the entire Pacific and its scattered constellations of islands.

Polynesians became the greatest maritime voyaging society in the history of the world, achieving unimaginable feats of navigation long before Columbus stumbled across the New World. The word *wangka* evolved into Franck's *va'a* and shares that same meaning and similar pronunciation in Hawaiian. In Maori it's *waka*. Elsewhere in Polynesia it's *vaka*. It's *wongka* in northern Australia and *vahka* in the Rapa Nui language of Easter Island. This one word unites a proud and scattered nation of explorers. And now this *va'a* carried us to the edge of the lagoon and the verge of the great ocean that Franck's ancestors had conquered.

He anchored on the edge of the lagoon near the channel leading to open sea and spent an hour unloading sections of net from the boat and carefully tying them with the bark strips in a giant V in a coral channel to intercept the fish on their run toward the deep water. Once set, he and his nephew patrolled the edges of the net with harpoons to chase off sharks and eels that could easily slice it to ribbons and also to remove the smaller fish that became entangled, waiting patiently for the big fish to arrive as had been promised by the moon and Franck's father.

Just as the sun slipped to the edge of the horizon, they appeared: brilliant blue and red parrotfish, black unicorn fish with their sharp tail spines, spotted groupers, bright triggerfish, yellow goatfish, four-eyed butterfly fish—a kaleidoscope of colors flowing into the channel like Manhattan commuters heading for the subway. Franck dove down and grabbed the fish with his bare hands as they clustered at the tip of the netted V, tossing them up into a floating tub tethered to a rope tied around his waist. It was physical work, like farming, picking fruit, or digging yams. When the tub was filled, he swam it over to the boat and dumped it over the gunwale, where Houtu sorted the fish by species into separate bins.

To witness this river of sea life appear on cue—as it has for generations—is to sense the power of traditional knowledge. It also helps us understand how precarious a tightrope we humans walk. One too many coastal development projects dumping sediment onto the reef, one more pineapple plantation spilling its excess nutrient fertilizer into the lagoon, one degree of temperature warmer, and the corals might bleach on Franck's reef. The spot he's been fishing since childhood would be reduced to a field of slimy rubble. The river of life would dry up and a complex system studied for generations would reach its end.

The bins filled with fish, we motored back to the shore in the darkness, the only light coming from Houtu's flashlight as he lay across the bow and shouted back to his father to steer us away from the surfers paddling back from the reef break we could still hear crashing at the edge of the lagoon. The ragged island peaks looming above us were empty black shapes outlined by starlight.

Since humans first settled Mo'orea more than a thousand years ago, its luxuriant volcanic peaks wrapped in bonnets of cloud and encircled by the lagoon's pale blue aura made it the perfect calendar art image of paradise. The first Polynesian voyagers to settle here were as smitten by its beauty as we are today. To them, the green-clad hillsides promised not a dream vacation but fertile slopes for the taro and breadfruit stock they carried in the twin hulls of their voyaging canoes. There were no endemic snakes or mammals or other predators to prevent their livestock—dogs and pigs—from flourishing. And the lagoon with its coral nursery promised an ample supply of fish and a barrier to protect coastal settlements from the violence of storms and hurricanes.

But such coral lagoons present an intellectual puzzle: some of them encircle volcanic islands like Mo'orea, yet others form atoll rings with no mountainous islands in the middle. Scientists have been considering this discrepancy for a long time. Hiking

in Peru, Charles Darwin came across fossilized sea life—bivalves, shells, and corals—embedded high in the Andes mountains. Geological forces, he reasoned, had lifted the mountains, carrying fossils skyward. So if mountains rose, mightn't they also subside? Later, when he visited the Pacific islands, Darwin hypothesized that the coral lagoons were formed by volcanic mountains that rose from the sea, their very tops forming islands. As they reached their maximum height, the rocky slopes of these islands attracted coral recruits where the cooled basalt rock kissed the sea, the perfect hard substrate for corals to start their construction projects. Then, over millennia, as the islands subsided again, the coral reefs continued to build and form the fringing reef, indicating the outline of the volcanic island at its extremity in the distant past. Subsidence, Darwin theorized, was the key. This meant that one day, high islands like Mo'orea with a large lagoon marking the outline of its maximum shoreline, were slowly sinking and would lose the rest of their peaks below the waters, leaving only the coral ring behind as a ghost of what once was there.

Later in his voyage, as he scaled the mountains of Tahiti, Mo'orea's larger neighbor, he gazed across the channel that separated the two islands. The sight of postcard-perfect Mo'orea nestled in its tidy lagoon affirmed his belief in subsidence. "I was much struck with this fact, when viewing from the heights of Tahiti, the distant island of Eimeo [Mo'orea], standing within smooth water, and encircled by a ring of snow-white breakers," he wrote.

This theory would cause a stir. Some embraced it, including Darwin's mentor, Charles Lyell, who found poetry in Darwin's notion and would write to a friend that coral atolls represented "the last efforts of drowning continents to lift their heads above the water." Others, like the scientists Louis Agassiz and his son Alexander, would devote entire careers to disproving it. It wouldn't be until the 1950s, when navy scientists drilled thousands of feet into a Pacific atoll and found volcanic rock, that Darwin's theory was finally proven.

While Darwin may have figured out the mechanism by which mountains and corals are associated, Franck's Polynesian ancestors had intuited this connection much earlier. Through trial and error, Polynesian settlers had established an effective system of land division and management known as *rahui*. These divisions, similar to the *ahupua'a* system in Hawai'i, stretched from the mountaintops to the deep ocean beyond the reef crest, dividing the island into pie-shaped districts that kept ecosystems functionally intact. Chiefs of these wedges of territory instituted rules on how best to use natural resources, including proper farming techniques and restrictions on fishing. They understood that the resources were finite. Such connectivity was revered, and the tops of the watersheds were sacred, lofty heights where gods dwelt, adding the weight of divinity to the natural systems that sustained the lives of the islanders. The moon-based system that Franck had shared with us fit into that framework. And for centuries, Mo'oreans managed their reefs sustainably in this way.

But then came European contact, and this elegant system was shattered. Along with naturalists like Darwin came outsiders driven not by curiosity but dominion. Missionaries of various faiths brought their religions, which supplanted mountaintop deities, chipping away at the foundations of a culture that had struck a sort of balance with the natural world. Colonizers brought schemes and diseases. The French wrested control from the other colonial powers in the nineteenth century and brought missionaries to begin the work of suppressing and extinguishing the old ways. The connected *rahui* divisions were sliced up into disconnected plots of private property, with foreign people and companies

Waves break across the reef crest on the outer edge of Mo'orea's lagoon, a sight that convinced Darwin his reef theory was correct.

acquiring much of the coastal land. By the 1950s, when France needed a place to test its burgeoning nuclear weapons program at the height of the Cold War, remote atolls in Polynesia were chosen for this dubious honor. The Society Islands were then flooded with workers, civil servants, and others wanting to cash in on the "bomb economy" boom. Nearby islands were blasted to smithereens in the ultimate desecration of a landscape once held sacred.

The colonization continued. Schoolchildren learned the departments of faraway France before they learned the names of other Polynesian islands. They were forbidden to use their own language and share their old stories. Those who dared to speak Tahitian were forced to pick razor grass in the sun until their fingers were swollen and stinging. Danielle, Franck's mother-in-law, told us these details over breakfast. Her French name was evidence of how deep was the push of cultural eradication: even their names were stolen. It is only in the most recent generation, that of Franck's son Houtu, where Polynesians are beginning to reclaim their lost identity.

Given such history, it's easy to understand why Western scientists and resource managers are regarded with skepticism when they try to inform Tahitians how and where to fish. In recent decades, as fish stocks began to decline, a new regime of marine protected areas (MPAs) was introduced with an earnest goal of protecting fish populations. These MPAs were resisted by locals as another form of top-down colonial imposition. What could science tell them that their grandparents couldn't? Despite the best efforts of colonial regimes to squash traditional knowledge, Mo'oreans had been able to pass along their wisdom so that fishers like Franck knew the reef to an astonishing level of detail.

Western scientists are just now beginning to shed the old colonial arrogance, learning that the untapped wealth of Franck's ancestors can be an asset that informs research and management, thanks to the work of Hinano Teavai-Murphy and others like her. The two communities have much to learn from each other. The toughness of these reefs—and their ability to bounce back from disaster—surprised visiting researchers like Pete Edmunds and Rebecca Vega Thurber. Part of the secret to such resilience might lie in the ecology. And part is likely hidden in the mysteries of their microbes. And yet more of the answers are likely hidden in a cultural knowledge that is struggling to endure.

For the rest of the evening and the following day we ate the fish. *Poisson cru* is cubed, raw parrotfish with onions, cucumbers, tomatoes, and coconut milk. *Fafaru* is raw fish soaked in long-fermenting saltwater brine until it takes on a pungency that is off-putting to the uninitiated but a lip-smacking delicacy to Tahitians. *Taioro* is a sweet coconut paste mixed with raw, cubed fish or shellfish. We boiled unicorn fish and ate them with salt and butter, nibbling their meat and skin from the bone like corn on the cob.

But most of the fish were sold. "Fish paid for our house, our car, my school," Franck told us. So we awoke at three in the morning and joined Franck's in-laws, Danielle and Alexandre, as they hung stringers of multihued fish on racks alongside the island's ring road. A dozen fish cost the equivalent of twenty dollars. It was Sunday morning, and epic family meals were planned where fish would be the main course. Sweet voices spilled out of open church doors and Franck's stringers of bright fish sold out even before the last parishioners emerged in their Sunday finest. Men and women bicycled past with bouquets of fresh baguettes in the baskets, leaving the fragrance of baked bread in their wakes.

On the way back for our own meal, we made a diversion to visit the family's *fa'apu*—their farm plot in the highlands. We drove to the end of a dirt track and then hiked up a muddy path in the steaming heat as trees closed in around us. The jungle grew dense and Danielle pointed out plants and flowers. Danielle also told us stories of gods and mortals, of stones and spirits. Through a break in the trees a peak appeared in a halo of mist. It was said that people born within sight of that mountain would grow up to be promiscuous. Another mountain was the domain of hopeless gossips. The people drew their qualities, good and bad, from the land around them. Beside a large stone that squatted next to the path like an altar, Danielle explained that here was where a young god had ridden a lightning bolt down from a nearby peak and bedded a mortal woman with whom he'd been smitten. After a brief and torrid coupling on the stone altar, he disappeared again, leaving her pregnant with a child who would someday be a chief.

I reflected on this tale. I thought of Danielle as a child forced to pick razor grass in the hot sun for speaking the old language that kept these legends alive. Stories are our most precious heirlooms. They are our immortality, our religion, and our wisdom. And like coral reefs, stories can be resilient despite a battery of threats and pressures.

There is so much we can learn from island people, especially now as our planet itself becomes an island with limited resources crowded with eight billion souls and spinning in the dark sea of the universe. For too many years we've come to Polynesia armed with our notions of conquest, with the arrogance of our culture, religions, technology, and science. We came to transform it, enrich ourselves from it, or just to gawk at its opulence in hopes of absorbing some of its spirit.

But what we need to do now is listen. The past still lives, in bits and pieces, through people like Danielle and Franck and someday his son Houtu. There are more than just scientific questions to pose.

There are answers here, too—how the phases of the moon can tell us when to fish and plant yams and make love. Or how to grow a *fa'apu*, a farm that exists in harmony with the natural world. And the connected *rahui* system that describes how everything from the top of the sacred mountains, down through the forests to the coast, across the broad lagoons and the deep sea beyond is all connected. Now more than ever we need a *rahui* system for the whole planet.

"I have so much knowledge," Franck said more than once over the course of the days we spent with him, holding his hands on either side of his head as if struggling to lift a swollen aura. He wasn't bragging about his own wisdom, but rather emphasizing the precious burden with which he'd been entrusted. "From my father. From my grandfather."

What would Franck's grandfather tell us about climate change? The resilient reefs of Mo'orea are now facing their biggest challenge since the Pacific Plate slid over a hot spot in the earth's mantle one million years ago, spawning a volcano that rose from the depths and eventually recruited corals to build their industry on its flanks.

In 2016, not long after Justin and I left Mo'orea with our carpetbag of Franck's stories, there was a modest bleaching event. Then another much more dramatic event in 2019. "It looked like 60 to 70 percent of the corals have died off," Pete Edmunds told me over a video chat. I imagined those rows of perfect little corals I'd seen with Rebecca Vega Thurber. Now many of those hopeful little colonies would be transformed into algae-slimed rock. More bleaching followed in 2020, and Edmunds was eager to return to study the result of these back-to-back events. But COVID had other plans, leaving him stranded in California.

Would Mo'orea's famously fast-rebounding corals finally lose their mojo? They've resisted so much for

Franck's son Houtu helps his father by sorting the fish by color for sale the next morning.

so long. This island's reefs, like its people, are tenacious survivors. There is a striking amount of diversity in the corals there, and diversity is a sign of ecological strength. The reefs have survived colonization and the bomb economy. They've survived supercharged outbreaks of crown-of-thorn starfish and hurricanes. They've so far survived industrial tourism. But it's not just the resilient reefs that have survived and bounced back after years of onslaughts; it's also the cultural connections handed down from Franck's ancestors that have defied occupation, missionary zeal, heavy-handed regulation, and the advent of Western-style private property and capitalism. There are still threads of culture that Franck can trace back through thousands of years of voyaging history to that bold and ancient seafaring nation knit together by the word va'a and shared language, customs, gods, and stories.

One day, hundreds of thousands of years hence, the ragged peaks of Mo'orea will slip below the waters as Darwin had forecast. But if we start to take better care of our island Earth, if we can somehow cure our addiction to fossil fuels and buy time for corals to adapt to climatic change, preventing mass bleaching and acidifying oceans from becoming barriers to the work that corals do, there will still be the ring of an atoll left behind where Mo'orea once was, built by little coral polyps upon the bones of their forebears. And perhaps, if we're very lucky, there will also be fishers like Franck who hear the whispers of their ancestors and who still know the old names of the moon.

Part II

Wonder and Devastation

"If I had to choose the most interesting and important time in all of human history to live, it would be now. As never before, and perhaps as never again, the choices made in the near future will determine mankind's success, or lack of it."

Sylvia Earle, *A Sea Change*

"In the deep glens where they lived, all things were older than man and they hummed of mystery."

Cormac McCarthy, *The Road*

5

Island of the
Super Corals

O'ahu, Hawai'i

AFTER FOLLOWING SCIENTISTS to far corners of the globe, I was heartened by their drive and effort. They scoured the world's reefs looking for clues to coral survival. They shared what they learned with local communities. They produced voluminous reports to guide resource managers and governments.

But I also saw that their data was rarely heeded. And I learned that the process of discovery and publishing was achingly slow. It didn't keep pace with the dire news flooding my news feeds. One report showed that since the 1950s, reefs globally had lost half their ability to feed and sustain people. Another showed that nearly sixty species of hard corals had vanished from Lizard Island's reefs alone. The collapse of these ecosystems was relentless, continuing unabated. I fretted. Wasn't there more I could do? Was there any single person anywhere who could make a difference, light a spark, inspire the level of change we needed?

On Mo'orea, I'd met a researcher named Ruth Gates. She was visiting for the cultural celebration at the Atitia Center. On the veranda of the Gump Station guesthouse, within view of the island's reefs, we had a lovely discussion about coral symbiosis, punctuated by her hearty laughter. She was solidly built with a rugged charisma that drew you in. Within minutes, she felt like an old friend. "If you're ever in Hawai'i," she said nonchalantly, "stop by." A few months later, I would pay a visit to the magical island where she did her work. I had no idea that I'd just met someone who was turning the world of coral research on its head. Here was the spark I'd been seeking.

~

The pier where we caught the launch jutted from a rim of houses stacked on a hillside overlooking the water, windows hungry for a view of Kāne'ohe Bay. The dock was like a portal to another realm, a world of turquoise flats and telltale dark, mottled shapes of

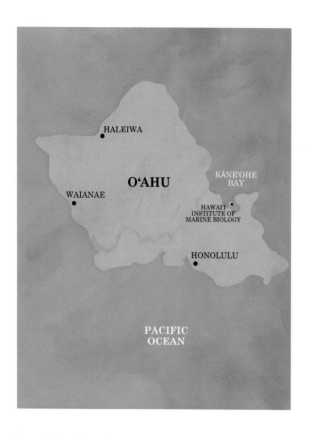

Page 76: Ryan McMinds and
Rebecca Vega Thurber check
the health of corals off the
north shore of O'ahu, Hawai'i.

patch reefs that began at the paved edge of humanity. The crossing would take us to Moku o Lo'e, also
known as Coconut Island, a small and eerily familiar
cluster of palms and buildings in the heart of the bay.

The launch arrived. The ferryman was no grim
Charon but a short, solidly built man with a trim
mustache and a cheerful Hawaiian patois. Even after
we loaded our gear into the boat and cruised toward
the island, my sense of déjà vu lingered. I'd eventually learn that the island was featured in the intro-
ductory sequence for the television series *Gilligan's
Island*. I had gazed upon its swaying palms every
afternoon after school as I knelt on the floor before
the altar of our television.

As the boat eased against the dock next to the
tiny ferry terminal, we unloaded our gear. I'd come
with microbiologist Rebecca Vega Thurber and graduate student Ryan McMinds, who were adding O'ahu
coral microbes to their collection for the Global Coral
Microbiome Project. Cinematographer Darryl Lai and
I were also drawn here to learn about bold, controversial experiments that had gained mythic proportions
and quite a bit of press, along with the intriguing
scientist leading it. I was learning that Ruth Gates, the
affable woman I'd met in Mo'orea, was a rock star in
the world of coral research.

The island and surrounding bay were no strangers to coral reef experimentation. Hemmed in by the
corrugated green luminescence of the Ko'olau Range,
which catches the precipitation on the windward side
of O'ahu and provides abundant rainfall, the entire
region is a garden. The first Polynesian settlers here
transformed the island's pristine landscape by inten-
sively farming it. Villages prospered and populations
surged, and the health of the bay and the health of
its corals declined. The Hawaiians responded to the
pressure they placed on the landscape by innovating.
Using a pie-shaped land-division system that
stretched from mountaintop to ocean, known as

ahupua'a, they kept watersheds intact. They implemented strict land- and water-use regulations, with powerful stewards appointed to enforce them. They introduced terraced farming innovations called *lo'i'kalo* that used systems of berms to improve water quality and prevent sediment and nutrients from running into the bay. Massive fish ponds were also created along the edge of the bay, catching estuarine runoff and raising a supply of fish to feed the exploding population while reducing fishing pressure on the reefs. Humans and corals eventually struck a sort of balance in the bay, and coral cover rebounded.

But then came European contact. The *ahupua'a* system was upended. The land was carved up into disconnected parcels for private property and plantation agriculture. By the 1960s, dredge-and-fill operations, sedimentation, and sewage had fouled the bay's waters and decimated the coral cover so that as little as 5 percent remained.

The tiny island Moku o Lo'e had witnessed it all. By the 1930s the island had been sold and resold. Now dubbed Coconut Island, it spent years as a playground estate, complete with private lagoons; a menagerie of exotic animals; a bowling alley; and a giant, floodlit saltwater pool grand enough to make Jay Gatsby jealous. When the island's last private owners agreed to lease a corner to the University of Hawai'i free of charge to serve as a research center, the Hawai'i Institute of Marine Biology (HIMB) was born.

Having the institute located in the middle of the bay to study and monitor the unfolding pressures helped lead to a rebound, which unsurprisingly mirrors what the first Hawaiians had figured out generations ago. Sewage no longer freely flows into the bay. Fishing is more closely managed than in the recent past. The island is also home to a boat called the Super Sucker, which uses four-inch hoses to vacuum up invasive algae that smother the corals.

After the Super Sucker hoovers up a section of reef, native urchins are deployed as bioremediation while the algae is bagged and shipped to farmers for use as fertilizer. Slowly, the reefs have begun to recover. Coral cover has returned to 65 percent of historic levels.

Enter climate change.

In 1996, the bay's corals experienced their first recorded mass bleaching event. A second event followed in 2014. Now all signs point to bleaching becoming a regular phenomenon, tracking what has been happening elsewhere in the Pacific.

After large human populations lived alongside the corals of Kāne'ohe Bay for a millennium, the corals seem to have become tougher. They have adapted, surviving conditions that would kill corals elsewhere. And humans have learned, more than once, to change their own behavior to lessen the pressure on reef ecosystems.

But now, with global forces driving warming and bleaching that is outpacing corals' ability to adapt, it may be time for a more radical intervention.

Some experiments taking place at HIMB, the sprawling complex on the southern end of Moku o Lo'e, were causing a stir. Depending on who you spoke with, the research from the Gates Coral Lab was either bold, dangerous, ingenious, or pure folly. In the bubbling tanks and aquariums scattered around the compound, scientists were rumored to be working on what were breathlessly called "super corals" by the press. Was this research the salvation of reefs? Or was it dangerous tinkering with the basic systems of life? The truth, it turns out, was a lot more complicated.

Hollie Putnam, a postdoctoral scholar and our guide into the coral breeding facilities, led us into a low, nondescript building in the shadow of the main administration offices. Inside we found rows of aquariums stacked from the floor to the ceiling under bright fluorescent lighting, each tank containing coral fragments, tubes, bubblers, wires, and solenoid switches that clicked on and off. At the head of the long room was a control panel with dials and knobs, plus a computer monitor with squiggling lines and numbers. There was a sound of hissing and bubbling, and wandering undergraduates with clipboards purposefully squinted through the glass at small colonies, captive in their clear encasements.

Hollie explained the experiment: they were exposing brooding corals—a kind of coral that hosts its fertilized gametes inside of it—to higher levels of carbon dioxide. Their test species, *Pocillopora damicornis*, more commonly called "cauliflower corals" because of their perfect bouquet-shaped heads, are hearty corals you often find colonizing slimy algal rock on Hawaiian reefs where other species struggle.

What they've learned from these experiments is astonishing. And also hopeful. Putnam told us that from their first experiments in 2011 onward, they found that when they exposed the adults to higher temperature or acidity during brooding period, their offspring actually performed better when they were reexposed to those same stressful conditions.

As I studied the knobby heads of the expectant coral parents, I thought how we humans sometimes perform similar experiments on ourselves, playing Mozart on speakers next to an expecting mother's swollen belly hoping to stimulate a fetal brain (and maybe tastes) in utero so that one day the child might pick up the violin or develop musical or mathematical abilities. Putnam likened the conditioning to a bad sunburn versus a suntan. The first exposure to extreme temperatures and sunlight causes skin to burn, blister, and peel. But ensuing exposures darken our skin without the stress of burning. Corals seem to be able to adapt to bleaching temperatures or high

levels of carbon dioxide in a similar way. And it appears that they can pass such resilience along to future generations.

The Gates Coral Lab was working to strengthen this ability to adapt even further by adding genetic research to the mix. By looking at what genes are expressed in these changing conditions, and analyzing the genetics of the corals that show the most promise for adaptation, the team hoped to identify and cross-breed the strongest corals, eventually planting them in the wild.

This was the heart of the controversial plan to develop "super corals" that might fare better in an ocean already experiencing higher temperatures and increased acidity. Tinkering with genetics can be concerning, however. Some fear that releasing genetically manipulated corals into the wild might have unintended, horror-film consequences, disastrous outcomes like the famous folly of introducing poisonous cane toads in Australia to feed on sugarcane pests, a bioremediation experiment in the 1930s that devastated local fauna. Hawai'i has had its share of invasive species—introduced intentionally or by accident—and this has helped make the archipelago the extinction capital of the world. In Hawai'i, the Gates Lab researchers were discouraged from even applying for permits to introduce these corals, hardened through their genetic work, onto local reefs.

But this type of crossbreeding is actually more mundane than movie monsters suggest, more akin to the hybridization that we have been performing for centuries. Putnam put it to me in this way: "So plants, so corn, so dogs...they're selectively bred for certain traits. Here we're thinking about the same thing. This has been done for thousands of years...selective breeding...but selecting for traits of resilience in the face of increase in temperature and lower pH and the stressors that are impacting these reefs."

Though this genetic work is fascinating discovery science about corals, much of the controversy around super-coral research comes from the scientific community. Critics fault the concept for its inability to scale up to an area the size of the Great Barrier Reef. Or that helping to engineer a few hearty varieties will reduce biodiversity. Others feel that there just isn't enough time for this type of manipulation. Some suggest it offers a false hope and even a fig leaf to fossil-fuel companies and other corporate polluters that might finance fanciful coral research projects as a way of greenwashing their own role in causing climate change.

But Putnam rejected such criticism. "We can't just stand by and watch," she said as she led us out onto a broad, concrete patio filled with round vats with solenoids and filters, larger versions of the small aquariums inside. Like many who study corals, Putnam's fascination with these animals stems from an epiphanic experience. A native Minnesotan studying marine sciences in the upper Midwest, she joined a research trip to Belize. She still recalled her first dive in a thicket of branching *Acropora* corals and described floating through the surge of waves as walking through a beautiful cathedral.

Hollie thrust a pH meter into the first large, green tank to check readings of acidity. She wasn't daunted by all of the criticism. She belonged to a new generation of scientists who came of age watching the mass bleaching crises unfold and whose careers have been defined by the search for solutions. This is what attracted her to the Gates Coral Lab, bringing her to this little island of wonders in the middle of a battered but still resilient reef. And living on Kāne'ohe Bay makes her work even more personal.

"I get up every morning and I look out my window, and I can see the reef," she told us. "It's a privilege. And I can also view the changes. I can see the bleaching happening."

A live *Pocillopora damicornis* magnified by the Hawai'i Institute of Marine Biology's confocal microscope and illuminated by ultraviolet light.

Like many tropical research stations, the Hawai'i Institute of Marine Biology has the atmosphere of a summer camp, but for erudite adults. There are small apartments near the docks with the ambiance of a 1960s motel. Our flat came with a wicked, foot-long centipede guarding the door. It was comfortable enough, though not luxurious. The open-air kitchen was a few hundred yards away, built on an old deck overlooking what I'd come to call the Gatsby Pool, a saltwater swimming lagoon that welcomed the occasional hammerhead through the sluiceway.

Around the island there are coves, beaches, and lagoons where you can slip into the water for a close-up view of the corals on the fringing reef. Many of the colonies you find are tagged for experiments. There's a small headland where you can scan the channel for cruising sharks under waving palms. There are enough tranquil corners that you can almost imagine yourself one of the castaways from *Gilligan's Island*.

But a short ramble across the remains of the former estate brings you to the main building with modern labs, and in a clinical corner there is another innovation that the Gates Lab has brought to the field of coral research. This is where Amy Eggers operates the lab's scanning confocal microscope. It has a unique configuration, tuned to scan live animals and specifically to make images of tiny coral polyps and their tinier algal partners.

Eggers showed us spectacular images on a monitor: coral polyps blown up to enormous size and shaded green by a combination of ultraviolet and halogen light. Inside the green tissue we saw tiny red dots. These were the individual zooxanthellae, normally invisible to the naked eye but in aggregate providing corals with their color.

Because the microscope scans living corals, it can capture a time series, a movie of how a coral waves its tentacles, how it feeds, and how the tiny plant cells circulate around in its tissue. The researchers can also subject the corals to stress, increasing temperature and acidity, and watch how the corals and their algae partners respond.

Eggers played a time-lapse series of a stressed coral as it slowly lost its color. The tiny red dots fled their host until the coral was pale white. The sad drama was stunning. The idea of an incrementally warming planet, despite the reams of documentation and data, is still abstract. Seeing a bleached reef makes it less so. But there is no more visceral and intense way to watch the consequences of climate change than viewing these images. What Eggers loved most about this powerful microscope was the way it could bring corals alive to the public.

If Moku o Lo'e, with its labs and tanks, gadgets, brilliant microscopic images, cruising hammerheads, and halo of scrappy reefs was a sort of circus of coral experimentation, then Ruth Gates was the ringmaster. She had reached celebrity status uncommon for a scientist. Darryl and I had fretted over gaining an audience for our interview. We were visiting during a busy time. The International Coral Reef Symposium, the world's premier gathering of coral researchers that takes place only once every four years, was underway in nearby Honolulu. Gates was president of that organization as well as keynote speaker. Writers cruised the island like the sharks. Articles sprang up in leading publications. Other film crews were also prowling the island. But despite everything, Gates cleared two hours for us on her schedule.

We filmed the interview in her sparse office on the upper floor of the research station. It projected a sense of efficiency and organization, the only adornments a lovely white bouquet of a coral skeleton that she'd rescued from a corner of the library and an abstract painting of brilliant and calming marine hues made by her wife, Robin, a visual artist.

Gates's trademark full-bodied laugh transformed her office into a comfortable space for our conversation. I began by asking her about the buzz surrounding her work and the controversy over "super corals." Was it revolutionary? Was it dangerous? Was it overhyped?

"We've never tried to do this before in coral reef systems—to take the strongest members and breed them. It's called selective breeding. It's not rocket science," she shrugged.

I asked her about the criticism that this distracts from the more important issue of mitigating climate change. She explained that if we have stronger offspring, we can use those corals to stabilize coral reefs that have been hit by, say, a very severe bleaching event, while we mitigate the larger driving forces that are causing the decline—fossil-fuel burning. "This might help give nature a leg up to get through this," she said, "to pick up the ball and run with it."

Gates was an optimist, and what gave her hope was not just the adaptability of the systems she has been studying but what our own species can do to help. "I am incredibly stimulated by where we are. People say, 'Don't you get depressed by it?' And the context is depressing. But you can either lay down and die or say this is a challenge that needs to be solved. It's a big problem, but we have enormous capacity with people. People are astonishingly creative."

This attitude separated her from doubters. For one group of scientists, humans are the root cause of all problems. But for Gates, we are also the ultimate solution.

"Can a lab like my own do it alone? Absolutely not. Can we generate information that can be distributed to many people who start doing the same thing in their place, engendering a sense of ownership of their own natural resources? Yeah, I think we can do that. I'm thrilled by that thought. Because it's not paralyzing."

She understood people. Whether it was the donors who'd funded the microscope we'd seen, a press hungry for a scoop, or students seeking inspiration amid a flood of grim data and dire news, she offered a way forward. She was fascinated by corals. But she was motivated by people, believing that we're preserving corals for humans; that they serve us, feed us, protect us, and are an economic driver that supports our species. She placed humans, not nature, at the center of the universe.

But I wanted to know if they could scale up this process. Could we outplant enough selectively bred corals to save a reef?

"I'm not interested in saving one reef here or one reef there, I'm interested in building a movement of people around the world, all working in concert to breed corals and save reefs in their place on the globe," she said. Then she paused and looked out the window. "I feel so much more comfortable in my soul, about trying to act myself."

Speaking with Ruth Gates made it easy to understand her celebrity. She was a gifted orator. She learned your name quickly and used it as if you were an old friend. She didn't abandon anyone in her orbit, whether it was a student or Darryl behind the camera.

She could motivate entire audiences. And while she dismissed this gift as a product of her British boarding school accent, she could have delivered crackling halftime remarks to convince even the most overmatched team they had a shot at winning the game. But digging back into Gates's history, there is little to suggest she would become the world's most recognizable coral scientist.

She was born in Cyprus. Her father was a hard-drinking, swashbuckling British diplomat and

Moku o Lo'e, also known as
Coconut Island, houses the
Hawai'i Institute of Marine
Biology. In its former life it
was a playground for the rich
and location of the television
series *Gilligan's Island*.

intelligence officer whose frequent postings left her to fill her time with sports and Jacques Cousteau films, sparking her curiosity in the natural world and marine ecology.

At university, she seemed bent on following in her father's rowdy footsteps. She was drawn to sports and drinking, not deep intellectual pursuits. Barbara Brown, then a charismatic young researcher at the University of Newcastle who would become a lifelong mentor, told me that early in her college career, Gates was "sort of a wild thing."

But it was a lecture by Brown that hooked Gates. She couldn't believe that any plant could live inside an animal cell. This intellectual lightning bolt, the puzzling blend of plant and animal, helped change her trajectory. Then came the death of her father, hastened by alcohol. She became more serious about research. And hints of her power as a communicator and advocate for bold action began to emerge. Such enthusiasm won her two years of funding from a foundation to research coral bleaching at Discovery Bay in Jamaica, where she delved into the mysteries of bleaching. Her time there coincided with a major bleaching event in 1987, allowing her to examine the troubling phenomenon *in situ*. This led to a ground-breaking paper that would put her among the first researchers to tie coral bleaching to warmer water. While in Jamaica she also visited the Rio Bueno Wall, a great submerged cliff with massive corals growing out of its side, and witnessed firsthand how runoff from a development project clouded the wall. The resulting sediments destroyed the reef in less than two weeks.

After Jamaica and formative experiences in that crucible of coral research, Gates joined another cohort of up-and-coming researchers where she spent a dozen years as a postdoctoral scholar under the tutelage of another pioneering researcher, Len Muscatine, an expert on symbiosis, that mysterious process that had first attracted Gates to the field. For scientists, a "postdoc" can be an uncertain time, surviving from appointment to appointment searching for a permanent home and a lab of one's own. But at UCLA, Gates delved into molecular genetics, building skills and insight that would directly lead to her assisted evolution projects.

In 2003, Ruth finally established her own lab at the University of Hawai'i, where she would work to redefine the symbiotic landscape and the roles of microbes in the coral holobiont. This was deep science. Egghead stuff. But buried within the lab administrator she'd become was still the boisterous athlete, the same idealistic warrior shocked by the devastation she'd seen in Jamaica that had been wrought by human shortsightedness. She couldn't shake the sense that she had to do more than simply explore intellectual puzzles. By the late 2000s she found herself stagnating, following a conventional scientific routine, writing papers, taking on graduate students, and dodging teaching responsibilities so she could hide in discovery science.

And then in 2010 she took a sabbatical, spending a year in Santa Barbara at a research institute dedicated to solution-based science. By the age of forty-eight, she'd crossed the likely midpoint of life, that place where we all begin to call into question the grand existential themes. Why am I here? Where does my path lead? She realized that the young iconoclast had been subsumed into an arcane system of research and discovery and publishing. The connection between what she was doing and what she'd seen happen in Jamaica was now a yawning gulf.

She reflected on a trite statement that she often included at the end her grant applications, the kind of thing most scientists copy and paste without so much as an afterthought: "And this work is directly relevant to the conservation and management of coral reefs because…" the refrain began. She realized how hollow those words rang. It was an idealistic fig leaf used to secure one more grant, to run one more set of experiments, but without ever changing the trajectory of collapsing reefs.

Realizing the shortfalls—her own as well as those of the entire research enterprise—she decided to change. Inspired by her new perspective, she decided to act. She convened a conversation with scientists and conservationists and they spitballed a list of eight projects that could have a real impact on saving reefs. As you might guess, Ruth Gates—the athlete, a double black belt in karate, the former college wild child turned pioneering researcher—was attracted to the most audacious and riskiest project on that list: assisted evolution.

This epiphany rekindled Gates's fighting spirit, and the years that followed were a whirlwind as the pieces of her career, her personal life, and her overriding ambition to make a difference began to fuse, resulting in unexpected celebrity.

In 2013 she received a $10,000 prize from the Paul G. Allen Family Foundation for a proposal, coauthored with Madeleine van Oppen of the Australian Institute of Marine Biology, that suggested adaptive evolution as a solution to addressing ocean acidification. The pair eventually received a $4 million grant to pursue the concept, launching a flurry of experiments, including those we'd seen on Moku o Lo'e.

In 2014, Gates met her wife, artist Robin Burton-Gates. She became the first woman to serve as president of the International Coral Reef Symposium, the premier organization in her field, which had been cofounded in 1980 by her old mentor Barbara Brown. The following year, she was selected to lead the entirety of the Hawai'i Institute of Marine Biology, with Brown serving as a reference. Channeling the same confidence and vision that had secured the funding of her graduate research in Jamaica, Gates launched a wave of renovations to the facilities at HIMB, including the confocal microscope that had produced the stunning visuals Amy Eggers shared with us.

Gates's reputation soared. The press came calling. Reporters, writers, and indie filmmakers flocked to Coconut Island, and she was gracious to all of us. She hadn't asked for fame, but she recognized her innate gift for evangelizing the plight of stony corals and the imperative to mobilize the broad research front required to save them.

Sometimes her exposure attracted criticism, as when she spoke at the Aspen Ideas Institute and the United Nations. As the term "super coral" began to take on a Frankenstein connotation, she plunged forward undeterred. She gave a World Wildlife Fund lecture tackling her critics head on. "It's my favorite thing to deal with," she said with relish in a video of the talk. Then she systematically addressed every critique. Can humans change the trajectory of corals? "I say yes," she said, "Because I think people can do anything."

This was what defined her. It's what made people like her. She loved corals, but she loved people more. Her affection and belief in her fellow humans was completely genuine.

So with her star on the rise and her time in demand, her research charged forward, managed by a team of idealistic young acolytes. She was beginning to reach the pinnacle of her profession. She broke gender barriers. She assembled a team at HIMB of unprecedented diversity. She fused academics with advocacy in a manner that some found refreshing and others saw as dangerous. She inspired a new generation of coral researchers for whom solutions-based research was an imperative, not an add-on. She was making coral science exciting.

Then the exuberant and unstoppable Ruth Gates, who had traveled the world speaking about the plight of corals and come home to pommel the practice bag in a karate studio she cofounded, began to show signs of wear and tear. Her colleagues began to think that the strain was too much. At a conservation meeting hosted at HIMB, her lab's project manager, Kira Hughes, spotted her in a room by herself. Hughes asked her if she was okay, and Gates insisted she was fine. But Hughes was persistent. She could tell that something was wrong. Gates finally admitted she was experiencing frequent migraines.

Shortly after that, Gates confided in a few members of her team that she'd been diagnosed with brain cancer, and in October of 2018 she died in surgery from complications with diverticulitis. She was fifty-six.

As Pete Edmunds told me, "We lost the most capable, most charismatic, most accomplished spokesperson for reef biology of this generation. And you can only dream and weep at what we lost. I think in the remaining twenty years of Ruth's career she could have changed the coral world and the broader world in so many ways. And so it's just hard to come to terms with the tragedy of that loss."

Shortly before she died, Gates sent an email to Barbara Brown in which she pensively reflected on her career and accomplishments. Perhaps her legendary optimism was beginning to wear thin. She admitted that, in a field where discovery, publication, and intellectual prowess were prized above all else, her greatest strength was something for which she hadn't been trained. She wrote, "I stepped back from everything at the moment. And in thinking about what my unique skills are, I think it is in the arenas of science communication, the development of teams, and fund-raising." Her greatest gifts weren't driven by her intellect. They were driven by her heart.

There's a moment six minutes and twenty-one seconds into my second interview with Ruth Gates when she laughs. She was teasing cinematographer Darryl Lai for taking an excruciatingly long time to set up the two-camera shot. You wouldn't know how busy she was, hosting a global conference, her research station flooded with scientists from around the world on top of an already bustling cohort of students, postdocs, faculty, and researchers.

"That's an interesting shot," she told Darryl, seeing her face in his monitor. "Does it look good... will it ever look good?" And then burst out with her wicked belly laugh. It was her hallmark, a full-throated and mischievous howl at the wonder of life. Now that she's gone, I often go back to that point in the recording and play it over when I need a dose of inspiration or a few tears.

I knew Gates for a matter of six or so hours over the course of two interviews and a few conversations on two different tropical islands in 2016. But I still feel as if I've known her all my life. And I'm not the only one. I've met a lot of people who knew her. Many spent less time with her than I did, and all of them commented on a sense of familiarity and connection that she exuded, leaving the encounter feeling they'd met a lifelong friend. This was her gift. She liked to joke that it was her proper English accent that gave her credibility, and her ability to explain science in simple terms and unabashedly pitch big ideas. But ultimately it was her laugh that won you over.

My biggest fear following the news of Gates's death was that this movement she had helped to spark might never fully materialize. That her flame would fizzle. How would her lab continue without her larger-than-life personality? Would the audacious scheme of assisted evolution fade without its most charismatic proponent?

Kira Hughes told me of attending the Reef Futures Conference in Florida in 2018 shortly after Gates's death. Hughes discovered at that meeting that many people around the world were already working on their own variations of assisted evolution projects. The movement that Gates had hoped to inspire was already underway. The Gates Coral Lab still exists. The team has had to split her leadership role into two parts, with coral ecologist Crawford Drury overseeing research while Hughes handles grant writing, outreach, and communication. Gates's audacious vision marches forward.

In Hawai'i, the lab has recently been funded to outplant corals in three sites. The lab also received a second round of funding from the Paul G. Allen Family Foundation. They are working with partners on restoration and resilience projects from University of Hawai'i engineers, airports, military bases, local Hawaiian communities, canoe clubs, and state agencies.

And Gates's influence has spread far beyond the lab. High school students who heard her speak to their classes are now pursuing higher degrees at HIMB. I've since met young students and researchers from Florida to Arizona who told me they chose marine biology because they heard Gates speak or saw her in a film.

Jennifer Koss, who directs the Coral Reef Conservation Program at NOAA, knew Gates well, and after her death made a passion project out of establishing a coral restoration grant named in her honor. In its first year, the grant awarded funds to projects in Florida, Hawai'i, and the Mariana Islands in the western Pacific. Madeleine van Oppen is continuing assisted evolution work in Australia in concert with the Gates Coral Lab. Florida is fast becoming a hub of restoration research inspired by her work from Tampa to Miami and down the length of the Keys. In the Bahamas, a company called Coral Vita developed a business plan around a private, for-profit venture to restore reefs using the technology and raised large amounts of investment funds.

A happy, healthy *Pocillopora damicornis* coral enlarged under a confocal microsope large enough to see the tiny algal symbionts that are invisible to the naked eye.

nology and raised large amounts of investment funds.

Some of these projects will fail. Disasters, both natural and man-made, will continue to devastate reefs around the world. But where only despair existed in the past, Gates lit the spark. That spark has ignited a brush fire that is circling the globe. Even her death couldn't extinguish it.

"I see a world in ten years," I remember Gates telling me, "where thousands have joined in a mission of stabilizing and building back reefs with corals that can withstand the changes that are coming."

Given all the criticisms that I had heard, plus the drumbeat of dire news, the back-to-back global bleaching events and the intractability of climate policy, I still harbored doubts.

"Now, is that lofty?" she concluded. "Yes! Should you have a big dream? Abso-bloody-lutely!" Her bright smile crackled like lightning.

And with that I saw a glimpse, if only for a moment, of the promise and potential that exist within all of us.

6

Ex Situ

Moloko Reef, Oregon

I PEERED THROUGH THE WINDOWS of Moloko, a bar in Portland, Oregon's gentrified North Mississippi neighborhood. Too many people search in vain for hope from a bar stool, and given the dire prognosis for the world's coral reefs this was either a dangerous or inevitable place for my quest to lead. It was not yet open, but I saw movement inside, behind the shadows and upended bar stools. The neon tubes were cool and dormant. Bottles lined the shelves behind the bar. But this isn't what drew my attention. It was the large, glittering tanks filled with darting fish and the pulsing neon of fluorescent corals.

A sign next to the locked door offered insight: "Portland's Only Coral Reef Cocktail Lounge." It read like a brochure for a dive resort: "Look closer...the creatures of coral reefs come in every shape, size, and color. The seafloor is a hive of tiny crustaceans, worms, mollusks, and tentacled beasts—all of which you'll find here, in the Moloko Reef."

I rapped on the window and a man who'd been standing on the bar hunched over a 200-gallon tank pulled his arm out of the entrails of the filtration system and jumped down to unlock the door. This was the owner, Christian Fitzpatrick. He wiped his arm on a towel and shook my hand. He wore a plain white T-shirt and studious glasses. He seemed more like a researcher than a nightclub owner. Maybe that's because walking into Moloko feels like entering a coral lab. The bar top was strewn with tools of the trade: pliers, a Dremel cutter, and plastic containers with racks of coral fragments glued to cement plugs. A hatch in the bar's floor led to a cellar that whirred with the sound of pumps.

Moloko opened in 2006, back when the storefronts on North Mississippi Avenue were largely vacant and rent for the space was five hundred dollars a month. Now the street was lined with posh boutiques and eateries. Christian named the club *Moloko*, Russian for "milk," in homage to its slang usage in the novel *A Clockwork Orange*. He installed the first aquarium as an adornment because he wanted a "cool" water feature.

What had started as a whim evolved into an obsession, and years later it wasn't the bar that was the reason for the aquariums but the other way around. As the nightclub business took its toll on Christian, the aquariums gave him a reason to come in every day. When I met him, he was spending up to forty hours a week maintaining them.

Christian became an indoor naturalist and Moloko was his Galapagos. Unlike Darwin, though, he had the ability to control his environment: maybe two of the fish weren't compatible, or a certain crab had grown aggressive and was munching on the coral. Were two corals starting a slow-motion turf war by sending out threads of their stinging nemato- cysts to attack their neighbors? Should one of the colonies be moved? In the wild, human activity is destroying reefs. But within the walls of Moloko, the godlike human hand engineers the subtle corrections that keep everything in balance. One false step—a failed pump, a misplaced decimal in a chemical addition, or the introduction of a diseased fish—can wreak havoc on a habitat. Christian had a major disaster early on when a troupe of captive-bred clown fish introduced without a proper quarantine brought along bacteria that spread to all of his interconnected tanks, wiping out the fish. He bought off-the-shelf remedies, but then these potions killed some of the corals. A shadow eclipsed Christian's face as he recalled those events. "It was a dark time," he said.

Most corals survived, but he was filled with guilt over the lost fish. It piqued his sense of responsibility and drove him to become a more careful aquarist. He picked up Bob Fenner's bible on tank steward- ship, *The Conscientious Marine Aquarist*, which Fitzpatrick credits with opening his eyes to the ethical aspects of this hobby. He spoke of the author as a sort of prophet. "I met him once when he came to talk to our reef club," he mused. "I actually got to shake his hand."

When I reflect on the massive experiment we're currently conducting on the world's wild reefs, the metaphor for what is happening in the closed systems of Moloko is sobering. But also somehow hopeful. After witnessing Christian's passion for the life within his tanks and his careful stewardship, it was not a great leap to imagine that humanity at large might feel the same moral conviction to protect our global reefs after our repeated screwups. Maybe, like him, we will collectively pause, take stock, and vow to do better.

Christian Fitzpatrick is just one of thousands of obsessive coral hobbyists around the world, each a master of the high-wire act of balancing chemistry and biology to keep coral ecosystems alive *ex situ*. I wondered: Can these people become ambassadors for reef ecosystems? Can their scientific knowledge and engineering prowess be used to address threats that wild reefs face? As I stared into a Moloko tank featuring the busts of Artemis, Apollo, and Hermes encrusted with corals, my optimism surged. Apollo sported a bristly fingered coral that gave him a ragged, Don King hairstyle. Here was a fusion of art, wonder, and human ingenuity.

Christian next demonstrated the process of "fragging." This obscene-sounding term describes a method of taking one healthy coral colony and divid- ing it into multiple parts to asexually produce clones. On the bar in front of one tank there was a dish fea- turing a piece of mounding coral. Christian plucked the fragment out. He used the spinning disc of the Dremel to slice through the soft tissue and into the hard aragonite skeleton as easily as if it were butter, sending up a puff of powder. He then picked up a cement plug and glued the new fragment on, drop- ping it into a rack in the tank. What was one coral

colony became two. The process had taken about fifteen seconds.

Hobbyists grow their collections by fragging corals. There are events known as "frag swaps" where aquarists can trade species without having to pay the steep prices of shops or online retailers. Rare corals in the hobby can fetch hundreds of dollars for a piece the size of your thumbnail, though most seem to be around twenty bucks.

As Christian arranged the new coral fragments in his tank, I asked him about wild reefs and climate change and how that relates to his hobby. "It helps me understand it better," he said. "But the way I feel about it comes more from a political deep feeling." He's seen plenty of climate change denial on the reef tank forums he scans online for advice—even among

Page 90: The author's reef tank one year into a coral-growing experiment is a thriving habitat and home to a captive-bred clownfish named Franck.

Above: Christian Fitzpatrick spends up to forty hours a week maintaining the extensive collection of tanks in Moloko.

people who've lost corals due to accidentally driving up the acidity in their tanks. Before I left the bar, Christian showed me the largest and most impressive tank. "It's weird to think someday this might be something that can only exist in this way," he said. I felt an involuntary shudder. As lovely as the display was, I didn't want to consider the likely possibility the world's last reef might be in a tank.

I didn't expect to find any answers when I first entered Moloko. But neither had I expected to find so many new questions. And as long as there are more unanswered questions, there is still room for hope.

After Moloko, I wondered where I should search next. It didn't take me long to decide that I should try to contact Bob Fenner, the man who'd written the bible on aquarium stewardship. It wasn't difficult to track him down. After wandering through a few narrow internet side streets and into the back alleys of reef-tank-hobby bulletin boards, I found his email address with disappointing ease. I'd expected at least a few hurdles on a trip to visit the guru on the mountain-top. It would make for a better story. I became even more cautious when I dropped him a note and he responded within minutes. He said he'd be happy to meet, and that I should look him up if I was ever in San Diego.

A few months later I was in Southern California filming at an oceanography conference with my coproducer, Saskia Madlener. I dropped another email and asked Bob if he'd meet for dinner. Within minutes, he'd shot back a response, suggesting we meet at the Brigantine in La Mesa, a sprawling, old-school suburban seafood palace festooned with nautical nicknacks.

The place was packed and Bob showed up late, suddenly appearing table-side. He was a small, squarely built fellow. Maybe it was the Captain Ahab

decor around us, but with his wavy gray hair pulled back in a nub of a ponytail, plus an unplaceable accent, he had the bearing of a sailor just arrived from a far-flung port. He bowed and presented us with his business card with both hands before squeezing into the booth alongside Saskia.

Bob told us he'd acquired his speech and mannerisms in Japan and the Philippines. He'd been a navy brat, and his early access to coral seas ignited his lifelong passion. He'd worked in all levels of the aquarium trade, taught college courses on biology, and written extensively on the business and science of ornamental fish. His fountain of chatter, peppered with scientific terms, flowed easily, all the more enjoyable for his smirks, winks, and eccentric mannerisms. At times he clasped his hands together and leaned forward, as if sharing a secret. Saskia is a marine scientist, so she could follow his stories better than I as he dropped taxa of fish and invertebrates into his monologues with such regularity that at first it seemed like an affectation, but after an hour I realized this is just how he saw the world. He cited papers and scientists and history and policy. And he generously pretended as if I understood most of what he said.

Bob referenced everything from Pliny the Elder to the latest Netflix documentary about cartels controlling the avocado trade in Mexico. He paused occasionally, carving out space for a question or two. I asked about the ornamental fish and coral trade's impact on wild reefs. He said that it could be good or bad. Collecting fish for the trade, or practicing coral mariculture—growing coral fragments *in situ*—can encourage communities to adopt ecologically sustainable practices. "People are far more given to treasure the reefs if they can identify them with the pursuit of their livelihood," he said. Sometimes people turn to destructive or unscrupulous practices like dynamite fishing out of desperation if they lose the ability to subsist through the ornamental trade. And some collectors used cyanide to stun fish for the trade.

I asked his opinion on the solution for a sustainable aquarium hobby. He said he believed in the power of market forces and had a ranking system for suppliers and collectors in the trade: He only dealt with "A-players." The others, he said, should be driven out of the business. I asked if hobbyists and the aquarium trade could collaborate with the academic community on conservation efforts. He was less optimistic about this.

"There's no Venn diagram between the three, and to me, that's a great shame," he said. "I'm counting on you to erase those lines." He winked and laughed. I felt like he was giving me an assignment. I asked if people in the trade were concerned about climate change, bleaching, and destruction of wild reefs. He assured me that all of the A-players were absolutely concerned about the state of the reefs.

Bob painted a swashbuckling portrait of his career in the trade in far-flung locations. He told us of finding new species, of small subsistence collectors struggling to feed their families, about innovative operators pioneering new coral restoration technology. He invited me to the next industry conference and offered to introduce me to some of his contacts from around the world.

Afterward, I mapped out our conversations on note cards. I drew up an itinerary that included visits to some of the "A-players" in far-flung locations and sketched that Venn diagram showing hobbyists, the ornamental trade, and university researchers. Somewhere in the world, they must overlap.

Researchers estimate that up to thirty million fish of 2,300 different species are shipped out of the tropics every year, most winding up in tanks in the West.

While Bob Fenner's bible claimed that marine aquarists could become ambassadors for ocean conservation, how sustainable was this level of wildlife extraction? I reached out to an expert to help me understand the numbers.

Andrew Ryne, a marine biologist at Roger Williams University in Rhode Island, is a data-driven wildlife detective. He helmed a prizewinning project developing software to keep tabs on the global market in a range of endangered species, but he's especially knowledgeable about ornamental fish. If you know the numbers, you can hold an industry accountable.

I called and asked him if the ornamental fish industry was a part of the problem in global reef destruction. He told me that it is a small biomass trade, and that the real issue was climate. The trade had a negligible impact. So if the ornamental trade wasn't a major culprit in reef destruction, could it actually help reefs, incentivizing poor communities to prize the health of their local reefs? Ryne told me that many of the fish species collected are especially fecund, able to quickly rebuild their populations, offsetting collection for the trade and propping up local economies. As long as it was not destructive in its nature of harvest, and wasn't overharvested, then it could provide a lot of income. I also wanted to know about harvesting wild corals. Does the trade harm reefs in that way?

"There's a fraction of illegal corals in the trade," Ryne told me, "and they sell for thousands of dollars so there are not many of them. And they're probably not necessarily threatened in the wild." Ryne thought coral mariculture—farming corals *in situ*—could actually help incentivize habitat preservation. The live coral trade offered opportunities for coral reef ecosystem conservation and sustainable economic benefits to coastal communities. I asked him if he shared Bob Fenner's belief that the aquarium hobby can spur a mass movement in coral reef advocacy. "There's good data that people care about things they know about," he said, noting that it was not just the private aquariums that mattered. Large nonprofit aquariums were also part of the trade. Public aquariums educated millions of people every year, and many people's literacy came from their aquariums at home.

Another benefit of the aquarium trade comes in the form of technology. The industry's innovations spill over into the cash-strapped research enterprise. "There's a multibillion dollar industry out there that people are developing new technology to make money on, and that's one way you get technology into the system," Ryne said. I asked if all this meant that the aquarium trade could be a force to help turn the tide in reef destruction. But he dashed my hopes, pointing out that a lot of people in the trade are climate deniers who don't admit the impacts of climate change even though they know full well what increased temperatures and acidity will do in their own tanks. "What I do is ask them just to put their tank in those conditions for a couple of weeks and then just report back how well those corals are doing," he said.

So far nobody has taken him up on it.

Pushing the aquarium trade toward sustainability and ethical practices is a worthy cause. But keeping fossil fuels in the ground, according to Ryne, is the only hope for the future. "I think the important thing is for people to understand how dangerous of a point we're at right now and that we have such limited time to get on top of it. I honestly think that in the near future and possibly in my lifetime, there'll be more corals in people's houses than there will be in the ocean."

Despite Ryne's worries, I still held out hope of finding the sweet spot of my Venn diagram, where researchers

With hundreds of gallons of thriving reef tanks, Moloko, a bar in Portland, Oregon, offers patrons an unexpected glimpse into tropical marine habitats.

overlap with passionate hobbyists like Christian Fitzpatrick and also the aquarium trade in an effort to help beleaguered coral reefs. I reviewed my notes and drew maps and pinned them to the wall like a cop stalking a serial killer in a television drama. With Fenner's and Ryne's help, I now had contacts in Fiji, Australia, Europe, and Indonesia. I circled a date on my calendar to attend MACNA, the Marine Aquarium Conference of North America, which draws legions of hobbyists and professionals. After years of covering coral conservation and science, here was a new frontier. The world of indoor coral reefs was a visually rich horizon populated by art and an obsession with a dash of science and engineering know-how, plus a whole lot of money to be made. I packed my bag and camera and prepared for a deep dive into this undiscovered country.

But just as I returned from my visit with Bob Fenner, there were rumbles about a new virus identified in Wuhan, China. Within weeks, travel screeched to a halt. Restaurants and bars shuttered. Schools closed for one month and then another.

I waited. I read Darwin's *Theory on the Structure and Distribution of Coral Reefs* and Charlie Veron's *A Reef in Time*, hoping that by the time I finished, I'd be off to Bali. But the virus had other plans. Many island nations went into lockdown and guarded their borders. More businesses closed, some for good. The summer MACNA conference was canceled. My window into the ornamental fish and coral trade was closing. And then, in May, there came another blow. I learned that Bob Fenner, my guide into the strange and arcane world of swashbuckling collectors, intrepid reef entrepreneurs, and obsessed hobbyists, had passed away from heart failure in his sleep.

Unable to travel, I hunkered down in my home office, where I occasionally paced and pined for the tropics. I interviewed researchers by video chat and phone. I mourned the loss of John Prine, Eddie Van

Halen, and my new friend Bob Fenner, a rock star in the world of "reefers." I reflected that, housebound for COVID, I was living in a sort of aquarium of my own.

I thumbed through Fenner's book, pausing at passages I'd highlighted, and one line held my attention. "Aquariums can and do serve as a paradigm for our own lives," he'd written. This was a clue. I heard Bob's voice in my head. I knew what I had to do. It was time to start my own tank.

I rushed to my computer and searched the web. I selected a sleek little aquarium which, if it delivered on the promise of its marketing photos, could support dozens of species of corals and other critters. It held 13.5 gallons of saltwater and sold for $160. If I couldn't visit a reef, then I could bring one to me. How hard could it be? My plan was to learn what it takes to raise a single coral colony, hoping that this might add to my understanding and appreciation of reef ecosystems as Fenner's book suggested.

My tank arrived and I opened the box. The gleaming quadrangle with its pumps and filters and two-phase light mimicking daytime and night illumination was a work of art. I placed it on my office desk so I could view it from multiple angles—perfect to distract me from my writing and other such tedium. It was magnificent in its unadulterated newness. It was also calling out to be filled. I felt an itch, something deep and primal. I had no idea what I was getting into.

Out of sheer luck, coincidence, or destiny, there happens to be a coral shop a few miles from my house. I'd driven past its mysterious blue actinic-lighted windows a number of times. Bob's book told me that, before introducing my coral colony, I had to do a few things to get my tank ready. I needed some type of substrate: usually sand or rock. I also needed base rock to create structure on which to attach my

coral. The project also required saltwater, which shops will sell by the gallon. And finally I needed something called live rock, which is a chunk of coral rubble or stone that is cured in a likely spot in the sea so that all manner of life grows in and on it: microbes, plankton, algae, tiny worms and starfish, and other small sea critters that help make your artificial ecosystem happy. Live rock turns your sterile aquarium into a thrumming ecosystem.

I went to my local shop and marveled at the tanks and gawked at the fish, the waving soft corals, and the fluorescent rows of frag plugs with their hard coral jewels, trying to decide which one I would select. But the owner cautioned me that it was too soon to add corals. Instead, I left the store with just a box of live rock, a bag of gravel, and three five-gallon buckets of saltwater.

I assembled my tank, setting up the pump and filters, pouring in the gravel and arranging my live rocks. I added the water, fired up the heater, and waited. I was eager to add my single coral fragment, but it was still too soon. First I would have to "cure" my tank. This meant creating a stable, balanced environment with just the right temperature, amount of nutrients, acidity, and microorganisms. Corals are fickle. They don't like change. That's why they only live in those few spots on the globe with perfect conditions and die en masse when those conditions change.

In weeks, tiny creatures called diatoms bloomed and covered all the rock in a brown sludge. This was the "brown phase" I'd been warned about by the shop's proprietor. He'd told me to be patient. So I waited, testing the nutrients with a mail-order chemistry kit and turning the light on every morning and off every evening to imitate a natural cycle. The nutrient levels shot up to create an environment far too toxic to sustain corals. The water turned cloudy. And I waited.

Next came a "green phase"—a bloom of green algae. This was a good sign. The water clouded up more and the rocks were now covered in bright green fuzz with a few clumps of hairy macroalgae. This meant that the tank was almost ready. I checked the nutrients again and they'd dropped to an acceptable level. The biological engine was chugging to life. Now it was time to change some of the water. I went back to the shop and told the owner the good news. I mentioned the unsightly green algae. He recommended some critters to help. I left with pails of clean saltwater, four snails, and four tiny hermit crabs. I changed the water. The crabs and snails cruised the tank and climbed over the rocks, mowing the algae down.

A few weeks later I returned to the store. Since I had crabs and snails, I needed to keep them healthy. They'd munched nearly all the algae in the tank. I didn't want them to starve. So I picked out a fish. A fish would help the tank from getting too sterile. A base level of nutrients are needed to keep the algae growing, which feeds the invertebrates. The crabs and snails also clean up the extra fish food and poop. Plus, I'd read that keeping fish was easier than keeping stony corals. I figured that if I could keep a fish alive, I could move up to corals after that. So I bought a tiny, captive-bred clownfish and another pail of saltwater.

A couple weeks later I returned to the store. My algae were under control; the tank was happy; my invertebrates were scurrying around; and the clownfish was full of energy, attacking my hand like a miniature shark every time I reached in to adjust something. I decided he needed company, so I picked up another fish, a slender, elegant goby with orange trim. I looked longingly at the stony corals in the store's raceway, a glittering, shallow display tub with coral fragments arranged like gems in a case at a jewelry store. I wondered aloud if I was ready for a notoriously fickle stony coral. The owner suggested I add a couple soft corals first. They're easier to keep alive than hard corals, plus they provide cover for the fish. So I left the store with the goby, a pail of water, a toadstool leather coral (which looked like a cross between a mushroom and a pincushion), and some zoanthids—soft-bodied cousins of hard corals that resemble tiny bouquets of glow-in-the-dark daisies.

Two weeks later, I returned to the shop for another pail of water. My tank had remained stable. I was keeping fish, invertebrates, soft corals, and all manner of microbes alive. I was changing a portion of the water regularly without disrupting the nutrient levels. I was finally ready for my stony coral colony.

I spent a long time looking at fragments. There were so many shapes and colors to choose from. Some were plating. Some grew in fingers. Some fluoresced under actinic lights like neon lights in a bar. There were maze corals and brain corals and marbled corals. While it had been my initial goal to raise a single coral colony, now I couldn't make up my mind. So I picked three. Then, in future trips to the store, I selected a graceful, spider-like cleaner shrimp and an ungainly conch snail with an elephantine trunk and two comical eyes perched on stems. And I bought more hard corals.

I started to spend hours staring into my tank, studying each coral colony as it popped out new polyps, expanded to cover the rocks, or built its own spiraling, jutting, and plating structure. I started to understand this slow-motion dance of growth in a way that I couldn't when parachuting into random reefs around the world. I saw the corals create ledges under which fish can hide or that catch spilled food, a delight for the crabs. In the evening, I'd switch from daylight mode to the neon-blue lighting that causes the corals to glitter like a miniature galaxy trapped in a box.

These pillar coral fragments in the aquarium at Frost Science in Miami represent the last surviving members of the species in Florida.

I recalled Christian Fitzpatrick at Moloko telling me how he'd spent countless hours every week just staring into his tanks. I'd found that somewhat extreme at the time. But I was clocking at least a half an hour a day gazing into my cube, largely to avoid sticky writing situations or the dreaded flood of email. But I was also studying the health of the animals. Did the snails seem sluggish? Was there an outbreak of dinoflagellates, tiny algae that are usually helpful but can become problematic? Was that a patch of bleaching on a coral colony, and if so should I move it lower in the tank, away from the lights?

I originally planned on raising a single coral colony, like those lonely colonies I'd seen in researchers' aquariums in Ruth Gates's lab in

Hawai'i. But what I'd learned was that corals don't belong in isolation. They require an ecosystem. I'd done an audit of all the creatures that had either arrived as stowaways on the live rock or that I'd added along the way. I counted thirty-seven. And when it comes to microbes, that number likely increases dramatically.

I was coming to believe that Bob Fenner was right: I did have a greater appreciation for what makes a coral reef ecosystem tick and how tenuous is the balance that keeps such systems alive. As he had written: "Exposure to the living world fosters appreciation and caretaking."

But there were no epiphanies. I learned that, with a little ingenuity and lots of tedious work, humans could keep small fragments of corals alive in captivity, but I still hadn't found a solid relationship between this hobby, the industry, and the struggle to save wild reefs. I was beginning to doubt if it even existed at all.

I worried a lot about Moloko. Many restaurants and bars hadn't survived the pandemic's winter surge. And I drove past and saw that the club's sign had been removed, with only the faint outlines of the letters remaining. What would happen to Christian Fitzpatrick's fish and corals in the hundreds of gallons of habitat if the place were shuttered?

But as vaccinations increased and the virus began to subside, I stopped by to find that Fitzpatrick had only taken his sign down to paint it. He was ready to reopen. He'd nested during the pandemic, installing a new floor in the bar, building a new deck out back, and even adding a number of new reef tanks. These latest were tall structures with curved arcs of glass, each sporting a classic Greek statue he'd scored on Craig's List. "These are great for dates," he said, pointing to a table for two with a coral-clad Aphrodite

in its own private tank. "If it's not going well, you have something to look at instead of the other person."

I left pleased that Christian's life work was still intact. He said his tanks had even helped him weather the pandemic, providing him with meditative time in the empty bar while he waited to reopen. The continuous labor gave him a reason to come in every day even while the bar was closed for months on end. I now had a new appreciation for the effort needed to maintain such a system. Even my 13.5 gallons required hours of work every week to keep running.

But I was also still haunted by the idea he'd raised at the end of my first visit: what if the last reefs in the world existed only in tanks like these? In the wild, reefs were still in decline. Mass bleaching events continued. Ports were dredged through healthy reefs. Pollution and sedimentation flowed onto corals. Coral cover declined. Couldn't all of the ingenuity required to keep corals alive in captivity play some sort of positive role in conservation?

I finally found an answer in Miami.

A few weeks later I was staring up through a thirty-one-foot oculus in the ceiling that offered an unusual perspective into the great Gulf Stream Aquarium. People gathered below the oculus, standing, sitting, and even lying on the sloped floor, immersed in this unique view, a perspective you could otherwise get only when diving. I was standing next to Zach Ransom, the curator of animal husbandry at the Miami Aquarium at Frost Science. His title meant he was responsible for the large tuna and hammerheads we could see through the oculus above us. He was also responsible for all of the corals in the floor-to-ceiling reef aquarium behind us. In total, there were more than fifteen thousand animals in his care. But one species in particular kept him up at night.

After I had a chance to ogle the massive exhibits, Zach led me through a side door and then down some stairs. Of the thousands of different kinds of marine animals in the aquarium's menagerie, there was one in particular that I'd come to see. These were fragments of *Dendrogyra cylindrus*, or pillar corals. This species was functionally extinct in Florida waters. Only a handful of examples remained in the wild, scattered and dying and too dispersed to breed. A devastating blight called stony coral tissue loss disease (SCTLD) has been mowing through Florida corals since 2014, and pillar corals are especially susceptible.

So a coalition of aquariums, conservation organizations, and universities pooled their resources to keep the Florida genotypes of *Dendrogyra cylindrus* from going extinct. Clones existed in multiple facilities, *ex situ*, to keep replicates for genetic diversity: if a storm, power outage, or human error wiped out the pillar corals at one site, their DNA would still live on in another.

Zach led me through the catacombs of the aquarium's substructure to a room with huge floor-to-ceiling pipes, tubes, and pumps. This was the impressive pulmonary system of the aquarium exhibits above us. In the middle of this chamber, like a sort of altar, stood a coral basin the size of a large billiard table. Through the rippling surface of the tank's water I saw a collection of flesh-colored coral fragments the size of grapefruits. Unlike other coral fragments, these were fuzzy, like scleractinian muppets, their extended polyps pulsing in the tank's artificial current. Pillar corals are one of the few species that keep their tentacles extended in the daytime, and it's part of their charm. In the wild, they grow into huge colonies that send up thick stumps as big around as your thigh, forming clusters of distinctive shapes like columns of ruined Greek temples. These examples were just bits and pieces of that lost world.

It's hard to describe the sensation of seeing the last surviving members of a population of animals. Sadness? Relief at the technical wizardry that still

allowed them to survive? It was a feeling somewhere between awe and sickness. In the tank there were 112 fragments with 65 distinct genotypes—all the genetic diversity that remained of these Florida corals.

Zach pointed out the sensor panel on the end of the tank. It tracked water temperature and chemistry. It was connected to his phone so he could monitor conditions from anywhere. "I haven't slept in years," he said. He was smiling but not joking.

An intern was measuring and photographing each fragment. Other staff hovered in dark corners of the room, reading dials, checking monitors, and taking notes. Zach pointed out the pumps, lights, and skimmers of the raceway. They were state of the art but not that different from my little tank at home.

Zach led me to another lab where there were more raceways with other species of corals. These were part of research taking place through a partnership with the University of Miami. More tanks held baby *Diadema* sea urchins, spiky, long-spined pincushions that are beneficial to corals because they devour algae. And in one large basin, there was a specific coral fragment that Zach wanted to show me. It was another pillar coral fragment, scruffier than the others.

This was Lonesome Larry, Zach told me. A crew with the Coral Restoration Foundation in Key Largo had just brought the fragment in. They'd discovered an isolated colony tipped over in the Upper Keys and on the verge of collapse, one of the last pillars in the wild. They were given permission to add it to the captive collections around the state, thus increasing genetic diversity by one more individual.

Lonesome Larry was still alone. He had to be kept in quarantine to ensure that he didn't have any diseases or other harmful hitchhikers that could endanger the rest of the captive pillar corals. At least he was well cared for and fed in his solitude.

Zach explained that these corals ate a lot; the corals in the other basin had doubled in size over the past year. His team fed them Reef Roids and the usual commercially available stuff. Also some frozen mysis shrimp. This was the same diet as the corals and fish in my own tank. I told him about my tank, its make and model, and he was pleased to be meeting a fellow "reefer." I asked him what success looked like in ten years for Lonesome Larry and the pillar coral program.

"That's a difficult question." Then, after a long pause, he said that "the pessimist in me tends to win out. I guess success is an increase in the genetic diversity, creating new corals from these corals and spreading them to more facilities." As for reintroducing them into the wild, "over the long term, the Florida Reef Tract's survival depends on large-scale changes." This was a diplomatic way to say that such things were out of his hands. The only world he could control was the one inside these walls.

As I made to leave, Zach led me through back passages into a loading dock near the garage. Like the rest of the labs and facilities there, even this storage area was pristine. There was a beautiful, rimless showcase tank next to shelving, filled with branching, colorful corals. Any hobbyist would have been thrilled to show off such a project. I asked him why it was hidden away in the loading dock. He told me they bring donors through here, so they wanted it to look nice. There were other corals in small basins. These were also quarantined before going into exhibits.

I asked him if he kept any tanks at home and he said that he had just one now. When he was in college, he was out of control and had eighteen tanks in his apartment. Had his hobby informed his work here?

"Hobbyists are much better at husbandry than academics," he said. He pulled a container of insecticide off the shelf, something you could find at your local garden store. "For example, we use this to dip our corals when they come in to get rid of parasites. The people in the hobby figured this out."

I realized that here was the link I was looking for. Zach existed in some middle space between academia and the aquarium hobby. Indeed, he maintained one of the biggest aquarium collections in the world at Frost. And he was as passionate about the natural world as he was about the ones he manages *ex situ*. As an accomplished underwater photographer, he crossed the globe to capture images of animals *in situ*. He was especially fascinated by sharks and had worked with great whites in Australia. He had traveled to the Red Sea to photograph marine life on reefs. I recalled what Bob Fenner had written. How by controlling approximate versions of wild reefs, "we gain an awareness of the magnificent diversity and beauty." Without Zach and other aquarists, many inspired and informed by the hobby and with the husbandry skills needed to keep endangered and even functionally extinct animals alive indefinitely *ex situ*, the already uncertain future of corals would be even more tenuous.

So here was the overlap in the Venn diagram Bob Fenner had sketched in the air, the place where academic research, hobbyists, and the aquarium trade all come together. Zach Ransom had sharpened his animal husbandry skills in the reef tank hobby. All of the endangered pillar corals he kept in the back rooms and basement chambers of the aquarium ran on systems developed and pioneered in the aquarium trade. Researchers were now partnering with the aquarium on coral restoration projects. At best, it's a tenuous overlap, but without it Lonesome Larry and others of his species kept here on life support in back rooms would have vanished into history.

7

Coral Seas of the American Southwest

Nevada and Arizona

THE BASIN AND RANGE PROVINCE of the American West is a rumpled otherworld of soaring mountains and broad, arid valleys that occasionally fill with ephemeral lakes from snowmelt and spring runoff only to dry into cracked playas again, the baked phantoms of freshwater seas and saltwater oceans that once covered this land in ages long before human memory. It's a landscape that was born of violence. Once a shallow continental shelf and coastline, Nevada was hemmed and augmented, slammed by the foreign terranes that made California and the Sierra Nevada Mountains, island arcs like ancient Japan or the Aleutians drifting across the sea and piling up against North America. Now it's like a rumpled bedsheet of rock heaved upward, spilling the stony viscera of the ages on the hillsides. This country harbors most of America's gold, silver, barite, and copper, the stuff of vast fortunes for a lucky few and backbreaking futility for the rest.

Occasionally, from the belly of deep time, this geological mayhem has heaved up other miracles:

the tracks and impressions of sea creatures that tell stories of ancient oceans, stony corkscrews and clamshells and dark smears of sponges turned to stone, encrusted bivalves, and strange, spiral-shelled animals called ammonites. There are also the bones of the occasional ichthyosaur and the leavings of ancient coral reefs.

It was to examine this lost marine world that I entered the desert where Oregon meets Nevada. The sun was dipping toward the flank of the western range by the time I rolled into Mina, Nevada, population 151, in the heart of the Basin and Range. I was dusty, tired, and hungry after the drive from Oregon. I stopped at the only place open in town, a tavern, ordering a basket of fried grease and a beer as I took a stool next to a miner.

We talked about geology and strata and marine limestone. He asked me what I was looking for and I told him that I sought corals. I said that some of the best examples of Triassic reefs and Jurassic corals in North America were nearby. He nodded knowingly

and told me I could find crinoids and other fossils up by an old copper mine. And then he scanned the room and spoke in a low voice: "Are you with the folks drilling up there?"

Miners can be coy and secretive, still seeking clues for new ways to pull primordial riches from the ground. I told him I wasn't looking for gemstones or heavy metals but rather what ancient reef formations could tell me about climate change. Then he asked if I was a journalist. By this time, other men at the bar were looking our way with suspicion.

I told them I was a science writer, which seemed more palatable to them. With a belly full of grease and beer, I headed for the door and drove into nearby Dunlop Canyon, climbing a ridge and unrolling my bedroll on the crest. I slept in fits and starts despite a comfortable breeze. Maybe it was the weight of what was below and around me, and its strangeness. I was in a coral sea, but like none I'd experienced before: there was no damp salt tang in the air, no gentle lapping of waves, no foaming break roaring over the distant reef crest. There was just a stir of desert air and mute rock.

Embedded in limestone layers in the canyon walls beneath and around me were the remains of a coral reef. This reef had flourished in an ancient sea called the Panthalassa, a superocean that dwarfed the modern Pacific and covered 70 percent of the planet during the late Triassic some 240 million years ago. These reefs edged the shallow shelf of a super-continent known as Pangea. This was an age when the continents we know today were crunched together. Everything about this world looked different. There were no flowering plants on land. No roses, palm trees, or grasses. No cottonwoods or mangroves or orchids. There were dinosaurs, though their ages of dominance lay millions of years ahead, in the Jurassic and Cretaceous. There was no polar ice. The only mammals were tiny, unimpressive

Page 104: The Biosphere 2 complex in Arizona has a long history of cutting-edge coral reef research.

Above: Early Jurassic corals like this one were solitary animals, not reef-builders, but they mark a step in a million-year journey toward reef recovery after the end-Triassic extinction.

shrew-like creatures tucked in low, hidden places. The skies were empty of birds and would be for tens of millions of years to come.

But in the seas, reef-building stony corals were already harnessing the power of evolution and sunlight to construct their submerged cities, and the structures they built were extensive. They left evidence of their magnificence that you can still see today in stripes in the Austrian Alps, the Italian Dolomites, the Atlas Mountains of Morocco, and also here in the Nevada desert.

Strange creatures prowled the waters. Giant ammonites, squid-like animals that built concentric circular shells the size of wagon wheels, drifted through these coral seas. Ichthyosaurs, or "fish lizards," flourished, dolphin-like reptiles that gave birth to live young.

But the extensive reefs, plus this alien and wondrous life that surrounded them, were perched on the very edge of collapse. The corals would suddenly and dramatically disappear from the fossil record for millions of years. Something happened on our planet to destroy them, and after they collapsed, so did most of the rest of life. The knowledge and mystery of this, finally, was what set me on edge through the restless night.

I awoke at first light. The sun popped over the far rim and flooded the canyon with morning fire. As I drove out of Dunlop Canyon, there were angled strata of rock stacked one on top of the other, reaching up the cliffs, what geologists like to call a "layer cake." This was evidence of a Triassic reef, but it was written in a language I couldn't understand. I'd read the literature and knew that scientists who'd studied this site were able to determine that the diversity that had flourished here would have been recognizable to us today, with mounding, branching, and plating corals. I could see the line where one layer ended and another began. This was a line, one

of many, that marked the boundaries between the end of the Triassic with its flourishing reefs and the Jurassic, when corals suddenly vanished from the Earth. The event that created that boundary is known as the end-Triassic extinction, which wiped out 70 percent of life in the sea along with 60 percent of terrestrial life. What happened to these reefs? Why did they suddenly vanish and take so much of the other life on the planet with them? How does that time more than 200 million years ago compare to the loss of reefs we're experiencing today? And what happens next if we continue to burn carbon and transform our atmosphere and oceans with reckless abandon, reaching levels of CO_2 not seen in at least 3.6 million years?

These were questions I couldn't address alone. But fortunately, about ten miles away in another desert draw, I'd be meeting a geologist who could shed light on a few of them.

The paleontologist stepped out of a green SUV with large Jurassic Park logos on the doors and a sticker featuring a T. rex happily devouring a nuclear family on the back window. The vehicle looked like a prop from the popular films.

"People smile when I drive up," she said.

I supposed it's healthy to have a sense of humor when you study mass extinctions for a living.

In boots and cowboy hat, a white bandanna around her neck, a white shirt to ward off the baking heat not quite hiding colorful tattoos, and clutching a rock hammer, Montana Hodges embodied her profession in a way that few people do. Even her name had the ring of paleontology about it. And like any good character, she even came with a sidekick. Her dad, Chris, ambled around the side of the truck wearing a floppy, wide-brimmed hat and clutching a pair of hiking poles for balance on the uneven terrain. He was already hungrily scanning the sides of the canyon for his next geological fix.

Montana teaches geology at Sierra Nevada College, writes books about rock hunting, and combs the landscapes of the Southwest, Mexico, and Alaska in search of Jurassic corals. Chris, a physicist by training and a rock hound by passion, plays the role of field tech for his daughter and has even been credited on her research papers. They share a lifelong passion for things etched in stone and baked into rubble, which they can read like the runes of an ancient language.

"Which way should we head up to the ridge, Monty?" Chris asked. It had been years since they were at this spot and had discovered corals together. They both were eager to return to the site. Montana checked the GPS on her phone and pointed up a rocky draw.

"I think it's this way."

And with that I followed the pair up into New York Canyon. It was slow going. The ground was loose and crumbly. But that's not what really held us up. Chris and Montana had their eyes on the stones underfoot. At turns they stopped to pluck fossils from the dust. I recognize the corrugated shells of bivalves. Stranger to me were the ribbed spirals of ammonites. We climbed toward a ridgeline. What these fossils told us was that we were walking along an ancient seabed. A layer of marine sediment had been pressed down toward the earth's mantle, exposed to heat and baked into limestone, and then uplifted and broken and continually eroded until it lay scattered across these ridges and draws. Now these fossils provided clues to what the ancient world was like.

We reached the ridge crest and took in a breathtaking view of the yellow playa below, the ramshackle town of Mina twinkling in the distance like a metropolis. Then we descended a draw where seasonal water had washed the rocks downhill in a natural sluiceway that continually revealed more fossil treasure over time.

Chris pulled a small, twisty gray tube from the dust, thinking he had a fossil. False alarm. It was just dried coyote scat. We worked slowly downhill and then Montana picked up another twisty brown tube, striped with little ridges like a bent, rusty bolt. "Jurassic coral," she said with reverence, handing it to me. Encased in grayish limestone, the curving tube was broken at one end, revealing a cross section that looked not unlike a broken finger of the branching corals we see today. I took it and studied it. This was a coral that lived after the end-Triassic extinction. It marks a sort-of recovery for scleractinians. But this species didn't build large reefs. It wasn't even colonial: the stony skeleton was manufactured by a single polyp. But it did tell us something important. After the obliteration of Triassic reefs, this specimen indicated a return of hard corals to the fossil record. Life was finding a way. And that piece of broken coral offered perspective on what's currently happening to our reefs.

At the end of the Triassic 202 million years ago, Pangea began its breakup into the puzzle pieces of today's continents, and the Atlantic Ocean started to form in the rift that tore them apart. Massive volcanic activity in a region called the Central Atlantic Magmatic Province (CAMP) ensued, creating the largest lava floods on Earth. This volcanic activity released enormous pulses of carbon dioxide and sulfur dioxide into the atmosphere. Increases in atmospheric carbon, back then just as today, sent temperatures soaring and changed ocean chemistry, making the seas more acidic. Animals that produce skeletons and shells from calcium carbonate, like corals, collapsed, vanishing from the fossil record.

Extinction followed, wiping out three-quarters of all life on the planet.

Taking a class on mass extinctions from renowned geologist George Stanley at the University of Montana is what turned Montana Hodges into a paleontologist. She'd been an aspiring environmental journalist. Always a rock hound, hunting gems and fossils with her father since childhood, she suddenly saw, in these ancient tales of upheaval and slow geological violence, parallels with today's extinction crisis.

The atmospheric carbon reached stratospheric levels over a period of thousands of years near the end of the Triassic. We are expected to reach similar conditions thirty to sixty years from now. But instead of supervolcanoes emitting the carbon dioxide, we humans have been responsible for the increase through our targeted extraction and burning of fossil fuels.

When Hodges began thinking in deep time, understanding how millions of years of evolution went into the production of those flourishing reefs and how they could be wiped out relatively swiftly, it put our current crisis in perspective. She learned that "swift" extinction in geological time meant hundreds of thousands or millions of years. And today's extinction event is happening a thousand times faster than anything that has occurred in the long, long, long history of time. She grew both fascinated and alarmed. And when she tried to use deep time to convey the urgency of the environmental crisis in her journalism, she found that editors were asking her to dumb down the science. They didn't trust readers to do such heavy thinkwork.

That's when Hodges switched from journalism to paleontology. And she's never looked back. As a professor of geology, she doesn't have to dumb down anything. Her students amaze her. They get it.

The heat was radiating up off the baked earth now. She crouched and picked up more corals. They were twisting tubes about as big around as an AA battery. But these Jurassic corals didn't build anything we'd recognize as a reef.

"They were simple corals hiding in the mud. It was nothing like what was happening in the Triassic," she said.

"What does that tell us?"

"It tells us that reefs just weren't being built."

According to projections, unless we immediately reverse course on fossil-fuel burning, we'll reach levels of atmospheric carbon matching the end-Triassic extinction sometime between the years 2050 and 2080. And even though it's happening at a rate that feels achingly slow to us, that's blazingly fast on Earth's clock. "Everyone's waiting for a false apocalypse," she said, describing an Armageddon where we might look out the window to see nature in sudden, smoking ruins. That happens at times, in climate-strengthened storms or forest fires, or in a mass bleaching event on reefs. But most days, we can't see the shifting climate out our window. It's happening slowly and steadily by our meter but in the blink of an eye according to deep time. But the extinction *is* happening now, Monty knows.

This is a difficult lesson to process from fascinating things in the rocks. When I asked her what the world of these corals—and the biodiversity of marine creatures in general—was like after the end-Triassic extinction, she told me that it wasn't like a coral reef or even like a city, that common metaphor for reef ecosystems. She picked up some more little brown fragments of the solitary Jurassic corals. "It was more like rural Nevada," she said, pointing out over the basin, "with one neighbor here, and the next one way over there."

As we started back toward the cars, we left the coral layer behind. We picked up the occasional spiraling ammonite or tiny washboard bivalve. Chris pointed out a sooty black stripe of exposed rock, identifying it as a layer of sponges. Today, sponges are opportunistic organisms, colonizing areas where corals have been wiped out. They're colorful and often beautiful. But they don't create the marine structure that stony corals do. Someday, in unfathomable eons ahead, subduction, faulting, and orogeny will push up new mountains and reveal layers made from today's reefs. And unless we can find a way to keep carbon in the ground instead of releasing it into the atmosphere, there may be a line in the rock marking where today's reefs vanish and sponges inherit the wreckage.

Just as I was beginning to feel that these Jurassic corals painted a dark picture of the future—lonely animals struggling in the murky bottom of an empty sea that had once been decorated with vast reefs—I asked Montana if there was any way to put a positive spin on my pocket full of fossils.

"What I see in these corals is recovery from the extinction," she said. There is beauty and resilience embedded in the rock. She pondered the fossil-studded rubble. "But it makes me see that we're getting the bum end of the deal. We get to be here for the biodiversity loss but not for the recovery, which will take another couple million years."

We crested one last rise and the cars came into view. I saw the Jurassic Park SUV again, and the sight lightened my spirits. I said as much. She smiled. "I tell my students that I'm going to take them to the real Jurassic Park. I lure them in with dinosaurs and then we come out here looking for corals and bivalves. Pretty soon they forget about the dinosaurs."

Montana had to leave. She'd be catching a plane the next morning bound for Alaska, where she would explore a rugged coastline for more Jurassic corals. They had a four-hour drive ahead. She would catch up on sleep while her father took the wheel. The fossils she sought had lain in wait of discovery for

Ancient, slow-moving geological forces take on a new urgency for paleontologist Montana Hodges and her research associate and father, Chris.

nearly two hundred million years. But now there was a new urgency to reveal them to the world.

As I left New York Canyon, I continued south. I spent the night near the summit of Mt. Charleston in a grove of cool pines on a marine limestone bluff that had once been an ocean floor but now perched ten thousand feet in the air. The next morning I descended and drove through Las Vegas, with its forest of casino towers and a surprising number of billboards advertising personal injury attorneys. Was this also a sign of the apocalypse?

I passed Hoover Dam, that false monument to our command of nature, and then skirted Lake Mead, America's largest reservoir, with its bathtub ring of drought indicating a high-water mark not reached in decades. The baked playas of Nevada gave way to rumpled ranges of Arizona studded with saguaro cactus. A sign advertising a combination burger joint and machine-gun range heightened the sense of impending end-times.

I was now seeking a different coral sea from the one I'd found on the slopes of New York Canyon. I was interested in a glimpse not into the distant past but into the future. What might a coral reef look like in sixty years when we reach atmosphere carbon levels that shoved Triassic reefs out of the fossil record?

Early the following morning, I drew close to my destination as I climbed to the high deserts near the border with Mexico. I saw the first glimpse of the white domes tucked at the base of the Santa Catalina Mountains, which were illuminated by the pastel light of dawn. As I descended a low rise, I saw a sprawling complex of gleaming white-vaulted arcs and triangular glass plates: towers, domes, a pyramid, and massive greenhouses. This was Biosphere 2.

Built between 1987 and 1991, the original intent of this three-acre enclosure was to create a self-contained world, a proxy for a space colony, a sort of reverse Noah's Ark with thousands of species of imported plants and animals and people. Eight humans would lock themselves inside for two-year stints, sealed off from Earth (aka Biosphere 1), with everything they needed to survive, including the very air required to breathe. It was a grand project that would become the largest closed-loop ecological system ever attempted. The "Biospherans" would maintain the five biomes, grow their own food, and conduct experiments on this artificial world and on themselves. There was an indoor desert, farm, mangrove forest, jungle, and—of most interest to me—a coral sea.

From the start, the project was controversial and audacious. When you added the colorful personalities behind the original concept, including a Texas oil billionaire and an eccentric theater director turned environmentalist, things became more interesting. After the Biospherans were locked inside, personal rivalries emerged. The group was challenged by declining oxygen levels, spiking carbon dioxide, dramatic weight loss and hunger, rumors of opened windows, and midnight escapes for smuggled food. Add events outside the bubble, including accusations of embezzlement or endangerment of the researchers, mismanaged publicity, and finally the takeover and eventual dismantling of the whole enterprise by investment banker Steve Bannon (who would later rise to fame as a far-right media executive and Donald Trump adviser with white nationalist leanings), and the project became quite the media circus. All of this distracted from the many successes of the project, not the least of which was the fact that it largely worked. The Biospherans not only survived, but became healthier. Enclosed ecosystems thrived, including the ocean and its corals. The agricultural biome became the most productive farm on the planet.

The initial project ended abruptly in 1994 as the private company managing the program collapsed while the second crew of Biospherans were sealed inside. Management of the facility was taken over by Columbia University, which ran the project for nearly a decade, converting it from a self-contained biosphere into a series of flow-through laboratories. The property was next purchased by real estate developers and threatened with everything from demolition to conversion into a spa or shopping mall. But in 2007, the University of Arizona stepped in to run the research program, eventually acquiring the entire facility. Today, the university operates it as a research and outreach facility dedicated to the study of Earth systems. Researchers from around the world collaborate on projects there.

Through all of the drama and upheaval, a particularly fascinating experiment was taking place—the establishment, destruction, and restoration of a fully self-contained 2.6-million-liter coral ocean. Here was a coral sea about to be reborn.

Restoring the self-contained Biosphere 2 ocean can offer important lessons—and warnings—for conserving wild reefs.

I met University of Arizona researchers Diane Thompson and Katie Morgan at a back door to Biosphere 2 set in a giant glass and steel wall. Following them inside was like entering a giant terrarium, and instantly the parched Arizona landscape vanished and there was a musty, indoor tropical tang to the air. I followed them through a lobby under giant beams, through hatches and over catwalks until we emerged onto a boardwalk set on a forested slope edging a cliff overlooking a sunlit basin a bit larger than an Olympic swimming pool. The water bubbled and churned as pumps simulated wave surge. A small rowboat bobbed at a mooring. There was a dock and a tiny beach. And through the greenish water, I saw the dark mounds of a structure below the surface. It looked exactly like a tropical reef.

Thompson began her career as an ecologist studying how ecosystems worked, but then she altered her trajectory to study how they collapsed. This change was prompted by a shock she'd experienced years before. She'd returned to a beautiful Caribbean reef off St. Croix, where she'd studied as an undergraduate. Five years had elapsed since her first visit, and she was so eager to return that when her boat drew close, she began shaking with anticipation as she pulled on her fins, mask, and snorkel.

"And I jumped in the water and saw that it was completely decimated. It was like nothing I'd ever seen. My snorkel fell out of my mouth and I was crying," she told me.

As a young scientist, Thompson had heard plenty of stories from old geezers about how the reefs had degraded over their lifetimes. The shifting baseline was a well-understood, generational phenomenon. And there she was, in her early twenties, already experiencing it. It was a life-changing experience.

That moment led to the division of her research in two directions. She started examining past ocean conditions by drilling core samples on coral skeletons around the world to read the layered cores like tree rings showing how they responded to stress. She wanted to understand what killed them and why. And what made them survive. She also began looking to the future, at ways in which humans might better understand coral survival in predicted ocean conditions and how we can help with that survival. To shed light on this, she was bringing the world's largest, closed-loop, human-constructed coral reef ecosystem back from extinction.

There were no longer any living corals in the ocean basin below us. I knew that the dark shapes I saw below the clear green water represented dead reef and patches of algae. The only survivors of the original experiment were a few hearty fish. But I also knew that another chapter was about to be written in Biosphere 2, that other-Earth that had once faced the threat of bulldozers and had teetered on the edge of oblivion.

Katie Morgan, who had been at Biosphere 2 since she was an undergraduate intern, shared some of the history of the ocean as we followed catwalks and descended a stairway hidden behind walls of artificial rock. We left the soaring, cathedral-like chambers and entered the guts of the place, with giant tubes and ducts and whirring pumps that drove the ocean's waves and currents.

The original iteration of this coral sea was a sort of Frankenstein ocean, made with manufactured seawater combined with ocean water trucked in from the Scripps Institution of Oceanography in San Diego, which contained essential plankton and microbes. To this soup of Pacific microbes and artificial seawater, 1,465 Caribbean corals were brought up from the Yucatán in Mexico, some of them massive old colonies with their own contingents of microbes and critters. In all there were thirty-four species of stony corals shipped on a four-day journey to Arizona in specially designed aquarium trucks that included lighting and current flow. Then the corals were cemented in place with epoxy in an artificial ocean built at four thousand feet of elevation in a temperate climate with a strong seasonal diurnal variation at the base of a mountain range nearly a thousand miles from the nearest tropical reef.

Abigail Alling was the marine biologist on the original project in charge of the ocean. During the course of the first closure, she had mighty struggles to maintain the health of the reef. Algae threatened to choke out the corals and had to be removed by mechanical scrubbers and often by hand. In the winter, the coral colonies adapted to the low light and short days. Then spring happened. "It was remarkable to see how the shallow corals that had been in such low light during the winter months started to show bleaching," she told me via video chat from her new project in Bali. Back then, she'd had to move the bleaching corals lower in the basin by hand to keep them healthy. She learned to actively manage the ocean to keep its corals in balance.

More challenges ensued. Diseases, latent hitchhikers from the Caribbean, began to emerge with the increases in light and warmer weather. Octopuses that had also hitched a ride from the Yucatán munched through helpful invertebrates, threatening the health of the reef, and had to be removed. But with her ongoing labors, the ocean stayed healthy. "We really learned from each other. We were working together...me and the ocean," she said.

By the end of the two-year experiment, this symbiosis led to a dramatic success. Of the original thirty-four species of corals, all but one species survived, and 75 percent of the corals survived overall. Most notably, there were thirty-eight new coral recruits. These corals were not only surviving,

they were breeding. The scientists knew they were recruits, Alling told me, because they were living on the tank walls, and they hadn't put any corals there.

After the collapse of the overall Biosphere 2 project, the ocean was neglected. No one expected the corals—animals that thrive on consistency of conditions—to survive the mayhem happening inside and outside the facility. But they endured. And when Columbia University stepped in, the corals received a new purpose, though not one they would have asked for had they been sentient beings. Chris Langdon, a researcher at Columbia, chemically altered the carbon dioxide levels of the ocean basin over a three-year period to study coral response under simulated future scenarios. One of those scenarios was pH levels our oceans are expected to reach later in this century under a "business as usual" model of carbon emissions. The results weren't good. Coral skeleton calcification declined by 40 percent. These findings convinced Langdon that under current fossil-fuel consumption scenarios, acidification will push our oceans to a point of no return, relevant to coral reefs, around the year 2075.

After those experiments concluded and Langdon moved on to the University of Miami, the ocean basin languished. The corals, battered by experiments, smothered by algae, neglected, finally died off after more than a decade of stubborn survival. The Biosphere 2 coral sea had undergone a phase shift, as so often happens in the wild on degraded reefs. It was now an eroding algal habitat, not a growing coral reef.

The algae grew and thickened. And then Ruth Gates entered the picture. Along with University of Arizona researchers, Gates suggested using this huge ocean basin to test novel ideas, like her adaptive evolution work and other aggressive schemes, including the large-scale use of probiotics. The large, self-contained ocean mesocosm would be a perfect proxy, an interim step before moving such high-risk experiments to the open ocean.

As I followed Katie Morgan into a bunker of a room in the basement level of the facility, I saw one such project in action. Raceway tubs with racks of coral fragments rippled with artificial current under neon-blue lights. The little corals were from the Mote Marine Lab in Florida, which has been doing research on stress-hardening corals adapted for future ocean conditions. These plugs of fuzzy colonies would resurrect the Biosphere 2 coral sea.

But first, the ocean itself needed be restored to conditions that allow corals to thrive. Morgan was part of a team hard at work rebuilding the habitat. When she began, the ocean had turned into a pea-green pond. "People would look at it and say, 'How could that ever have been a tropical coral reef?'" she told me.

So they hauled algae out by the fistful. On one of her favorite dives in the basin, Morgan recalled ripping out thick strands of the stuff, pulling off a full sheet and finding a cluster of brain corals massed together underneath. She'd never seen the skeletons of these corals.

We made our way from the bunker filled with raceways of growing coral, through tunnels that felt like the corridors of a submarine, to the beach on the Biosphere 2 ocean. It suddenly wasn't hard to imagine being on the shore of a tropical island. Diane Thompson explained that there were three phases to the project. First, they wanted to fully understand this degraded reef. She and her students would be drilling cores into the old, dead colonies to analyze their history, much as they did with colonies on wild reefs. In the "tree rings" they'd be able to see the impacts of the colonies' relocation from the Yucatán to this mountain ocean, to see evidence of the changes in morphology that Abigail Alling had witnessed when the corals adapted to the diurnal

Katie Morgan and Diane Thompson stand on the Biosphere 2 beach inspecting a tank filled with urchins, animals that devour algae and help keep reefs healthy.

Perched on the edge of the Santa Catalina Mountains near Tucson, Biosphere 2 still serves its original research mission even after a tumultuous history and threats of dismantling.

swings of winter and summer, and then to see what damage Langdon's chemical acidification experiments had ultimately wrought.

Microbiologists were also studying changes in this basin's tiniest critters. There were hundreds of species of microbiota to analyze, including some never seen before. Thompson also was sampling the sediment, taking cores of the floor of this artificial ocean, again with techniques long used on the outside and not possible in any other human-made habitats.

The second phase of the project was also underway: ecological restoration. After the messy work of hand removal of the algae, the researchers were introducing such herbivores as beneficial fish, shrimp, crabs, snails, and urchins to help keep the system in balance. From a large round tub at the edge of the beach, Thompson fished out a tiny urchin and held it up in the palm of her hand for us to see. It was a killer algae eater, Morgan told me.

Once the system was stable, the corals I'd seen in the raceway would be introduced, and the next chapter of the Biosphere 2 reef would be written. Some of those corals would be outplanted right over the old dead colonies, where they would add their own layers to the story. This also happens in nature, as Thompson's coring work had demonstrated. "Sometimes it's one species of coral and I get halfway down and it's a totally different species," she said. "So you see evidence of death and destruction followed by a sort of rebuilding, and you see that over and over again."

The final phase of the project will be to subject this reef to stressors again to mimic the world that lies ahead. Some of the inhabitants may be "super corals." Some might be hybrids of Pacific and Caribbean species, opening a lot of possibilities for experiments deemed too risky to test in the wild.

It's hard not to feel inspired, standing in a coral sea in the high desert, dwarfed by the scale of this indoor world that was built from a combination of vision and hubris. Something here in Oracle, Arizona, fed such imagination and inspired innovators like Abigail Alling and Ruth Gates. After witnessing a destroyed reef, Diane Thompson had picked herself up with a new sense of purpose in pursuit of a bold idea. I asked her if she dared to hope that the work here could make a difference.

"There's a tremendous amount of hope in being part of a great team," she said. "I can feel things shift."

Indeed, the idea of intervention, which had until recently been seen as risky or ineffective, was gaining momentum. If they could fix this ruined ocean, wasn't it only a matter of scaling up to put back the shattered pieces of the world's broken reefs? Or was such thinking the result of the same sort of hubris that had inspired the first Biosphere 2 project, which had ended so calamitously? Might the last healthy reef in the world someday exist in a manufactured facility like this once the industrial overdose of carbon rendered the wild oceans too acidic? I asked Thompson.

"We're working hard to buy us time," she said. "It's time to do something. We're not going to let this sadness overwhelm us."

Thompson's determination echoes that of the ocean's first manager. Abigail Alling, who had ripped out algae by hand and moved colonies one at a time to avoid bleaching, had learned decades ago that it was time for humans to take an active role in maintaining the systems that sustain us. "By living in there, we became Biosphere 2. We wore it," she told me. "Our whole life became focused on understanding our world and being supportive and managing it as a steward."

For the eight researchers locked inside Biosphere 2, ruled by the limitations of a three-acre world, they needed to maintain balance with their environment to survive. They needed to learn to "wear it." And this is a lesson that the eight billion of us living on Biosphere 1 must rapidly embrace if we hope to have a shot of ending the same calamity that was written in the stripes on a Nevada hillside two hundred million years ago.

8

The Heroic Reef

Bocachica, Colombia

VALERIA PIZARRO HOPED to save a few corals. She was in the front of a skiff, the pilot in the back steering them away from the towering white condominiums of Cartagena's posh Bocagrande neighborhood across open water dotted with a few low-slung islands and clusters of mangroves. They motored toward the mouth of Cartagena Bay, where murky water fans out into the blue Caribbean in a smudge of brown that you can see in satellite photos. To her left, the skeletal fingers of port cranes loaded containers onto massive freighters. Refinery towers smoldered farther in the distance. Ahead, a queue of massive freighters waited to run the bay's lone shipping lane, forming a line that stretched to the horizon. To Pizarro's right, an ancient fortress drew into view, ominously guarding the mouth of the bay, a reminder of Cartagena's colonial past and its nickname—the Heroic City—earned through centuries of conflict.

Pizarro didn't suspect her mission might become part of this heroic tradition. It was just a day's work.

A marine biologist and refugee from the university system, she had recently hired on to an environmental assessment project. Tired of the bureaucracy and politics of academia, she wanted to get her hands dirty, to do something practical. Her job was to survey the floor of the bay's mouth for coral cover before the port authorities began the dredging of a second shipping lane to ease the bottleneck of sea traffic constricting the port's growth. She wasn't expecting to find much. Maybe a few sorry coral colonies hiding below the polluted water. She would identify these stragglers and oversee their relocation to cleaner, clearer waters where they could thrive. She felt good about this mission. Instead of huddling in a darkened lab, crafting arcane papers that only her peers could understand and fighting academic politics, here she was doing something real. After years of coral devastation across the Caribbean, this was a simple action that would help at least a few colonies survive.

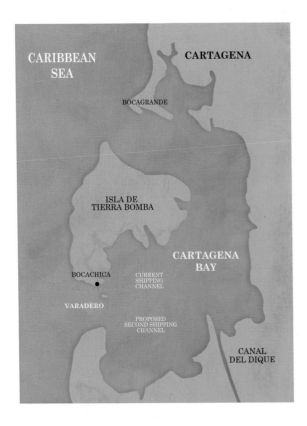

Page 118: Varadero, a reef near the Colombian city of Cartagena, has astonishing levels of coral cover not seen in other parts of the Caribbean for decades.

The launch slipped through the mouth of the bay, dogging the freighters that lumbered toward the port. The city faded into the distance. The small fishing village of Bocachica came into view: a cluster of concrete houses and thatched huts on an inviting strand of beach perched on the edge of the shipping channel. Terns and cormorants circled, swirls of black and white sea-slick feathers, plunging and skimming the murky water and emerging with wriggling prizes. A few dugout canoes bearing fishermen from Bocachica bobbed in the tumult: signs that there was at least some wildness at this juncture where industry meets nature.

Pizarro checked her handheld GPS for the location and cross-referenced it with a map in a plastic sleeve on her lap that showed the proposed path of the new channel. She guided the pilot forward to a spot marked on that diagram where she would begin her survey. A little to the right. A few meters to the left. They circled to find the exact location.

It wasn't deep. Corals thrive in shallow water. Pizarro pulled on her worn gray-and-black wet suit, veteran of hundreds of research dives. She looked doubtfully over the gunwales into the brownish soup. Were there corals down there? Probably not. Still, in an act of optimism, she strapped on her scuba gear and rolled over the side. Bobbing on the surface, she checked her air, fixed her mask, flashed the "thumbs down" signal and submerged into the turbid water as the pilot looked around, wary of the freighters and speeding tourist boats.

In the water, Valeria felt claustrophobic, the visibility less than a meter. She sank slowly. The water turned from brown to green and then a greenish blue. She realized that the murk clung only to the top few meters. A sudden vista opened up below.

And what she saw next shocked her.

After a quick look around, she surfaced again. "We have a problem," she told the pilot. "There is not just one coral; there is a reef here."

The pilot was baffled. He cross-checked the charts and the GPS. They were right where the new channel was supposed to go.

This seemed impossible. Corals prefer clear blue water. They don't do well in polluted, sedimented estuaries. But what Pizarro saw was not the bleak, muddy landscape or seafloor of her expectation, dotted with a few struggling corals and heartier sponges. Instead she saw a vista of massive coral colonies stretching in all directions, huge boulders and elkhorn thickets as far as she could see below the cap of cloudy water. These corals formed the densest, strangest reef she'd seen in the Caribbean. It defied all logic and scientific consensus. She knew the discovery would shock her colleagues. And it would greatly complicate the dredging plans of her employers. But what she didn't know was how completely it would change her life.

The story of what Valeria Pizarro found in the cloudy water at the mouth of Cartagena Bay only makes sense in the context of more than five hundred years of conflict, exploitation, and revolution.

Cartagena des Indias was founded in 1533, during the theft and slaughter of Spanish conquest, by an adventuring thug named Pedro de Heredia. The first great exports of the port city of Cartagena were gold and precious metals. Heredia was an exceptional grave robber, but he failed to properly fortify the city. A string of humiliating raids at the hands of British and French pirates followed.

After a couple centuries of raids, the Spaniards finally got serious about defending the city. They began construction of the imposing walls and fortresses that give Cartagena its tourist charm today.

They also expanded on the city's natural defenses. The large island of Tierra Bomba plugs the opening to the horseshoe-shaped bay, and ships wishing to enter for trade or invasion had to sail through the passage on either side of the island. Those gaps, perhaps due to a cartographer's stunning lack of creativity, are simply called Bocagrande (big mouth) on the north and Bocachica (little mouth) on the south. Bocagrande was shallow and dotted with shifting sandbars that frustrated invaders, so engineers built up these natural defenses with a submerged levee that prevented them from sailing into the bay and surrounding the city. This meant that the only passage into the bay was now the narrower channel through Bocachica. That shipping channel was dredged and widened through the centuries. Fortresses were constructed on either side of it from which defenders could bombard invaders with cannon. To further frustrate entry, a massive underwater chain connected the two fortresses. During times of siege, it was drawn from the channel floor by a great turnstile. This defensive formula worked, leading to a stunning victory over the British in 1741. When the city declared its independence in 1810 after 275 years of Spanish rule, it used these same fortifications to resist the loyalist troops sent to reclaim it, earning the title of "Heroic City" from revolutionary hero Simón Bolívar.

If conflict and defense shaped the channel and built the fortresses between which Pizarro and her pilot motored that morning, it was trade that created the conditions for the murky cap of water. Cartagena grew to become the hemisphere's largest port. Every gold-filled Spanish galleon bound from the Americas to Spain sailed through this channel. In 1713, Spain also signed a contract with Britain to provide slaves, and Cartagena became the hub of that inhuman trade for all of Spanish America. Slaves built the fortresses guarding Bocachica and manned the huge turnstiles that lifted the chain across the channel in times of siege. Their descendants still live in the shadow of the fortress today, and semiautonomous communities on islands in the surrounding archipelagos still bear a rich Afro-Caribbean history.

Because no natural river flowed into the bay, early engineers created the Canal del Dique to connect Cartagena with the Magdalena River. Built in 1582, the canal brought more trade goods from the interior, along with massive amounts of sediment spilling into the bay. The canal fell into disrepair until it reached its current defunct state. Today it is most noted for the continued flow of murk and its role as a set piece in *Love in a Time of Cholera*, the novel by beloved Cartagena native Gabriel García Márquez.

While the canal slipped into disuse, Cartagena's importance as a hub of trade only grew. In 1926, a pipeline was completed bringing the modern equivalent of gold: crude oil. Today, refineries encircle the bay and tankers make regular runs through the channel, along with ships carrying cargoes of platinum, coffee, and sugar.

There has been pressure to create a second shipping channel through the bottleneck of Bocachica. In 2012, the Colombia government began formal peace negotiations with FARC (Revolutionary Armed Forces of Colombia) rebels, the largest of the leftist guerrilla armies that have been occupying Colombia's rugged mountain interior for the last half century. This bloody conflict stunted Colombia's development, largely because the rebels held areas most rich in natural resources. The FARC had even made an industry of kidnapping and holding for ransom oil engineers and mineral prospectors.

With the subsidence of the conflict and talks of peace, plans to extract the natural resources accelerated. In the year after the signing of the 2016 peace accords, increases in logging and mining surged. And the Port of Cartagena desired to resume

its role in sending Colombian riches abroad, no matter the ecological costs. Plans for the second channel forged ahead.

Until Pizarro made that dive.

What she found wasn't a few straggling corals, but a flourishing reef that had adapted to five hundred years of human engineering. It defied the odds. There was much to be learned. How had it evolved? Was it the ocean conditions, or the corals themselves, or both? Were there clues in the microbes? Could such resilience be exported to other beleaguered reefs?

Theories of the reef's tenacity abound. Maybe the cap of silted water is helping protect these coral from a warming climate by providing a sort of sun shade. Maybe the five hundred years of increasing human pressure gave these corals needed time to adapt to a human planet. All of these thoughts rushed through Pizarro's head as she made more dives along the proposed path of the channel and found more and more flourishing corals, massive reef structures that teemed with fish. The extent of the reef was at least a square kilometer, and it had astonishing coral cover up to 80 percent.

But at the very moment that this marvel of coral was discovered by scientists, it was also slated for destruction. Local fishermen had long known of this resource, having dubbed the reef Varadero. Now their livelihood was being threatened. The reef is the perfect metaphor for the global collision of the natural world with modern development and exploitation of natural resources. Varadero was telling Pizarro something. And she was determined to listen.

Diving is like slipping into another dimension where the rules of color, light, gravity, pressure—and even breathing—are undermined in an instant. There's also something familiar about it. Down deep, a part of us belongs to the sea. Somewhere back on the tree of life, our predecessors crawled out of the water. Maybe that's why slipping back in always feels like a sort of homecoming.

But none of this prepared me for the disorienting contrast of sinking through the layer of murk above Varadero, emerging in a moment onto the wrinkled washboard canyons of coral. First there was the contrast to the surface world: massive freighters barreling past and sending fat, rolling waves in their wakes, the traffic of the bay's mouth, the smell of engine oil, the buzz of twin-engine tour boats mingling with cries of seabirds.

I tumbled over the side of the boat and splashed into the water. I submerged, and in that moment when the world turned cloudy gray and I lost orientation, I no longer knew whether I was sinking or rising. I lost sight of my team. I wasn't sure how deep I'd gone or if I'd ever find the bottom.

Then the light changed and suddenly I was below the soup. I looked up to see legs, arms, and cameras emerge from the cloudy membrane of turbid water, and I was reunited with my fellow divers in greenish-blue water clear enough to see twenty meters in any direction. There were canyons and crags studded with urchins, sudden explosions of schooling fish, and a lone puffer cruising the rills and valleys. The light was different in tone from any other reef I had visited, diffused and tinted by the clouded cap, bathing the reef in the sepia luminance of nostalgia for a lost continent under the sea.

My cameraman, Darryl Lai, and I had traveled to Varadero after meeting Valeria Pizarro and Mateo Lopez Victoria at a coral conference in Hawai'i. At lunch in the main hall of the convention center, we were prospecting for stories. Their table had two open seats. Once we had explained our project, Valeria stood up and circled over to us, showing photos on her phone. "Have you ever seen a reef like this in the Caribbean?" she asked. We hadn't seen anything like it—not anywhere in the world.

So a couple months later, we joined their team in the field off Cartagena to film them gathering data on this strange and wonderful reef scheduled for destruction. That's when I made my dive. Valeria Pizarro was project manager, having left her consulting job for those dredging the reef and joining another team hoping to unlock its secrets. The party included Monica Medina from Penn State University and Roberto Prieto from the University of Mexico.

They represented a growing coalition engaged in a mission extending beyond mere empirical study. This reef was unique and astounding, and so threatened that they knew there wouldn't be enough time to answer all the questions they were asking about it before it was destroyed. The scope of their efforts was fast expanding into territory that is often controversial for scientists—advocacy.

Monica Medina, a coral microbiologist by training, had secured a RAPID grant from the National Science Foundation, a program that allocates modest funds for urgent projects. The dredging of Varadero fit the bill. Medina was born and raised in Colombia before pursuing academic opportunities in the United States, and for her this was a chance to apply her talents to a critical project in her home country.

She'd grown up with a sense of pride in Colombia's astonishing biodiversity, one of the most ecologically rich nations on the planet. When she learned of Pizarro's discovery, she saw an opportunity to give back to the country that ignited her curiosity about the natural world.

Now she was building a coalition around her research. This included scientists and filmmakers from around the world and also locals from the nearby community of Bocachica. That's how Pablo Avendaño became a part of the effort. Avendaño is one of the *Ochos Hermanos* or "Eight Siblings" who eke out a living with their small fleet of boats, shuttling passengers to Cartagena, fishing, hosting tourists, and now bringing scientists to Varadero. They became more than just the group's official pilots—they added value, insight, and their own history working on the reef.

After our first morning of dives, Avendaño brought us to Bocachica so we could regroup after the unsettling spectacle that is Varadero. The tiny town was becoming a hub for the research activity. Its residents stood to lose the most if the reef were dredged. For generations, fishermen from the village have been plying these waters, perhaps unaware of the colorful landscape below the layer of murk, but absolutely certain that something down there attracts fish like a magnet. When I carried my camera ashore, a group of old fishermen gathered around me while I flipped through images on the small LCD screen.

"Ahh, look at the mountains!" one fisherman said with reverence, pointing at the massing colonies.

"Look at the fish!" another exclaimed. The men gathered close, murmuring in surprise and wonder. Varadero possesses the power to astonish even those who know it best.

Bocachica is tucked next to the seventeenth-century fort of San Fernando. If you arrive as a tourist and step onto the plush stretch of beach, someone will soon rush over to offer you an interpretive tour. You'll hear about the moat surrounding the fort that was once filled with ravenous sharks, where slave laborers were tossed as punishment for recalcitrance. You'll hear about the blood of the slaves mixed into the very mortar that constructed the walls. Slavery may have been abolished in Colombia more than a decade before it was in the United States, but the descendants of those who built the fort and who decided to stay and carve out a life in Bocachica certainly haven't prospered in their emancipation. The town's streets are made of mud and studded with broken glass. The houses are ramshackle or spartan, though coats of vibrant paint, the carefully restored fortress, and a glorious stretch of palm-lined beach give it the thin veneer of a tropical paradise. There are few services you'd expect to find in a modern city: no paved streets, no garbage disposal, limited access to health care. The arrival of electricity was so recent that even the youth recall the event.

Still, the villagers are savvy survivors. In addition to fishing, Bocachicans also subsist on tourism, playing host to occasional boatloads of travelers from nearby Cartagena who seek pristine beaches beyond the cloudy water of the bay but can't afford the trip to the more luxurious beaches farther along the archipelago. But since recent rounds of widening of the existing channel and the subsequent increase in shipping traffic, there has been a steady drop in visitors. Development of a second channel could prove disastrous, reducing the numbers of fish and tourists both.

"What's going to happen to us if they tear down the reef? Things are going to get more complicated. What will we live off of?" wondered Hector Avendaño, another of the *Ochos Hermanos*. He was a stocky fisherman with a generous smile and a business sensibility. Hector also owned a pavilion

Page 122: Fishermen from the town of Bocachica display their catch. The size of fish has been on the decline.

Above: Local fishermen from the island of Tierra Bomba who rely on paddle power are entirely dependent on the local reef for their catch.

This *Agaricia*, or lettuce coral, is a hardy species that forms razor-sharp ridges and grows in abundant thickets in Varadero.

with a thatched roof near the beach that turned into a restaurant or even a makeshift school when needed. It became our island studio for interviews.

For now, the *Ochos Hermanos* seem to be managing. Their boats are in good repair; their motors run reliably. And when they do break down, Avendaño and his siblings have the knowledge to fix them on the fly with only a length of cord and a pair of pliers. But like the tough reef that they fish, they're not so sure they can withstand the forces of progress.

I asked him what he had to say to the authorities planning to dredge the channel. "I'd ask them to put their hands over their hearts. Because how can they destroy something that's been planted here for years?"

The *Ochos Hermanos* appreciated their newest clients, the growing number of scientists Medina and her coalition have drawn to the reef. "For some reason these corals are doing well, and they are tolerating a lot of environmental insults," Medina said when we interviewed her in Avendaño's pavilion. She smiled at an old woman who wandered in, shyly offering bites from a tray of coconut sweets melting in the heat. Medina bought some out of politeness but also to savor a taste of home.

She told me that it was not only important to study the corals, but also important to protect them, because they were trying to find relics of reefs that are sturdy, that are resilient, that are really robust against climate change and anthropogenic activities, and this reef seemed to be one of them.

Indeed, while the loss of Varadero so soon after its discovery would be a stunning blow to science, Avendaño and his siblings stood to lose most if Varadero were dredged. They were the ones who fished its crags and canyons for red snapper and octopus. They were the ones forced to travel farther, work longer, and rely on more dangerous fishing practices to make ends meet. Their fledgling tourism industry would suffer if there was a doubling of the massive freighters chugging past. For Medina, exploring this reef and meeting the people who depend on it had become a career-defining moment.

"I always question, 'Why did I get a PhD?'" she reflected. She'd been drawn to her career because of the intellectual puzzles that scientists unravel, the thrill of being the first person to know some obscure detail about how the world works. But after we interviewed the local people about their lives on the reef and their concerns for the future, she saw that her work was serving a bigger cause. "This is why I got my doctorate," she said. Varadero, and the coalition she was forging for its advocacy, were bigger than science. She was worried about the future of Colombia. And of the children.

We spent several days on Varadero while the scientists collected samples and measured transects. The days were long, hot, and tiring. In the evenings the researchers shared their theories about this strange reef.

Mateo Lopez had also been caught off guard by Varadero. He literally wrote the book on Colombian coral reefs, and while he was traveling the entire coastline gathering information for that manuscript, his team took one look at the brown waters of the bay and didn't even bother to dive there. "In the textbooks corals like crystal-clear, deep blue water. But these corals are telling us, 'There's something wrong with your books, because we're doing well here.'" Lopez said.

Roberto Prieto was a coral physiologist who studied the shape and structure of coral colonies and how they respond to environmental factors. With a gray chin beard and a reputation for sagacity, he was the senior researcher on the team. The other scientists referred to him affectionately as "Dumbledore," the beloved wizard from the Harry Potter books. Prieto's specialty was investigating how living organisms respond to light, and he believed that part of these corals' resilience stemmed from how the murky layer fools them into thinking that they are living at a greater depth. "You can see these morphologies of corals when you dive very deep in the rest of the Caribbean," he said. "In some parts of Mexico you will find these types of morphologies at forty-five meters. But not necessarily at four meters." These corals grew with the light-hungry shapes of deeper corals but without having to contend with the colder water associated with greater depth.

Varadero proves corals are resilient. And surprising. That they can adapt to their location. That they can endure through hardships. But climate change is happening so fast that there's not much time for adaptation. A mass extinction is already underway. Past extinction events have wiped out reefs. If corals succumb en masse this time, they could eventually reemerge again from oblivion, but only after millions of years.

Mateo got philosophical. "I'm not worried about the corals…. Somehow, some way, they will find a way. In millions of years they will come back again. But what I'm really sorry for is us, for humankind. I'm worried that our children and the children of our children will not be able to see even half of what I have seen."

There are global pressures and local pressures. And then there are national politics and civil war. All of these factors shape the fate of Varadero. Colombia has been, in fits and starts, emerging from the hemisphere's longest-running conflict. A tentative peace between the Revolutionary Armed Forces of Colombia, or FARC, and the central government was signed in 2016, spurring development interest in the resource-rich areas formerly held by the rebels. This in turn created pressure for expanded port infrastructure, like the channel through Varadero.

Pizarro understood her country's troubled history well. Her uncle, Carlos Pizarro, was a founder and leader of the Movimiento 19 de Abril, or M-19, a rebel group that waged armed struggle against the government in the 1970s and '80s. A rabble-rousing law student with leftist leanings, Carlos Pizarro cut a dashing figure, and in photos he even resembles the bearded young Che Guevara.

The M-19 staged a series of swashbuckling, symbolic acts, like theft of the sword of Simón Bolívar from a museum. Other actions included breaking into the national armory to steal rifles and laying siege to the Dominican embassy, holding international diplomats captive, including the ambassador from the United States. They had a sense of panache, and Pizarro became a sort of rebel heartthrob.

The American ambassador survived, but the M-19's actions grew more reckless, eventually taking a brutal and bloody turn, as did the government's response. In 1988, the group began negotiations: in exchange for laying down arms, they asked forgiveness for their crimes and the ability to participate in the political process, not unlike the demands FARC recently negotiated. By 1989, the group returned the stolen sword and rebranded themselves as an old-fashioned political party. The charismatic Pizarro became their candidate for president. By 1990 he was leading in the polls, posing an even greater threat to the establishment than when he'd been a rebel commander. On April 26, 1990, while traveling on an Avianca Airlines flight from the capital to the Caribbean coast, he was assassinated. Suspicions of involvement in the murder ranged from political rivals to drug cartels, the CIA, or a combination of all three.

Given her family history, it was no surprise that Valeria Pizarro grew up with a focus on social issues. "The discussions within the family have always been how to improve and how things should be done, and how you should solve all the issues of the country,"

she said as we rode in a cab along the slip of road where the thick walls of Cartagena's old city meet the sea. Varadero might not be the sword of Simón Bolívar, but it was hard not to admire the rebel spirit in these besieged corals that continued to thrive and still remained part of Cartagena Bay's natural fortifications, defenders of the Heroic City that Bolívar liberated during the founding of a nation.

Pizarro and Medina took us to meet another member of the broad coalition of scientists, activists, and community leaders who were beginning to gather around the flag of the defiant corals. We were to meet the spiritual leader of the movement. We stopped at a convenience store to purchase a tribute: a six-pack of beer and a bag of plantain chips.

Then, in a cozy apartment tucked behind the Cartagena airport, we met Rafael Vergara. With long gray hair pulled into a ponytail and a booming voice paired with a sparkling wink that suggested we shouldn't always take him too seriously, he was a slice of living history.

Vergara's apartment was filled with Amazonian art, small fetishes, and statues and shelves of plants, so that we felt as if we were in the jungle. He gave us a tour of the flat. He was especially proud of a felt painting of topless mermaids above his bed and a large Siberian husky panting in the heat under his writing desk. In the hallway I paused, taken aback by a black-and-white photo on the wall that depicted Vergara in the jungle sitting next to the dashing Carlos Pizarro, complete with a beard and beret. Vergara was also an alumnus of the guerrillas. But he'd now channeled his revolutionary spirit into a role as an environmental attorney and journalist who used his column in the local newspaper to advocate for Varadero's protection.

"This is a heroic coral reef. It has resisted everything. It has resisted pollution. It has resisted sedimentation. It has resisted unclean waters. It has to continue resisting, but now it is our turn," Vergara said during our interview, pounding his chest like a rebel commander firing up his true believers.

That the utopian idealism of Vergara and Pizarro's generation has become the science-based, pragmatic form of environmental activism of Valeria Pizarro and Monica Medina is part of a hopeful trajectory in Colombia. Once violent armed struggle seemed like the only solution. But Colombians now feel that they can work within the system. While Vergara's language may still carry a martial tone, he is now fighting with words instead of weapons. "Now we have to come out in their defense because they cannot move," he says of the threatened corals. "Their strength is their beauty in survival. Our defense has to be an ethical imperative."

Cartagena is not only a flash point of the struggle to preserve Colombia's astounding biodiversity but also the symbolic home of another massive shift: the signing of the peace accords between the government and the FARC. On Monday, September 26, 2016, shortly after our first visit to the reef and nearly thirty years after the M-19 demobilized, president Juan Manuel Santos and FARC leader Rodrigo Londoño, both dressed in white, shook hands in agreement to end five decades of civil war. The event was drenched in symbolism. With the thick walls of the old city in the background, the crowds of observers, also wearing white, watched as a cloud of doves swarmed the air while jets zipped overhead trailing the gold, red, and blue colors of the nation's flag. Beethoven's *Ode to Joy* blared from speakers.

Valeria Pizarro was in the stands. "For me, being there was very exciting and emotional—a little bit overwhelming," she said. She sat among other survivors and victims of the conflict. "I couldn't stop thinking on how great and difficult were the times to come."

And she was right to be concerned. A week after the signing, voters rejected the peace accord in a referendum. Many felt the terms of the agreement were too lenient on the guerrillas who had waged the bloody struggle against the government for so long. She was depressed for weeks. It was the only thing she talked about with her friends and family.

The Colombian parliament eventually approved a revised peace agreement, providing new hope and earning Santos a Nobel Peace Prize. But then the more strident and militant government of Iván Duque was voted into power in 2018, and the peace accords have been on shaky ground again, with both sides reneging or failing to fulfill terms of the accords. Ironically, this stuttering end to the conflict may be aiding the cause of preserving Varadero while investors wait and observe the oscillation of the peace process before committing to massive infrastructure projects.

Varadero's future remains uncertain. Dredging has yet to commence. In 2018, the reef was designated as a "Hope Spot" by Sylvia Earle's organization, Mission Blue. There have even been public discussions of protecting Varadero as part of the regional marine park. It has been a major step for the government even to acknowledge the existence of the reef. But, conspicuously, no one has taken dredging off the table. Mateo reported from the latest round of discussions with a decidedly pessimistic view. He worries that even though they are entering negotiations about the fate of Varadero, the government's true end goal is to find a way "to destroy it quietly and nicely."

There are other options for a second shipping channel. A longer route could be carved for ships through the Bocagrande section of the bay that was blocked off centuries ago. But it would be much more costly to dredge the greater distance, and it would lead freighters past some of Cartagena's highest-priced real estate. At Bocachica there are no condos, only a ramshackle fishing village.

Varadero still crouches below its cap of muddy water. Bocachican fishermen still drift over its corals, fishing from dugout canoes and small launches. Medina, Pizarro, and their coalition of scientists, villagers, and even an ex-guerrilla perform surveys and transects, pen passionate editorials, and document and photograph the spectacular corals in an attempt to decipher the mystery that allows these colonies to thrive in such an unlikely location. They hope that having the eyes of the world on their nation as it stutters through its peace process might shed some light on their efforts.

The Heroic Reef has survived, largely hidden from view, through half a millennium of human exploitation and conflict. If there ever is a last coral reef, it may well look like this hidden wonder, defying the odds, sequestered below a murky veil of progress. But Pizarro now believes it's time to share Varadero's secret with the world. This reef gives scientists hope. At a time of global coral destruction, Varadero offers promise that some of its corals may survive the onslaught. But as the great freighters continue to rumble past Bocachica, the scientists and fishermen understand that any day the dredging on the second channel may start, and Varadero could become just a memory, an artifact, another part of Colombia's glorious and tragic history.

Valeria Pizzaro swims past a pair of massive mounding corals. While most other reefs in the Caribbean have less than 20 percent coral cover, Varadero averages 80 percent coverage. The reason for this unusual vitality remains a mystery.

Part III

Searching for Hope

"The world is a fine place, and worth fighting for,
and I should very much hate to leave it."
Ernest Hemingway, *For Whom the Bell Tolls*

"Humans only love what they know; and people
do not destory what they love."

Bob Fenner, *The Conscientious Marine Aquarist*

9

Lionfish Hunters
of Tom Owen's Caye

Southern Belize

WE CAME TO BELIZE TO kill fish and save corals. One of the most beautiful creatures on the world's second longest barrier reef also causes the most damage, so my daughter and I joined a strike team of spear-wielding conservationists on lethal expeditions to deep coral canyons in order to hunt down these lovely fish.

And eat them.

In this way we learned that conservation could be both delicious and fun. Especially when your base of operations is a tiny jewel of an island set in gradients of Caribbean turquoise, fully equipped with a dozen hammocks, a volleyball net, and a professional chef.

This adventure had begun years before, when I was packing for my first dive assignment to the Red Sea. My daughter, then ten, tried on my dive gear. She wandered around the house in fins, with my wet suit accordioned down to fit. "Take me with you," she said, as she often did before I traveled for work.

She wanted to learn how to dive. I promised to take her once she turned eleven, the age minimum for certification by the Professional Association of Diving Instructors.

But the years slipped by with that promise unfulfilled, and suddenly she was seventeen and no longer asking to tag along. In a panic, I started looking for a way to continue my research on struggling reefs and also bring her along for dive training. That's when I came across a program in Belize called Reef Conservation International. They offered five-day trips to a remote island where volunteers paid for the opportunity to learn about reef ecology, participate in underwater conservation, and even check off training requirements with certified instructors. The whole scenario sounded fascinating, idyllic, adventurous, and meaningful to boot. In short, it seemed too good to be true.

A few emails and exchanges of credit card information later, and we were booked. And thus

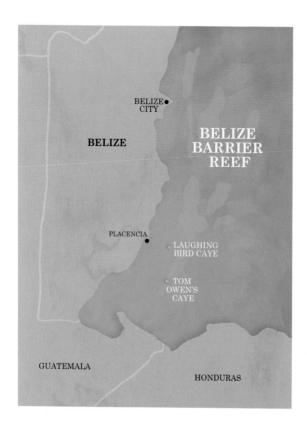

Page 134: A lionfish wriggles on the end of a sling spear. Tourists are enlisted in the effort to reduce their numbers in Belize.

began my first experience with the sometimes controversial practice of ecotourism.

It's human nature to seek wild, untrammeled places or immerse ourselves in new and fascinating cultures. Those of us who chase the unfamiliar are following an ancient tradition, from the Polynesian voyagers who settled a vast continent of scattered islands and atolls to the eighteenth-century geographers and explorers like Humboldt and Cook who trailed curiosity to the ends of Earth. In the nineteenth century, we began to set aside wild places like Yellowstone specifically for the purpose of connecting citizens to unspoiled landscapes. The early twentieth century brought safaris, favored by Hemingway and others, where reverence for wildness was often accompanied by an elephant gun.

By the 1960s, as air travel began to open up the last wild corners of the world to the masses, writers like Rachel Carson and Edward Abbey were making us aware that nature is finite and fragile. So a subset of intrepid travelers began to seek ways to visit remote places without ushering in a monoculture of resorts and a plague of T-shirt shops and parking lots. Could mass global tourism be tweaked to lessen its impact on remote wilderness? Maybe thoughtful tourism could even aid conservation, putting political and economic pressure on governments to protect pristine landscapes.

By the end of the 1960s, ecological scholars like Nicolas Hetzer were suggesting a set of principles to fuse tourism with conservation for the benefit of fragile ecosystems and traditional cultures. This friendlier form of travel, they suggested, should have five basic principles. It would be "nature-based, ecologically sustainable, environmentally educative, locally beneficial, and generate tourist satisfaction." By the 1980s, a name was given to this concept, and "ecotourism" had arrived. Here was a practice born of the optimistic capitalist conviction that the same market forces responsible for the relentless destruction of the natural world could be tweaked for its preservation and even restoration.

Reef Conservation International followed those five principles of ecotourism to a T, at least according to the website copy. I was eager to find out how it all worked.

Ecotourism is not without its problems. Travel in any form eventually brings development, which changes culture and puts pressure on vulnerable ecosystems. Citizen scientists from overseas enlisted on conservation missions perform tasks that could be done more deftly and cheaply by locals in need of jobs. Tourists from the developed north bring fat wallets that drive up prices, and locals end up having to pay more for goods and services they need to survive. Corporations sometimes use the ecotourism label to greenwash expansive and unsustainable resort developments. Trophy-hunting outfitters even claim the ecotourism mantle, and while there is evidence that hunting can create economic and political pressure to preserve habitat, that doesn't matter much to an unlucky lion.

More benign activities like diving still impact ecosystems. Recreational divers can take a toll on reefs, especially if they lack experience and education. Even the best diver will bump up against a coral on occasion, breaking off branches and opening up vectors for infections. Sometimes they can carry pathogenic hitchhikers in their gear. Plenty of studies show that heavily dived locations have stunted corals and more disease pressure than sites off-limits to divers.

And finally, in any form of long-distance travel, 90 percent of its contribution to climate change comes from the trip to get there. It would ultimately be better for the planet for all of us to stay home.

But staying home wasn't a choice or sacrifice I was willing to make. I wanted to get back into the water. I'd heard tales of wonder about the Mesoamerican Barrier Reef system, the world's second largest. I knew that the fabled reefs of Belize were also in decline. I wanted my daughter to learn how to dive and see healthy corals while there was still a chance. Plus I had a book deadline approaching and needed another chapter.

So that's how we wound up, after a red-eye flight from Oregon and a gauntlet of airports punctuated by a jouncy ride in a single-prop island hopper, standing on a dock of Hokey Pokey Water Taxi at the end of a sandy finger of land pointing south toward Honduras, waiting for a boat to take us to a speck of an island known as Tom Owen's Caye. Our intention was to help corals and have fun. Was this combination possible? We were about to find out.

It took an hour of slamming through large waves on the inner lagoon to reach the tiny island. As we pulled up to the dock, we could see a line of foam rippling out to the horizon as swells broke on the shallow shelves of the barrier reef. Our new island home was just a small exposed tip of a massive, submerged landscape.

We were now on the Mesoamerican Barrier Reef, a feat of coral construction second only to the Great Barrier Reef. It runs seven hundred miles from Mexico's Yucatán Peninsula, along Belize, past Guatemala, and down to Honduras. It's the home range of one of the largest surviving populations of manatees. Hawksbill and loggerhead turtles nest there. Whale sharks stop by for visits, along with five hundred other species of fish. There are sixty-five species of stony coral. Tom Owen's Caye, our home for the week, lay in the Sapodilla Cayes Marine Reserve in the southern reaches of the system.

Our tour group came from across the United States and Great Britain, along with the Belizean staff of cooks, boat pilots, housekeepers, and dive instructors. There were some other parents with teens, and I was pleased for my daughter that it wasn't a group of bird-watchers my own age or older, an early fear. We disembarked, and while the staff dispersed to their chores, the rest of us wandered about the little island charmed and awestruck. Palms swayed above, many strung with hammocks. A half-dozen huts and a sturdy central building with walls of mortared reef rubble seemed both cozy and comfortingly hurricane-proof. There was a volleyball court, a makeshift outdoor gym, and then what looked to be a cheerful little cemetery but upon closer inspection was a collection of signposts and conch shell rings indicating where sea turtles had recently nested.

As we were waiting for a second boat that carried the food and luggage, I followed some of the other guests a few dozen yards across the island to a stone pier with steps leading into the turquoise water. I jumped into this massive bathtub and paddled around. It was sheer bliss until I felt a sudden sharp scrape against my ankle. For a moment I thought I'd been bitten by something toothy, but then I noticed dark, massing shapes around me. I'd sliced my ankle on a stand of lettuce coral that rose to within a few inches of the surface. I turned in the water, hoping the blood oozing out in ribbons wouldn't tempt the barracuda that had suddenly appeared nearby. Despite the cut on my ankle, I was thrilled by the coral encounter. Here, within a few meters of the island's edge and within the shadow of its little buildings, was a dense stand of stony corals. Until that moment, I hadn't realized that it was possible for humans and corals could coexist in such proximity.

And then the bell rang. It hung in the courtyard of the main building. I hobbled out of the water and assembled with the group for our first briefing, where

The 1.5 acres of Tom Owen's Caye are perched on the edge of the Belize Barrier Reef.

we received our room assignments and learned the rules of the island—mainly that when the bell rang, you came running. That clanging would become our taskmaster. It would summon us to assemble our dive gear and load the boats for our early morning dive. Then it would muster us for breakfast. Next it gathered us for presentations on reef conservation, coral biology, or fish identification. Then the cycle would repeat for more dives, meals, and presentations. The bell kept us on schedule. It roused us from hammock slumber, swimming, reading, or sitting on the edge of the pier soaking up nature. The bell is what saved us from the indignity of being ordinary tourists. It transformed us from visitors into volunteers. It transformed us into ecotourists.

We were an easygoing, compliant bunch, though it's admittedly not difficult to encourage compliance when the most demanding task is a five-minute boat ride to spectacular dive sites. Or a graciously prepared and attractively plated meal by the resident chef, Bol, who proudly welcomed guests to his table with a personal description of each dish prepared "in the Belizean style!" and "made from scratch!" An army marches on its stomach, and though we were an army of students, writers, teachers, teens—plus a professional dolphin trainer and a union pipe fitter—we were molded over the week into a trained and not-so-elite fighting force. We weren't killers. Politically, we leaned largely as a group toward granola, with only a couple exceptions. But after training on land with sling spears and unsuspecting coconuts, we were ready for battle. We assembled our dive gear and loaded it onto the boats. We sped out to the theater of action, rap and reggae blaring on the boat speakers, the teens and dive leaders bobbing their heads. Sam, one of the dive masters, called orders to the boat pilot in Creole, and as the captain pulled back on the throttle we eased to a drift. Our leader stepped forward and gave us the briefing. Sam described the site and the depth, the sunken features, currents, and direction we would be swimming. He reviewed the hand signals. "Our mission on this dive," he finished, "is to kill lionfish."

Pterois volitans, also known as the red lionfish, is voracious, beautiful, fecund, easy to hunt, merciless, and tasty. In Belize, and everywhere else in its expanding range in the Atlantic and Caribbean, it is invasive. Lionfish exist in a baroque, feathery cloud of their own fins and venomous spines. Their orange, red, and rust candy-cane stripes both call attention and also make them difficult to spot against the varied topography of the reef bottom.

Hailing from the Indo-Pacific, lionfish made their Atlantic debut off the coast of Florida in 1995 and from there spread quickly through the Caribbean. They're now found from New England to Brazil. The first confirmed sighting in Belize was in 2008, and they quickly overwhelmed the Belize Barrier Reef and coastal mangroves.

How these Pacific predators made the leap to this side of the world, nobody knows for sure. Theories include their bumming a ride in the ballast water of transoceanic ships. They're also popular for home aquariums, and some suggest an intentional release or escape. The description on one hobby website hints at why it could go so wrong: "It is generally not recommended to keep lionfish in the same tank as smaller fish and ornamental crabs or shrimp unless these creatures are intended to be food for the lionfish."

Whatever the case, the Caribbean lionfish invasion was aided and abetted by humans. *Pterois volitans* joins a litany of other species imported by people to cause mayhem and extinction, whether that be foxes and feral cats decimating mammals and birds in Australia, dogs and rats imported to Pacific islands, carp muscling out other fish in American waterways, zebra mussels, emerald ash borers, cane toads—the dubious list is long and daunting. But lionfish are not just a threat to other species; they can bring down entire systems.

Red lionfish are lethal predators. They'll eat anything their own size or smaller as long as it fits in their mouths. And because larger predators in the Caribbean have not evolved to hunt them and don't quite know how to work around their eighteen venomous spines, and because their prey species have not adapted to evade them, lionfish and their insatiable appetites are the perfect killing machines. They're indiscriminate and opportunistic, and they'll snack on anything from juveniles of commercially important species like grouper and snapper or those that perform the vital task of reef algae removal, like surgeonfish and parrotfish. Lionfish seem to have a particular fondness for the critically endangered social wrasse. They can decimate reefs and put fishing communities out of business.

Lionfish thrive in the Caribbean, where they often have population densities greater than in their native Indo-Pacific range. Unchecked, they've been shown to destroy up to 94 percent of a reef's native fish populations. They can reproduce at a rate that puts rabbits to shame, reaching sexual maturity in less than a year and producing up to two million eggs annually. They're adaptable and live in a range of environments, from shallow reefs, mangroves, and sea-grass beds to depths of a thousand feet or more.

Given their fecundity, adaptability, and ferocious appetites, hunting lionfish didn't seem like some lark or novel greenwashing. It was serious work. Every dead lionfish reduced a serious coral reef threat.

While I was skeptical that a squad of newly trained spearfishers on Tom Owen's Caye could make much of a dent in lionfish populations, each dive leader optimistically carried two sling spears and a thick collecting tube into the depths on every dive. And we usually encountered our first lionfish within minutes of slipping below the surface.

Given the scale of their impact and their fierce reputation, lionfish are surprisingly easy to kill. While it does take skill to learn how to work a spear underwater as you control your buoyancy and avoid stabbing yourself, another diver, or sensitive marine animals like corals, lionfish patiently await their coup de grâce.

They're usually found in hunting groups of three or more, drifting near the bottom or edges of large corals. There they use their feathery, fin-inflated profiles to herd shoals of juvenile fish, slowly surrounding them before sucking the fry into their massive mouths with lightning-quick gulps. It's unsettlingly easy to sidle up to a lionfish and ready your spear. They won't dart away. It's almost like they're daring you to attack. Maybe they're overconfident in their venomous spines and camouflage.

The spears were four feet long with three sharp prongs at the tip and an elastic band looped at the butt end. When someone in the dive group spotted a lionfish, interlacing fingers and wiggling them to mimic our spiny prey, the dive leader handed a spear over. We then looped the elastic band around our thumbs and choked way up on the spear, stretching the band, gripping the shaft six inches behind the tip, loading the sling with tension. Then we drifted up close to the fish, within two feet, extending our arms and waiting for a clear shot where we wouldn't hit a coral head. We took a deep breath, exhaled and let fly. In an instant, the offending fish was wriggling on the end of our fork. Sometimes it was pinned to the rock structure and we had to work to extract it. Sometimes we missed or landed a glancing blow, and our quarry slipped away under the lip of a mounding coral. If there were other lionfish nearby, they usually hung out and watched, either baffled or morbidly fascinated, or both.

Once you had a lionfish on your spear, the dive leader brought the tube around. On one end of the tube was an eight-inch opening lined with forked tines. We shoved the fish inside the tube, and the tines kept the fish inside as we extracted the spear.

I felt bad the first time I speared a lionfish. They're pretty, and I felt the vibrations of their death throes running down the spear shaft to my arm. Stuffing their expiring carcasses into the tube filled with lionfish carnage also seemed cruel and brutal. But I quickly got over it. My Pleistocene instincts took the helm and I became a hunter, immediately scanning for the next fish. By my third kill, my tree-hugging, animal-loving tendencies were buried beneath a newfound aptitude for butchery.

After every dive, we returned with dozens of dead and dying lionfish. We emptied the catch tubes into crates while nurse sharks hungrily circled the pier. Caribbean predators don't know how to handle live lionfish, with their bristles and spines, but the lifeless carcasses are a delicacy.

There was a demonstration table by the pier, and a popular activity, especially with the teenagers, was cleaning the lionfish. Each specimen, no matter how tiny, was carefully filleted, with extra care taken to avoid the venomous dorsal spines. A sting can be extremely painful though not fatal to humans. The average fillet was bite-sized, about as big as a chicken nugget.

Every day, ten of the unlucky invaders suffered the added indignity of dissection. Their stomachs were sliced open and the contents were picked, prodded, and logged on a spreadsheet, noting the numbers and species of undigested prey. It was common to find shrimp, silver juveniles, gobies, and wrasses all in a rainbow of colors. Lionfish stomachs contained anywhere from a few fish to dozens.

Christmas tree worms settle on coral colonies and secrete calcareous tubes, which the coral eventually grows around. The worms emerge from their burrows in fanning spirals, filtering the water for phytoplankton.

Next, we trimmed off the tails and spines and set them aside to be used for making jewelry. And at night, our talented chef, Bol, served up the fillets fried or in curries. The meat has a dense texture, soft and rich. Locals compare it to grouper, a fish so tasty that the signal you use underwater to indicate that you've seen one is to rub your tummy and smile.

Throughout the week, our team grew more deadly with our spear work. I no longer felt a twinge of guilt when I impaled a lionfish. They even started to seem less beautiful to me. The daily kill tallies climbed. And as the new trainees gained confidence in their diving and joined more advanced divers in the open water, they earned their chances.

By the time we left the island, my daughter had earned her certification. She'd become a confident diver. And she had two confirmed lionfish kills. I couldn't be more proud.

I wondered how much positive impact our team of novice lionfish hunters might have on Belize's barrier reef. Did the few invaders we culled even begin to offset the carbon cost of our flights to Belize? Certainly not. But there is evidence that programs like the one we attended are having a positive impact overall.

A dive instructor from Reef Conservation International holds the record in number of lionfish killed in a single dive (120). The organization also boasted the largest invader ever speared (1.2 kilograms). The Belize National Lionfish Management Strategy lauds the organization's efforts, noting that they "can offer a sustainable and consistent source of income and manpower to contribute to lionfish management efforts."

Tourism that incorporates the spearing of lionfish is combined with lionfishing tournaments and developing a demand for the tasty invasive fish

in the restaurant industry. Creating a commercial fishery around the species has also been considered, but that can be problematic. What would the fishers who rely on the species do if mitigation is successful and numbers drop? Would commercializing their extraction lead to aquaculturing or re-release of the species? Tourism seems like a good alternative to establishing a commercial fishery.

Reef Conservation International harvests between four thousand and ten thousand lionfish each year. They study the stomach contents of forty fish per week and share the data. After a spike in lionfish populations in Belize occurred shortly after they first appeared, their numbers have declined and now leveled off. There's no doubt that our efforts reduced a direct pressure on the reefs we had come here to enjoy.

Killing lionfish was so much fun that it wasn't until our last full day of diving on the island that I looked closely at the coral cover on the fore reef, which is the massive outer slope of the barrier reef that faces the open sea. In the distance I spotted the columns of a pillar coral, a rare species that is functionally extinct in Florida. As I finned closer, I saw that the specimen was dead, its dozen columns devoid of living tissue. That saddened me.

I began to look more closely at the reef structure. Much of the intricate rock work on the slope was just bare coral skeletons, the living tissue gone. A few colonies grew here and there on the ghosts of massive colonies. Toward the end of the last dive, I saw a huge mound ahead, scooped and sculpted. It was a giant coral colony the size of a small cabin. As we drew closer, I could see that there were only a few patches of live tissue remaining. This great beautiful beast of a coral, which had been growing for hundreds upon hundreds of years, was dying.

A recent study found that only 17 percent of historic coral cover remains on the Belize Barrier

Reef, and that estimate matches what I saw on that last dive. There were thickets and patches of lush coral cover around our little island and in some of the coral canyons, but it was clear that overall this reef was fighting the same battle for survival as those the world over.

So I left the island with mixed emotions. Killing lionfish was necessary work. The program was part of a solution. The work we did was certainly better than sitting on a developed shoreline sipping daiquiris at a resort where sand is trucked in and dumped directly onto the fringing reefs. I was glad that my daughter was able to learn how to dive on Belize's wonderful reefs. But I was worried about the coral cover. I wanted more hope than 17 percent coral cover could provide. And fortunately, on our last dive in Belize, I would find some.

After returning to the mainland from Tom Owen's Caye, and before leaving Belize, I found the best stand of stony corals I'd seen anywhere in the world. It was surrounding a string bean of an island called Laughing Bird Caye that is a thirty-minute boat ride from the village of Placencia. Laughing Bird Caye is what's known as a faro atoll, a long narrow shelf with steep sides and just the tip of a reef protruding from the water. Its structure and formation make it ideal for a range of corals, from mounding species that build on the steep, deep sides to branching corals in the shallow waters of the island's edges. Laughing Bird's coral bounty has long made it a refuge, earning it designation as a national park and part of a World Heritage Site. Even after the rare namesake birds had abandoned the little sliver of land, the corals remained, strong and healthy. But in 2001, Hurricane Iris passed over and scoured the island's shallow shelf of surrounding corals. Overnight it was turned into a wasteland of coral rubble.

But, two decades on, its fringing reefs have returned. The edges of the island are thick with the *Acroporids* (elkhorn and staghorn corals) that have long vanished from most of the rest of the Caribbean. And this renewal all happened because of one person.

Lisa Carne is a native Californian who came to Belize to study corals and never left. This country, with its small population and vast jungles and reefscapes, has a long history of drawing refugees from the outside world, from seventeenth-century pirates to twenty-first-century retirees. Carne has now spent more than half her life in Belize and has a Creole lilt to her speech as evidence. I met her one afternoon on the second floor of a bar overlooking the pier at Placencia village. She'd carved out some time for me, a precious commodity for someone who serves as director and sole full-time employee of one of the most successful coral restoration foundations on the planet.

Carne traveled with an entourage. With her were a researcher, a board member, a chemist, an artist, and an aerial photographer. Like other conservation coalitions I'd seen, this was a ragtag cast of the truly committed. She was refreshingly frank, honest, and direct in a manner that bespoke some of the glowing press her efforts had rightly received. She was the subject of one recent article that gushed "How Belize saved its beloved coral." But she was not one to rest on her laurels.

Over a pair of drinks and a few cigarettes, we talked about her project, Fragments of Hope. It's been a registered nonprofit in Belize and the United States since 2013, but she has been doing restoration work since the devastating hurricane in 2001. After watching a thriving stand of corals wiped from the map, she began researching how to restore corals. Restoration work had been underway in other parts of the world for decades. It was a growing field.

Dissecting lionfish is a popular activity on an island without wifi and other digital distractions.

She'd read about the work of Austin Kirby, who had experimented with and documented techniques in the Pacific. She studied the efforts of Ken Nedimyer, who grew corals as part of his aquarium live rock business in Florida.

Carne borrowed from Kirby's and Nedimyer's designs and established nurseries in the water right at the edge of Laughing Bird Caye. She took coral fragments that were growing in similar conditions elsewhere and established them on the A-frame nursery structures in the water, then later on square-rigged wire frame tables. This was a key distinction between what she does in Belize and what happens in many other parts of the restoration world.

Other organizations, many with much larger budgets, lots of paid staff, and armies of volunteers, grow corals in labs or in huge nurseries, and then transport the fragments to the restoration location. But Carne's program grows the young corals on-site. "We grow them right on the reef. Then we see who our survivors are," she said with a shrug, flicking ash from her cigarette.

I asked why her project has been so successful on such a limited budget. She said that local support was the key. Fragments of Hope trains Belizeans in restoration techniques. They run classes in the evenings so that women and others with jobs and who work in tourism and fishing can participate. "If people aren't taken care of, they won't take care of the reef," she explained.

On this point, she was adamant. She decried "parachute science," and she backed up this criticism by example. She'd come and she stayed. She worked local. I asked if she was worried about global pressures like climate change.

"Climate change is out of Belize's hands," she said. She admitted to frustrations. They were a small foundation in a tiny country, and they needed to stay laser-focused on what was possible. Belize had been lauded for its environmental track record. But it was also called out for graft and collaboration with powerful global companies that dodged environmental regulations, often a problem in a small, poor country. Carne gestured across the water toward a new resort under development on a nearby caye, where the fringing reef was being damaged by construction.

"How do you maintain hope?" I asked.

"The corals give me hope. And the people. You want hope? Go out to Laughing Bird," she said.

So that's what we did. The next day, Bailey and I joined a dive tour out to the island. We met up with our friend Nick from Tom Owen's Caye and headed across the lagoon. In thirty minutes, a tiny sliver of sand and palm trees appeared on the horizon. We anchored nearby and slipped into the water.

Our guide, Harry, carried a short spear, but we didn't see lionfish. We saw eels, a huge nurse shark, and plenty of parrotfish and lobster. Laughing Bird Caye is in a marine protected area, off-limits to fishing. The regulations are strictly enforced. Ten thousand divers and snorkelers visit every year, and tour guides can kill lionfish on sight. The coral cover on the fore reef was greater than what we'd seen on the southern barrier reef, but it wasn't until we beached on the island and I jumped out of the boat to snorkel the shallows that I saw the thumbprint of Fragments of Hope.

Carne had now arrived in another boat along with her entourage. They were making aerial and underwater photo surveys to record the coral cover.

I snorkeled out to join them. After finning across fifty feet of sandy bottom, I came to the first patch of restored reef. It was a wicked thicket of staghorn with an entire school of juvenile grunts tucked under the reaching fingers of *Acropora*. It was stunning.

She called me over to another wide patch of corals, and pretty soon I was floating over shallow reefs completely covered in healthy corals. There were a few mounding and brain corals, but mostly thick stands of staghorn and then some massive, elegant elkhorn corals. Some of the outplants had been growing for fifteen years. I'd never seen coral anywhere so dense.

Carne broke away from the survey work to lead me on a tour. She showed me the nurseries. They were tall tables, like bed frames, secured to the seafloor with ropes running from one side to the other and fragments of *Acropora* tangled in the ropes. Their work largely done, the nursery beds were mostly defunct, but the remaining corals on the ropes were growing to healthy size, with some fragments broken off and now affixed to the substrate below the tables. The corals were taking over.

I saw patches of reef in various stages of growth around the caye. It was a magic, humbling sight. The numbers are impressive. The transplanted corals have survived for fifteen years. More than 82,000 corals have been planted, covering an area larger than a hectare. The work has been replicated across twenty-three nurseries at ten different locations on the Belize Barrier Reef. All this work was driven by the passion of one woman and a handful of volunteers and believers.

Ecotourism is still tourism, and it carries all the ecological baggage of international travel. It probably won't lead to the salvation of reefs. Perhaps it is only moderately less damaging than other forms of tourism, but it feels like a step in the right direction and it binds us to the natural landscapes that we love.

And for those who participate in ecotourism, the impact can be substantial. I've rarely felt so tethered to a wild landscape than those days I spent on Tom Owen's Caye. The naturalist E. O. Wilson's biophilia hypothesis suggests that we, as humans, have an innate need to be near other living things. On Tom Owen's Caye, and on Laughing Bird, we were certainly surrounded by life. We were hemmed in by corals and sea grass with glittering shoals of fish, scuttling crabs, and soaring frigate birds. It wasn't a surprise to see a pod of dolphin slip past. Nurse sharks circled looking for remains of lionfish.

One night on Tom Owen's Caye, a female turtle dragged herself up onto the island and painstakingly began digging holes, prospecting for the perfect spot to nest. Nick, the social spark of our group, went around pounding on doors, rousing us from our slumber. "You'll want to see this!" he effused.

We stood sleepily and patiently watching the mother turtle search for just the right spot. Mike, one of the Belizean guides, steered the tired turtle away from the volleyball court and other high-traffic areas as she searched like Goldilocks for the ideal spot to nest. Weary from diving, most of us eventually drifted back to our rooms. The next morning a guest named Chelsea told me that she had stayed up to watch the turtle lay seventy-eight eggs in the wee hours of the morning. There were tears in her eyes as she recalled how the weary turtle covered her nest and dragged her heavy body back toward the sea, trusting us with her secret. In Chelsea's recounting of the event, I saw the power and potential of ecotourism to bind us to wildness.

We need nature. E. O. Wilson was right. And there's good research that shows exposure to the natural world can improve our physical and mental health, relieve stress, reduce fatigue, enhance our mood, and even help us live longer. And while we need nature, we need each other more. We are a social species, and those of us who admire or fret about the health of the natural world benefit from being around others who share our hopes and fears. That's what the acre and a half of Tom Owen's Caye achieved. It threw a group of neophyte lionfish hunters together for a few days in a far corner of the world and knit us together in unified awe at the wild world around us, and at the human community that had suddenly formed there in the middle of nowhere.

Wildness had assembled us. Many in our group had been in transitions of disruption. I'd been mourning the anthropogenic changes that had been driving the loss of coral reefs for years. But my daughter had just discovered reefs and the wonders of corals. There were guests who were changing jobs, beginning or completing divorces, or taking a last solo trip before getting married. There was a woman who'd left a dying dog at home and another man who still mourned the dog he'd lost years ago. Nature is a tonic for past and present tragedies. There were teens just about to leave home for college. And there was a recent college grad desperately delaying adulthood. All of us stood at the crossroads. We all understood how precarious was this landscape that surrounded us. And all of us had come to Belize for the same reason—to be immersed in wildness. To be remote. Isolated. And to be together.

10

Songs of the Old Gods

Maui, Hawai'i

THE DEMIGOD MAUI, a notoriously lazy fisherman, tricked his brothers. Having snagged a coral reef, he told them he'd hooked the big one, goading them to row their outrigger and pull in a feat of enormous exertion. But instead of landing the promised fish, they drew the Hawaiian Islands themselves up out of the sea, bringing this verdant and most isolated of our planet's archipelagos into the world. The old stories don't say whether his brothers were disappointed by this duplicity, but I do know there are few things more satisfying than catching a nice fish.

It's the fishhook that is of special interest. In some tellings, it is made of coral. I can picture it: bone white and sharp, bent like a crooked finger fashioned from the aragonite heart of an ancient colony. Maui acquired it from his cousin Hina-'opu-hala-ko'a, the goddess of coral reefs and spiny sea creatures. She not only reigned over these submerged rain forests, but would sometimes assume the shape of an entire reef herself. I try to conjure an image of

this goddess, dressed in her baroque vestments pulsing with an aura of fish and studded with lobsters, long-legged shrimp, and pincushion sea stars worn like baubles and brooches.

Corals featured prominently in the oldest stories of the first Hawaiians. They knew the nature of these animals long before Western scientists. As Kahoali'i Keahi-Wood, a cultural expert with Chaminade University Honolulu, told me, "Early Hawaiians understood how corals worked and how they reproduced, and how they provided space for fish."

Hundreds of years ago, when Western scientists were bickering over whether corals were animals, plants, or minerals, Hawaiians were chanting the Kumulipo, an epic creation story in which the very first living creature mentioned is the coral polyp. Corals were offered as living sacrifices at shrines dedicated to sea gods.

Hawaiians knew a lot about the natural world and how to keep ecosystems connected. After years

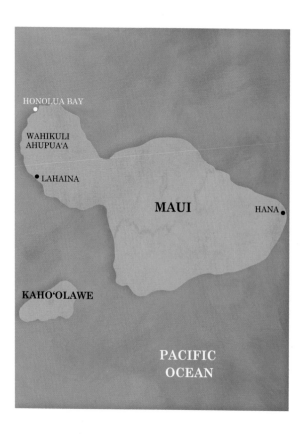

Page 148: A green turtle glides over *Porites* coral heads in Honolua Bay, a popular snorkel spot on the north shore of Maui.

of overtaxing island resources, they responded with innovation to keep systems healthy, including coral reefs. But little of this knowledge was passed to the Westerners who first came for exploration and then stayed for exploitation. This was partly due to Western arrogance, but also partly due to Hawaiian reluctance to share this knowledge. "We were always taught to not give out too much of our history, because what happens is that the outsider could use that against us," Keahi-Wood told me.

But for a moment in history while the old gods reigned, the Hawaiians learned, through centuries of trial and error and extinction of endemic species, to finally live in harmony with their island home. Using pie-shaped *ahupua'a* that kept landscapes intact from reefs to ridgetops, binding *mauka* (mountain) with *makai* (sea) through garden-like, terraced farming practices called *lo'i kao* that filtered the water working its way downslope, the Hawaiians had discovered a sort of balance. Indeed, to upset that balance was an affront to the gods. Dirty the rivers and you offended not only Lono, who gave the gift of rain and presided over the streams and taro plantations, but Kanaloa, god of the sea, who received those fouled waters. Keeping the system healthy and intact was to please the gods. In this way, the islanders were able to sustain large populations without further degradation. As archaeologist Patrick Vinton Kirch has asked, "Could the Hawaiians have been in a stable balance between population and resources, the kind of 'sustainability' that we all see for our planet today?"

While searching for answers to the question of coral reef survival in the face of anthropogenic pressures, I'd been speaking for years to marine biologists, aquarists, microbiologists, geneticists, oceanographers, and paleontologists. But maybe I'd been looking in the wrong place. Maybe the answers remain coded into legend and religion, in that shadow world of deities kept alive in the old stories whispered at the edges of our hyperconnected and carbonized existence.

~~~

Some old gods were on my mind as I stalked corals with a snorkel and underwater camera near a stream outlet next to a resort hotel on the western edge of Maui, the island named after a deity who had hauled it to the surface. In particular, the shark god Kamohoaliʻi had come to mind. Sharks are known to attack swimmers in sedimented brown water, and the nearby stream spilling runoff onto the reef was creating suspect conditions, bringing down silt from the desiccated highlands above the tourist fringe. The beaches of west Maui had been cleared because of an incident with a tiger shark a few days earlier. A lifeguard on a Jet Ski had chased me out of the water. I heard later that a woman was bitten on her ankle while snorkeling near another sedimented stream outlet to the north.

But on this morning I was back in the water to capture photos of the offending sedimentation and its impact on corals. I certainly didn't want to be surprised by a shark, at least not so early in the day, so I mumbled to Kāmohoaliʻi for mercy around the mouthpiece of my snorkel.

As I finned through the shore break and peered through the murky water, I saw leaves and kola nuts swirling in silted eddies. The first rocky substrate I encountered—spilled lava and coral rubble—was slimed with gray-green algae. As I finned farther out, fighting the surge of waves and the tug of a crosscurrent, this ragged mess became encrusted with the occasional outlier colony, a tenacious and perfect little cauliflower coral, *Pocillopora meandrina*, with its graceful bouquet of polyps, clinging to the algae-slicked edge of the degraded reef.

Farther out the water cleared, and I found more cauliflower corals along with great mounds of lobed coral, *Porites lobata*. I dove down and snapped more photos.

Yet farther away from the stream's mouth and its plume of sediment, the clarity improved, and here were great heaps of coral—smooth, irregular mounds with hearty color like vibrant lumps of melting cantaloupe gelato. This was healthy reef. It was a simple equation: the farther away from the little stream mouth and its payload of silt, the healthier the coral looked. I dove down and photographed more, relishing every second I could spend near these plentiful corals, surfacing only when I couldn't hold my breath a moment longer. After a week of snorkeling along Maui's fringing reef, this was my last morning before returning to the rainy Pacific Northwest. I wanted to linger in the presence of scleractinians. Like Hina-ʻopu-hala-koʻa, I wished I could cloak myself in coral vestments.

A movement in my periphery pulled my gaze away from the coral landscape. Was it a shark, drawn to feed in the brown water? No, to my relief it was a big green sea turtle rising to sip air. The sheer size and thick tail indicated that *it* was a *he*. He smiled at me, eyeing me sideways. And I believe he winked.

I drifted in the current a little longer and then reluctantly finned back toward the shore. I had a plane to catch. But my camera's memory card now held photographic evidence of the impact of sediment on reef health. And in that evidence, there was a story.

~~~

Earlier in that trip I'd made that same snorkel circuit alongside Jen Vander Veur, the Maui program coordinator for a nonprofit called the Coral Reef Alliance. On that morning the offending stream was bone dry and the water near its outflow was sparkling clear. As we waded into the water, Jen was a little disappointed that she couldn't show me the clouded water to illustrate the impact of sediment runoff, but a dozen yards from shore, as she began to rattle off the names of species of fish and invertebrates a dozen feet below us, it was obvious that she was reveling in this rare clarity.

She seemed part sea creature herself as she suddenly dove down and snatched a puffy starfish, bringing it to the surface to show me. "This is a cushion star, and it lives with a species of symbiotic shrimp," she said, pointing out with her pinky a small hole into which a tiny crustacean suddenly disappeared. "Sorry we got offtrack. We're supposed to be talking about sediment and corals." She returned the cushion star to its rocky perch below.

As we finned out farther, she showed me the gradation in coral health and the progression of sediment damage. She dove down to point out where the spires and pinnacles of coral heads had been scoured of living coral at their tips. We surfaced again and she explained the long list of effects that sedimented water can have on corals: it carries pesticides down from plantations upstream; it brings nutrients and fertilizers that spur harmful algae growth; it locks competing algae against the mucus layer that corals use to slough off invaders; it smothers corals so that their zooxanthellae can't photosynthesize and feed their hosts. Sedimented water can even scrub the delicate tissue right off of corals.

Farther out, the health of the reef improved. When we circled back toward shore and the progression reversed itself, the quality of corals again degraded. Closer in, Jen spotted one desperate and sad little bouquet of *Pocillopora* clinging to the side of a green mound of dead aragonite sprouting weedy algae.

"That little guy gives me hope," she said.

Where I saw a symbol of coral desperation, she saw optimism. I made a note to myself to spend more time with "glass half-full" people like Jen.

We left the water reluctantly. Jen would emphasize a number of times throughout the day that she was a marine biologist. The ocean is where she belonged, where she wanted to spend her time. But the key to the health and survival of these Maui reefs, I would soon learn, lay upstream. It was on the baked mountain slopes alongside abandoned plantations where she was executing her plan to save corals.

We dried off and joined Noor Dphrepaulezz, a restoration ecologist, on a walk from the beach parking lot to a culvert that escorted the stream under a four-lane highway separating the resort fringe and plush sand beaches from the scrublands upslope.

On this morning the stream was an empty wash. Jen crouched down to show me a float mounted on a metal bar that was bolted to the concrete bottom of the culvert. It was connected by wires to an expensive-looking tower alongside the streambed that sprouted cables and PVC pipe. The system measured fluctuations in water levels and volumes of silt carried down from the highlands, but today the float-and-bar system lay impotent in the dry gravel. If the work they were doing in the highlands was having a positive effect, reducing the sediments in the runoff, then the data gathered from this station is how they would prove it.

We hopped into Noor's four-wheel-drive pickup and crossed the highway. Soon we were bouncing upslope along the eroded field roads of a coffee farm. The neat rows of bushes gave way to empty land covered with eight-foot *kiawe* trees, tough invasive mesquite imported because introduced cattle like to munch on their large, flat seedpods. Soon we came to the edge of a broad gulch that harbored the same dry stream we'd seen far below. This was all part of the Wahikuli Ahupua'a, the same connected, pie-shaped watershed we'd snorkeled. There was a

A hawkfish shelters
in a cauliflower coral in
Honolua Bay in Maui.

red gash of bumpy road shooting straight up toward the peaks, tracing the edge of the gulch. The road surface was cut deep and packed hard, and it was one of the causes of the sedimentation we'd seen on the reef. Jen told me that this single abandoned dirt road dumped tons of sediment into the stream, carrying the loose soil down to the reef and dragging it along the coast in great cloudy plumes after every rainfall.

I asked where the water in the empty stream was now, and she told me that it was an intermittent stream, or it least it has been in the twenty years that scientists have been monitoring it. She added that old-timers said it always used to have water in it.

"Science is great, but the most accurate way to learn something is through three generations of watching it," Noor chimed in. He's Maori and from New Zealand. Despite hailing from the far side of the ocean, he felt a clear connection to Hawaiian culture. He explained that the Hawaiian language wasn't too different from Maori; just change a few letters and many words match. The great voyaging cultures that settled the far-flung islands of Oceania had common roots. Even explorer James Cook recognized the Polynesians as belonging to one great country scattered across this galaxy of islands in the Pacific. "How shall we account for this nation spreading itself so far over the vast ocean?" he wrote with awe.

It was more than language that made Noor feel at home here. There were many other cultural similarities. "I know that your mom and dad smacked you for the same reasons mine smacked me," he laughed. Both cultures shared a respect for the wisdom of elders. Such respect is what drives much of Jen's work, too.

We hopped out of the truck, Jen and I to tour the restoration sites while Noor fiddled with the irrigation system. Below us, the roadway alongside the gulch had been turned into a terraced staircase. Every few meters, there was a strip of native vegetation, each strip with a different configuration of species and barriers made either of sandbags or tubes of coconut fibers. The idea was that these strips, secured with native plants, would trap the sediment behind them, leaving a fertile bed of soil for the native trees and grasses to spread, recoloniz-ing the roadbed and transforming it slowly from a sluiceway dumping silt into the gulch into a strip of native forest, a riparian boundary where the water would instead percolate down into the earth, replenishing aquifers. Then the stream might again begin to flow permanently, and clearly, just as the elders recalled.

We walked farther upslope along the roadbed, where the plantings were thicker, older, and more mature. Behind every strip of vegetation that cut across the road, sediment had mounded up to form loose soil you could scoop with your hands and allow to run through your fingers.

Farther upslope, the trees grew thicker. Jen stooped to pluck bright orange seeds dropped by a wiliwili tree—her personal favorite. These hearty trees could grow into the large, twisty hardwoods from which the first Hawaiians made boards for their sacred practice of surfing. Jen slipped the seeds into her pocket. She would give them to volunteers to grow starts for future plantings.

The oppressive heat increased and we chugged water as we inspected the irrigation plumbing that fed the plantings. Even the hearty natives had trouble establishing themselves in the baking heat and depleted soil. So here was some of Noor's wizardry in action. A pair of large water tanks stood, sprouting tubes both uphill and downhill. On the uphill side, the tubes drained large plastic-lined catchments the size of suburban swimming pools that collected rainwater and fed the tanks via gravity. The tanks in turn fed drip irrigation lines downslope. This system extended a rain event, funneling extra water over time to help the scrappy natives get established and outcompete invasive plants.

We crouched down near a strip of native *pili* grass. One of the seed capsules, looking like the scruffy head of a stalk of wheat, had fallen to the ground on a patch of hardpan. The dried brown seeds in the capsule looked sad, desperate, and thirsty. Jen crouched over it and sprinkled the last of the water from her bottle onto the scraggly pod. Immediately the seed capsule bent to the ground as if alive, trying to bury itself into the earth in the interest of future generations, a tiny figure genuflecting as if in prayer.

"There's such determination in that native grass," Jen smiled. "They just want to survive."

I looked above us; the road was beginning to disappear, the strips of restored vegetation growing together. But then I squinted up at the peaks towering above us, the home of the gods in the old stories, off-limits to us mortals. I turned and looked downhill again toward the strip of road and hotels that the tourists know well, where the new gods of commerce and private property hold sway. Beyond this glittering fringe we could see the froth of waves curling over the reef.

"I truly believe that if you put native plants back in the ground, you can make a difference," Jen said. She expected that the plantings would hold back a little less than a ton of sediment in the first year and then another ton or a ton and a half every year after that.

Knowing how vast were the problems facing corals, I asked her if she really thought that restoring this one road could make that much of a difference.

"With only ten volunteers working for thirty hours, we did all of that," she replied with a shrug toward the disappearing road. "This is a landscape-scale solution for a landscape-scale problem."

Jen's ability to hold on to hope in the face of insurmountable odds stemmed, in part, from her experience working on the nearby island of Kaho'olawe. The smallest of the eight main Hawaiian islands, it was always sparsely populated due to lack of freshwater, existing as it does in the rain shadow of Haleakala, the volcano that dominates Maui. But settlement began to deplete the island's resources, and this pressure accelerated after European contact.

First came the beginnings of a goat infestation after a "gift" from sea captain George Vancouver to Maui's Chief Kahekili. This was a slow-acting Trojan horse of environmental destruction, peaking when the goat population reached 50,000, blanketing the forty-four-square-mile island with a herd of four-legged defoliant. Cattle ranching followed, further scrubbing the land of its vegetation and pounding it into hardpan like this decommissioned road on which we now stood.

And finally, for good measure, the navy started using Kaho'olawe as a bombing range after Pearl Harbor, continuing to blast it to smithereens until the 1990s. It's still unsafe to travel much of the island without an escort due to the possibility of unexploded ordnance.

After centuries of devastation, the assumption was it would take hundreds of years before new restoration efforts showed much improvement. But in the ten years that she worked on reef-restoration projects there, Jen saw progress. Where native forests had been restored, she found less terrestrial sediment in PVC traps out on the reef. With gnawed, stomped, and blasted Kaho'olawe as a measuring stick, making progress on the watersheds of Maui seems possible. But she understands it will take time. "I think that it will take five years to make a difference on land, and fifteen years to see the impact in the waters," she said. It seemed like a long time to me. She must have noted my impatience. "Because I've worked on Kaho'olawe for ten years in restoration biology, my brain has adjusted to the time line," she said.

Maybe it was due to the flood of depressing news about coral-reef decline, or perhaps because I hadn't spent a decade in the agonizingly slow restoration of an ecologically obliterated island, but I had yet to adopt Jen's sanguine outlook on the long-term efficacy of restoration.

After returning home from Maui, I dove into research again. I read how a project to create the first detailed maps of Hawai'i's inshore reefs "found vast areas of decline and degradation linked to shoreline development, overfishing and increasing water heat waves." And then I read a UN report stating that, if fossil-fuel admissions continue unabated, "annual severe bleaching (ASB) is projected to occur within this century for 100% of the world's reefs." The expected date of this yearly bleaching devastation? 2034. That is one year before Jen Vander Veur predicted that her road restoration project would yield visible results on Maui's reefs. I wondered how she could be so dauntless. She wasn't oblivious to the overarching threat of climate change on top of sedimentation, pollution, and a host of other pressures. She'd witnessed mass bleaching in corals she'd studied. "I was just swimming around crying. That was one of the saddest things I'd ever seen," she told me.

I needed perspective, a high-level view of how many small restoration ecology projects might add up to making a difference in the face of insurmountable odds. So I reached out to the ecologist Madhavi Colton, managing director of the Coral Reef Alliance. She was under pandemic lockdown in Northern California and pining for the tropics when I called her.

I asked her the same question I'd posed to Jen on the hillside. How can one road in this one watershed help protect a reef from climate change?

These corals on Maui's west shore create structure on the volcanic substrate surrounding the island, attracting large fish.

"Evolution can help rescue reefs from the effects of climate change," she told me, explaining that their projects aimed to buy time for evolution. This is the essence of the concept of "adaptive reefscapes" that underpins all of the work of the Coral Reef Alliance. Evolution and high genetic variability are the engines that drive adaptation.

I'd always thought of evolution as an agonizingly slow process, especially in long-lived and slow-reproducing animals like stony corals. But corals do have evolutionary levers to pull, many of them still mysterious. Perhaps they could change how they select and associate with zooxanthellae. Or the community of microbes they cohabit with. Red Sea corals had proven that, given enough time, corals could adapt to survive at higher temperatures and salinity. And Colton's research showed that preserving genetic diversity in corals, and doing so in key locations around the world, can aid that adaptation. Protecting large tracts of reef that are scientifically chosen for their adaptive potential, she has written, is the best way to allow evolution to work its magic.

This is quite different from the adaptive evolution approach of Ruth Gates and her team. The Gates Lab work focuses on a single species, and even individual corals: identifying those that show aptitude to resist climate change stressors and then crossing them in the lab with other hardy corals. But that approach involves humans picking the winners. Likewise, those doing coral restoration are also making choices about where and what to outplant.

But the Coral Reef Alliance is identifying networks of entire seascapes that show an aptitude for resilience and adaptation in the face of climate change. And West Maui is one of the regions they've identified. Colton turned our conversation back toward Jen's work: "We're helping reefs in West Maui survive and grow. Larvae from those reefs then spread to Maui Nui." Maui Nui is the four-island cluster on the eastern side of the Hawaiian archipelago. The thirty-thousand-foot view began to sharpen in my mind. It wasn't about one road, one reef, or one little coral struggling against a tidal flood of sediment. It was about an entire region's ability to adapt and then spread this resilience throughout the neighboring islands via its offspring.

But Colton did identify one problem with her approach: "We aren't advocating for a shiny, new, sexy tool in order to save coral reefs." This puts the work of the Coral Reef Alliance at a disadvantage. Engineered solutions or new technological fixes are sexier. Humans are attracted to novelty. And then there's the hands-on appeal of coral restoration—planting individual corals on a devastated reef shows immediate results. You can stand back and admire your work like a gardener. Adaptive reefscapes are more abstract. They identify regions and then work on watershed restoration or pollution control, in concert with local communities. Colton noted that "it's hard and it's slower than anyone wants it to be. But if it's done right, it reduces stressors and is creating the system in which corals can adapt to climate change."

"What if we continue to produce carbon at current levels?" I asked.

"Then it's game over for most coral reefs and all ecosystems. And our own species," she said. But she offered a way out: if we can find a way to mitigate climate change, and if we can protect and restore the reefscapes that show aptitude for adaptation, we have some hope that the engine of coral evolution can then keep pace with global change.

I asked what else gives her hope. And she answered that there are thousands, hundreds of thousands, millions of people working to protect their local reefs.

Like Jen Vander Veur and Ruth Gates, Colton shared the conviction that humans aren't just the source of the problem. We're also the solution.

Can we adapt? Are we capable of change? That's what Madhavi Colton and Jen Vander Veur were pinning their hopes on. And it's not unfounded hope. There's evidence that humans have been able to do it in the past, to adapt after centuries of depleting natural resources. But in Hawai'i, much of that knowledge has been lost—or more accurately, obliterated.

The old Hawaiian stories—and the deities that inhabit them—are infused with reverence for the natural world. The *ahupua'a* system divided the islands into sustainable wedges that determined the power and prosperity of its citizens and rulers. They knew that degrading their slice of the island meant hard times to come, not to mention displeasing the deities, so agricultural practices developed in ways that worked in greater harmony with the natural processes instead of against them. Fishponds, or *loko i'a*, were a major agricultural innovation. Constructed at the mouths of streams and rivers, they reared large quantities of juvenile fish, creating a supplement to the wild catch. Living coral colonies were plucked from the nearby reefs and integrated into the walls of the *loko i'a* to fortify their massive structures.

You can see the largest remaining traditional fishpond, recently restored, in Kane'ohe Bay on the windward shore of O'ahu. Viewed from the neighboring headland, it's a graceful arc of stone punctuated by the tide-driven sluice gates that trap the juvenile fish in the phytoplankton-rich waters where they grow rapidly until they're too big to exit the gates. On this overlook I met Hi'ilei Kawelo, executive director of the nonprofit that maintains the Paepae o He'eia fishpond as a cultural learning site and as a source of fish for the local community, much as it has done for centuries.

Hi'ilei told me that even while they were still fishing the oceans, her ancestors had the foresight to be innovative and contribute through aquaculture because they consumed so much fish protein. It was the responsible thing to do. I asked how the fishponds affected the reefs of Kane'ohe Bay.

"It alleviates the pressures on the reef, but it also enhances the system as a whole. The fish that are produced through the ecosystem are benefiting through overflow onto the reef," she said.

Herbivorous fish are the friends of corals, keeping algae in check. They're also the first to succumb to overfishing by people, which is a sure way to transform a healthy coral reef into a stretch of green-slimed rock.

Hi'ilei appreciated the ecological impacts of the fishpond she helped manage, but it was the opportunity to integrate the Hawaiian community into the process of growing and consuming these fish, and maintaining the pond, that drove her. She knew that every group of schoolchildren that came through would tell parents and grandparents about it, reintroducing the entire community to this heritage.

I asked about global pressures like climate change. She told me that a lot of the climate change issues came from problems that were too big for them, but that didn't mean they were not going to do something about it. "We could dwell on what's very difficult to address or might be impossible to change. Or we could do all we're able to do, which is, you see a problem and you fix it."

There's much we can learn from this island mind-set. And this is why, back on Maui, Jen Vander Veur went to great lengths to incorporate local traditions into her restoration efforts. When she gathered a group of volunteers, she often invited a local *kapuna*, or elder, to give an invocation before the work began. On the day we drove down from our visit to the Wahikuli restoration project, she took out

her phone and played a clip for me. When Noor heard it, he pulled over. "We should stop for this," he said quietly.

We sat in the heat of the truck on the side of the dusty road and listened to the haunting chant. Even from the speakers of a cell phone it was beautiful, the kind of song that raises the hairs on the back of your neck.

"When we don't have someone along to do the chant, I play this for the volunteers when we get started," Jen said. She believed that by restoring native plants, she was also restoring culture. Every seed, every shrub, and every tree had a story. Native plants provided the opportunity to learn about traditional crafts and medicines. And when the local people became engaged, that added some political muscle and reconnected locals with the *ahupua'a* that sustained them.

Outsiders used to come from the continents with a sort of arrogance grounded in colonial ignorance and grandiosity. Europeans brought their religions and their politics and their economic system, eradicating what was here before. Even the first Polynesians transformed the landscape, bringing invasive species and driving extinctions before settling in a sort of balance. But as the surviving native plants and animals disappear under the crush of modernity, so do the stories and the old gods that were linked to them. With recurrent mass bleaching events, corals may be next in line for extinction.

But two things are happening now that might finally be changing this dynamic. Kahoali'i Keahi-Wood described it to me as a "rekindling of the culture, the Hawaiian renaissance. The reacceptance of traditional practices and stories." Hawaiians were already reluctant to share, because these stories were seen as a source of a family's legacy power, which could be diminished over time if they were

Recently restored Heʻeia
fishpond rears fish through
traditional aquaculture methods.

told too often by strangers. Then later, the reticence heightened for fear that continental people would exploit the traditional knowledge for their own gain.

But now, because of this cultural renaissance, native Hawaiians are opening up, passing on their traditions. And people like Jen Vander Veur are listening and embracing them, and integrating them with the science of restoration biology to take small steps toward the global transformation needed if we are going to address the problems facing the world's reefs. We all need to think and act with the ingenuity and reverence of island people if we are to survive the Anthropocene.

In the days following my tour of the Coral Reef Alliance restoration project in Wahikuli, I continued my snorkel surveys up Maui's western coastline, rising early every morning to explore the mouths of rivers and streams with camera in hand. I made photos of corals, noting the damage from sedimentation and nutrient runoff, and seeing how coral health improved the farther I finned from the sources of runoff.

I experienced some brown-water days, when the sediment was thick in the water and visibility was low, and this always made me wary of sharks. One morning in Honolua Bay, renowned for its pristine corals and the world-class surf break shaped by the reefs, the sea was thick with silt. I'm as wary of sharks as any landlubber old enough to have seen *Jaws*.

I winced when the large shapes of turtles appeared suddenly out of the murk. A cluster of three chubs with eerie, doll-like faces tracked me along the reef, making me feel like I was part of a school of fat, delicious fish.

My fears were not unfounded. Indeed, only a week later, a surfer would be attacked by a shark near the corals I'd been photographing. A photo of his surfboard, with a bite larger than a basketball chewed through the hard epoxy, was splashed across the news pages. He later died from his injuries at the hospital.

I knew this sort of thing happened, though rarely. But also knowing the story of the shark deity was comforting. In the old tales, the shark god Kāmohaliʻi wasn't necessarily a danger. He wasn't known for devouring snorkelers from the continent. Instead, he was most often noted for guiding home disoriented voyagers. His method was to appear before a lost boat, splashing his tail to alert the confused sailors. And if they worked quickly to offer him a narcotic drink made from the native *kawa* plants, he'd lead them home as a reward.

As I finned farther from shore, the water cleared and massive colonies of *Porites lobata* corals materialized out of the murk. The water cleared more and I drifted over coral heads the size of large appliances and small cars, smooth shapes, spires, rills, and mounts smeared with the colorful melted ice cream of mounding coral. Momentary wonder was soon eclipsed by concern, however. What kind of shape would these corals be in fifteen years from now when Jen's restoration work will finally begin to bear fruit? Will we have reversed course on carbon emissions? Will we have embraced what scientific evidence and traditional cultures have been telling us for a long time—that we can't continue to follow a path of unmitigated exploitation of both *mauna* and *makai*, the great *ahupuaʻa* that sustains humans and corals and all other life on this planet?

As the water cleared more, I tried to will my admiration for the tiny corals and their massive construction projects to eclipse my concern for them. I looked around at schooling jacks, numbering in the thousands now. I was no longer afraid of sharks. Instead, I was even hoping to see one. I thought that our whole species, all of humanity, is like those lost mariners in the legends. We need the old gods now more than ever. Maybe it's time for Kāmohaliʻi to appear before us, slap his tail on the water and show us the way home.

If only we are willing to follow.

11

America's Reef

South Florida

THE FLORIDA REEF TRACT—running more than 365 miles from Martin County north of Fort Lauderdale, down the Florida Keys, past Key West to the parched cluster of islands known as the Dry Tortugas—is iconic. Corals are part of local identity. You'll find Cape Coral, Coral Ridge, Coral Gables, Coral Way, Coral Point, and a Coral Reef High School. Driving along Highway 1 to the End of America, you'll spot a Coral Supermarket, Coral Electric, Coral Title, and Coral Cleaners. Public buildings and monuments are tiled with polished "keystone," which clearly shows the shapes of fossilized coral colonies. These animals are literally and figuratively baked into Florida lore: longtime Florida bard of sunburns and margaritas Jimmy Buffett is backed by his Coral Reefer Band.

The tract is the only coral reef system that lies along the coast of the continental United States. It's been called "America's Great Barrier Reef," and our "Underwater Yellowstone," even though it's neither a barrier reef nor is it protected in its entirety as a national park. Still, tourists flock to a reef system edging one of the most heavily populated coastlines on the planet. There are forty-five species of stony corals, and the reefs provide up to $880 million in estimated flood protection annually. According to NOAA, Florida's corals have a collective value of $8.5 billion, provide for annual sales of $4.4 billion, and employ 70,400 people. The tract is an ecological wonder that drives an entire regional economy.

But along most of its length, the Florida Reef Tract is also functionally extinct. As little as 2 percent of historic coral cover remains. It has been hammered by climate change, pollution, dredging, dropped anchors, tramping tourists, surging development, and devastating outbreaks of disease. It is fast losing its ability to provide ecosystem services. With the Intergovernmental Panel on Climate Change predicting as little as 1 percent of global coral cover by the end of this century, I went to Florida for a preview of this grim future. Traveling the tract's

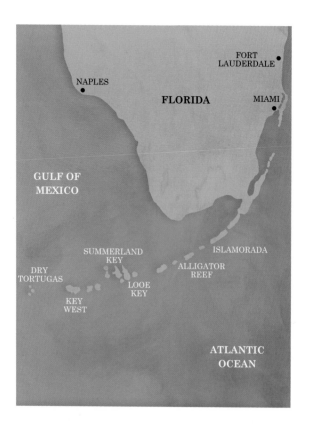

Page 162: Brooke Enright and Tommy Ingalls from Brian Walker's lab at Nova Southeastern University sample one of the few remaining "exceptional corals" amid a flurry of fish attracted by the massive colony.

length from north to south, I planned to stop at key locations to have a look at a world of lost corals. I braced for a disheartening journey.

So I was surprised to find myself, just a dozen hours after arriving, bobbing on open flats offshore from a line of condo towers in Miami Beach and hovering over one of the largest boulder corals I'd ever seen. This massive dome of an *Orbicella faveolata*, or mountainous star coral, might have begun growing before Ponce de León came bush-whacking through the mangroves in search of the Fountain of Youth.

Granted, this wasn't a reef. It was one large coral the size of an SUV in isolation in the shallows. But it bristled with life. I saw clouds of fish, wriggling nudibranchs, and even a nurse shark tucked under a ledge near the bottom. Temporarily added to the swarm of life were divers, a team of young research-ers led by Brian Walker of Nova Southeastern University, who had only recently discovered this large colony and many others like it. This big living boulder was Large Coral No. 16, listed in a database of what Brian calls "exceptional corals," stalwart survivors that had endured hurricanes, climate change, and the region's exploding human popula-tion, continuing to fill out their massive bulk while entire stretches of nearby reef succumbed to the battery of abuses.

I shadowed the team as they sampled their way through other large colonies in the database between Fort Lauderdale and Miami. They were retrieving bits of tissue and coral skeleton for use in a multiagency investigation into disease resistance and resilience. It had been a long, tiring day, but this last dip into the water was a "fun dive." Freed from the tedious duties involved in collecting and processing tissue samples, the students on the team circled No. 16, pointing out interesting features and critters tucked into the folds, rills, and valleys of the polyp-sculpted mass. Brian hung back, carefully studying the coral head. He was keeping an eye out for pale patches of dying tissue. There was a new disease spreading along the tract, one to which even these old survivors weren't immune.

Brian drifted closer and fanned away bits of sediment that had collected in the scoops and ridges the coral. It was an affectionate gesture, like petting a dog or brushing the mane of a favorite horse.

I was on the first stop of a journey where I expected to experience the devastation of a reef system slipping into oblivion, and instead I'd found a giant, healthy colony and the first members of a small army of passionate people I would meet in Florida. I'd been bracing for decline. I'd read about reef loss, hurricanes, and disease. But after visiting Coral No. 16, I learned that something else was stirring off the coast of South Florida.

I had yet to decide if I could call it hope.

In 2013, Brian Walker, a geospatial ecologist at Nova Southeastern University in Fort Lauderdale, received a federal grant to map the benthic structure of a stretch of the shallow seafloor from Biscayne Bay south of Miami to Port Saint Lucie to the north. Using a combination of aerial photographs and lidar (a technology that uses lasers to map topography on land and sea bottom), he created a detailed analysis of the bottom structure of the nearshore environment. This is useful information to have for communities and governments planning development, conservation efforts, dredging, locations for placement of piers and jetties, directing boat traffic, and preventing beach erosion. For a scientist like Walker, it was also a fascinating analysis of the natural history of the area. The lidar data revealed an ancient saga of shifting seafloors, changing reefs, ice ages, and cemented dunescapes dating back tens of thousands of years. Brian expected to use the data to learn where corals

had once been, particularly the fast-vanishing stands of branching staghorn corals. He was not expecting to discover massive boulder corals.

As the data came in from the overflights, Brian's team began to construct a 3D model of the nearshore bathymetry. To validate the models, they sent out divers to ground-truth what the aerial imaging was telling them. They examined a hard bottom of compacted sediment, sandy flats, and beleaguered stretches of reef that now held just a few scruffy stragglers plus soft corals, sponges, and a whole lot of algae.

But there was something else they noticed on the images, blips that looked like specks of coral reef. They were almost like blemishes, a spot of dust on the lens. They were too small to be fringing or patch reefs but large enough to indicate that something interesting might be there.

So they loaded dive tanks and gear into one of the boats bobbing in the basin of the Helmle National Coral Reef Institute, where Brian's lab was located, and motored out to investigate. And what he found surprised him. When they jumped into the water they spotted a massive, lone coral head forming a one-coral reef unto itself. And nobody had known it was there but the fish.

In the ensuing months, Walker visited more of these blips. And he found more monster corals— enough that he started assembling a database of the colonies.

"There was a sense of hopefulness because we started jumping on all of these targets and finding huge colonies that were still alive and had been alive for the entire history of Western culture that had developed in Florida," Brian told me on the day I joined him. "We thought, 'Wow, these corals are something. They're special.'"

Knowing that these corals could serve as great ambassadors, driving Floridians' appreciation for their urban waterways, he dubbed them "Exceptional Corals." He amassed a database of hundreds of colonies running from Biscayne Bay to well north of Fort Lauderdale. Something in their genetic makeup, their history of adaptation, or their immediate surroundings held clues to how humans and corals could coexist.

But then in 2014, unprecedented heat waves drove up the water temperatures, and corals all over South Florida began to bleach, even some of these Exceptional Corals. This was both a threat and an opportunity. How would these monsters survive a devastating heat wave? All up and down the tract that Walker's team had mapped, the corals turned white, expelling their algal symbionts. The team waited and watched for recovery.

Then things became complicated. A large expansion of PortMiami on Dodge Island—the massive shipping and cruise terminal that drives much of Miami's economy—began dredging new channels and stirring up sediments steeped for years in the region's effluent. Off of Virginia Key in Biscayne Bay, researchers noticed patches of intense and particularly devastating coral disease. Another wave of bleaching arrived in 2015, further hammering corals. It was hard to distinguish the bleaching from the effects of dredging, sedimentation, and the disease. But as the 2015 warming subsided and the disease outbreak intensified and spread, it was clear that a new killer had arrived on the scene and was here to stay. Theories as to its origins abound. Did the new bug find a banquet in the bleaching-weakened reefs, spreading like a forest fire through kindling? Had it originated in the muck stirred up by the port expansion?

But one sure thing was the disease's lethality. Once it infected a colony, the entire coral head was doomed. The disease steadily expanded its range, marching north and south along the Florida Reef Tract from its Miami epicenter. It targeted twenty of the region's

forty-five species of corals, mostly the mound-boulders like those on the Exceptional Corals list. Most infected corals died within months or even weeks.

The Exceptional Corals dwindled. Brian's database of hundreds of healthy giants had dropped to under two hundred survivors. These magnificent, newly discovered corals were disappearing. The new plague was dubbed stony coral tissue loss disease, or SCTLD, and it was a phenomenon that even these stalwart, ancient corals couldn't withstand.

But Walker's list proved invaluable. At least some of the corals on his list did show resistance to this disease. The map of large corals offered a broad canvas on which they could conduct experiments and test out possible treatments. State and federal agencies were alarmed. They funded disease research. The crisis and funding encouraged an unprecedented level of collaboration, which led to the multiagency effort I'd just witnessed—skilled student divers pulling samples in the form of seven small round plugs that would be sent off to labs at Nova Southeastern University, the University of Miami, Florida Atlantic University, the University of Georgia, NOAA, the Smithsonian Marine Station, and the US Geological Survey, where they would be analyzed for genomics, transcriptomics, proteomics, metabolomics, histopathology, microbiomes, and endosymbionts. This is all to say that a large number of very smart people were working together to map, understand, and treat the disease.

When I joined the crew that morning, Brian asked me where I'd been diving. I mentioned the Red Sea and Polynesia among other locations, noting that this would be my first dive in Florida.

"So, your bar is here," he said, holding his hand even with his head. "And what you'll see in Florida is here," he said, dropping his hand a couple feet.

I explained my thesis, that this Florida trip would be a preview for when the rest of the world hits the predicted 2 percent of historic coral cover.

"Well, I certainly hope not," he replied.

We motored from Fort Lauderdale to Biscayne Bay past Jimmy Buffett's Margaritaville Resort and more towering beachfront hotels and condos. We stopped at one exceptional coral after another and my appreciation for Florida corals increased. When I dove near them, I felt I was in the presence of sentient beings. Evidently the fish felt it, too, because they were drawn to these coral islands in billows of shoaling fish. And I was beginning to see that my thesis was flawed. A world of 2 percent coral cover isn't a blighted wasteland. There are glimmers of splendor and a determination to save the little that remains.

As I observed and photographed the students as they sampled the corals, clouds of sea life often obscured my subjects. The students hammered a marker nail into the coral head and then pounded the small round drill into the soft flesh and outer skeletal layer to collect their samples. The sound rang unnaturally through the water. They wriggled the drill bit and pulled out small buttons of coral tissue and skeleton ten millimeters thick. They placed each sample piece into prelabeled bags and shuttled them up to two students on the boat who would separate and pack them into freezers for distribution to the various labs.

The research team took samples from three different sets of coral colonies: those that showed resistance to SCTLD, those that faced moderate pressure, and others that had been significantly harmed by the disease. When the students finished the job on one of the colonies and moved on to the next, I lingered behind to examine the odd markings they'd left behind. The pattern of seven small holes trailed streams of mucus and white tissue into the water, seeping wounds spilling the viscera of the lonesome giant into the water column. I'd been told that corals don't feel pain. But still the wound felt raw to me. I knew that parrotfish often took wicked-looking bites out of healthy corals not dissimilar to these markings. I also understood that what researchers learned from their work could be instrumental in saving these colonies and helping treat the disease that was now spreading around the Caribbean. The team would eventually return to the corals, inspecting the wounds they'd left behind to assess the rate of healing.

It's not surprising that the disease had begun in the heavily populated region of South Florida. The pressures of such density may very well be the disease's cause. But the outbreak's proximity to this populous area, and the importance of the corals to this region, were also what prompted such intense focus, study, and treatment. Walker and colleagues at Nova and other institutions had already been applying novel treatments never before used on corals. Some of the techniques worked, including the use of antibiotic paste.

SCTLD is an existential crisis. From its first appearance in 2014, it had marched steadily up and down the Florida Reef Tract. It reached the last hold-out, the uninhabited Dry Tortugas, which lay in a national park seventy miles past Key West, just a few days before I arrived. Strike teams were ramping up to apply treatments to mitigate the damage. The disease has also appeared in Mexico, Belize, the US Virgin Islands, St. Thomas, Jamaica, and around the Caribbean. All of these countries were looking to Florida for answers.

Science is a competitive enterprise. But when I looked at the list of partners on Brian's project, I was impressed by the level of collaboration. As we unloaded gear and samples for the day, I asked Brian why, after the Florida Reef Tract had been hammered since the eighties, it was this crisis that had finally galvanized Florida researchers, turning rivals in the competition for scarce funding into partners.

"Because everyone cares," he told me. "Everyone wants to make a difference." This sense of purpose was something I would come to see rippling along the Florida Reef Tract as I worked my way toward the southernmost tip of the country.

I left Fort Lauderdale and headed south. When oil millionaire Henry Flagler, who built modern Florida, had the hubristic notion of carving a railroad through swampland to connect a muddy river town on the edge of the Everglades to the rest of the country, Miami was a settlement of five hundred people. Today the region's population is fast approaching eight million and has spread out to cover swamps, wetlands, and low-lying islands that are both natural and man-made. The mere existence of the city is a testament to the human impulse to transform nature. And no part of Miami represents such transformation better than Dodge Island.

Built from the dredge spoils of Government Cut, sliced through sandbars and mangroves to provide the city with access to the Atlantic, Dodge Island is home to PortMiami, the world's largest cruise-ship terminal and one of the biggest ports in the country. It supports 334,000 jobs and contributes $43 billion to the Florida economy annually. The riprap jetties of the man-made island may be the least natural coastline in all of South Florida. So it seemed like a strange place to look for corals.

But that's what I was doing the next morning as black thunderheads dropped sheets of rain and lightning zapped the horizon. I was following Colin Foord's SUV through canyons of shipping containers and over acres of open asphalt. We crawled like

insects beneath a row of massive cranes. We swerved around puddles the size of ponds. Huge freighters sprouting container cities sidled up to the artificial island and cruise ships lumbered past its rubbled shore. Port officers directed a dizzying stream of container-laden trucks as I squinted after Foord's taillights in brief glimpses of clarity left by the wipers smearing across the windshield.

Finally we reached a small parking lot at the far end of the island and Foord jumped out along with his friend Jake, whom he'd enlisted to help with his passion project. They began unloading dive and snorkel gear. Foord screwed a regulator onto a tank. In the canal beyond, boats chugged past.

Foord is cofounder of Coral Morphologic, an enterprise he describes as "an art and science hybrid that is powered by the coral." He conducts experiments, writes papers, and makes photographs and films that his partner JT scores with psychedelic soundtracks. He also consults on coral projects, creates art installations, raises corals in tanks, and occasionally sells fragments to hobbyists to help support this wide-ranging scleractinian enterprise. We'd come to PortMiami to visit his popular project Coral City Camera, an underwater livestream that he launched at the beginning of the pandemic. It attracts thousands of daily viewers who log on to watch corals, fish, lobsters, sharks, manatees, and a vibrant cast of characters that glide past the camera lens. And this naturalist's Mayberry is most impressive for being perched on the man-made rim of an artificial island in a body of water that's the marine equivalent of an expressway.

Wearing a rash guard covered in neon patterns inspired by the grooves of a brain coral, and with his dyed-blue brush of hair sticking up like the tentacles of a colorful coral polyp, Foord himself seemed to be in the midst of a Kafkaesque transformation into one of the creatures of his obsession. But despite his whimsical appearance, he was on a serious mission. Even the lightning wasn't going to deter him.

We climbed over the riprap wall and he slipped carefully into the water as I felt the thunder rumbling in my bones. Jake tended things from the shore and I snorkeled while Foord slipped with his scuba gear to the bottom to work on the camera, which was housed in a glass dome about a dozen feet off the riprap jetty and another ten feet below the surface. A cord snaked out of the water, connecting the system to power and a wifi.

For the past several months, Foord had been driving daily through the mayhem of the port to scrub the camera dome with a toothbrush so the viewers could enjoy an uninterrupted view of the sea from wherever they were in the world. The custom-built system's self-cleaning hardware, a wiper that was supposed to regularly clear the dome of sediment and muck stirred up by the passing cruise ships, had failed. Today he would be replacing the whole device with the help of a pair of security camera experts.

I watched Foord's bubbles from the surface, eyeing the wake-stirred water warily for a moment before slipping in. It was the last place I'd imagine taking a dip, during a storm or otherwise. But I pulled on my fins, mask, and snorkel and then dove down to survey the scene.

I was surprised by the number of fish. The huge marine limestone boulders of the riprap provided plenty of structure for them to hide. They shoaled along the bustling edge of the port. Fat and colorful parrotfish twisted through the water, nibbling on the rocky structure. The riprap was blotted with healthy little corals the size of grapefruit, recolonizing the human habitat that had long ago obliterated the natural landscape beneath it.

The camera sat in a sandy patch next to the riprap, and as I drifted above and watched Foord

Colin Foord's Coral City Camera project shares a livestream of the underwater life inhabiting the world's largest cruise ship terminal.

unbolt the system, I reveled in a scene I'd been viewing virtually for months. Like Coral City Camera's legion of loyal viewers, the project provided me with a window into the sea during the height of the pandemic lockdowns. It was a touch of wildness on my spare computer monitor during the stale routine that life had become. But what surprised me now was how this little patch of wilderness lay in the midst of an altered human landscape. The manatees, nurse sharks, sergeant major fish, four-eyed butterfly fish, dozens of other species, plus the clusters of corals had all recolonized the built environment and made it their own.

I shook the internet-fed feeling of déjà vu and scanned the wider area while Foord finished his work. A curtain of yellow-striped grunts parted before me as I circled. In addition to the mounding corals that had recruited onto the riprap, there was a cluster of spiny staghorn coral, *Acropora cervicornis*. This endangered species tends to be more delicate and bleaches easily from weather and pollution, but researchers at the University of Miami were partnering with Foord to test some stress-hardened, lab-reared corals in these turbid urban waterways. On a metal grid nearby, more mounding coral samples were attached as part of a different collaboration Foord has with researchers at NOAA, studying hearty hybrid corals that have colonized the city's waterways. Their research suggests that these urban corals have adapted to the more stressful conditions at a molecular level, allowing them to avoid pathogens in polluted water, derive more energy in the nutrient-rich environment rather than relying on the photosynthesis of their partner algae, and even team up with different zooxanthellae better suited for turbid waters. In short, they were naturally evolved "super corals."

Foord finally managed to detach the camera, and he climbed out of the water, carrying it carefully over the riprap wall. "This is my baby," he said, looking at it affectionately. This camera had connected him to thousands of marine-life fans around the world. An army of online volunteers tracked the sea life they saw on spreadsheets, chattering excitedly on social media about the changing conditions and plentiful creatures. Foord had captured and annotated more than 15,000 video clips, which he was now offering as data to any researchers interested in studying fish and invertebrate behavior in this bustling urban ecosystem.

I followed him back to his home and studio, a ramshackle building a few miles from the port. It was an old house inhabited by several species of termites and harboring a buzzing beehive in the wall. Inside, it was entirely devoted to corals. A giant macro photograph of coral polyps covered one wall. The dining room was a coral nursery full of tanks bursting with neon-colored colonies. Coral skeletons and shells lined the walls. There were monitors in every room to display the Coral City Camera feed, and boxes and crates of aquarium gear were stacked in the corners.

While the technicians operated on the camera, I chatted with Foord about his unusual career. He had originally pursued a path in academia. A lifelong coral hobbyist, he'd grown up tending the animals in tanks, and he thought those skills might translate to a university laboratory. But researchers at that time were more interested in jetting around the world to study remote reefs instead of looking at the animals up close in aquariums or investigating those in their own backyard. So Foord charted his own path to celebrate and understand Miami's mutant corals. Now, with SCTLD burning through local reefs and Florida corals collapsing, the crisis—and accompanying funding—has brought the research community a new appreciation for both keeping corals in captivity and studying the strange hybrid corals that survive in unlikely places like PortMiami. "Everyone's raising corals in the lab these days," he said.

I asked him if he regrets his choice to remain outside the establishment since the academy now seems to be embracing approaches he once championed.

"For a long time being independent was beneficial. But now the academic world is catching up," he said.

"Do you envy the researchers who have grant funding and squadrons of undergraduate students who can annotate videos or scrub equipment with toothbrushes?" I asked. He paused and I thought I saw a glimmer of wistful thinking.

"When you're a trailblazer, people can follow in your footsteps and they think, 'This isn't so hard,'" he said with more pride than bitterness.

Looking around his eclectic home and laboratory, the postcard picture of a mad scientist's workshop, I could see he'd found his niche. While others might not yet have given him credit, he had given it to himself. He'd done more to raise awareness about the coral bounty that exists in Miami's urban waterways than anyone. Through Coral City Camera, he'd built appreciation for marine life on a global scale. And in the process, he managed to inextricably link his own life with those of the ultimate survivors—those corals that were adapting to an uncertain and ever-shifting future.

From Miami, I drove south along the Florida Reef Tract to Bud N' Mary's Marina on Islamorada in the Upper Keys. I was sitting with a dozen people in an open warehouse on the edge of the water, watching a slide presentation about coral physiology and restoration given by two volunteers with Islamorada Conservation and Restoration Education, or I.CARE. It's a collaboration of coral scientists and dive tour

operators that allows the public to get hands-on experience in coral restoration. With Brian Walker keeping an eye on the health of the last beleaguered giants and Colin Foord highlighting scrappy survivors that are adapting to human pressures, here was another approach in a world of 2 percent coral cover: restoring what has been lost.

"Does anyone know what corals are? Are they a plant, animal, or rock?" Nathan, one of the educators, asked.

"Animals," the audience of volunteers said in unison and without hesitation. These were all experienced divers, including families, some father-daughter duos, a couple from Iowa, a veterinarian, and a university researcher originally from South Korea.

The presentation delved into the pressures that corals face in Florida waters, including disease and coral bleaching due to climate change, and then it covered the basics of coral restoration and how it works. Next we practiced securing coral skeletons to nails that we pounded into wooden blocks. This was a proxy for the work we would soon be doing underwater.

We toured a nursery under development at the marina, built and managed by the Mote Marine Laboratory, a nonprofit that has been in the restoration game for a long time and continues to pioneer new techniques. The land-based nursery featured a dozen raceways, broad, shallow, bathtub-like basins where corals would be reared until they're large enough for outplanting. The goal was to grow corals here that volunteer divers could take right out to nearby restoration sites.

During the break, Kylie Smith arrived with three five-gallon Home Depot buckets containing a total of sixty fragments of "super corals," echoing the term that had been applied to Ruth Gates's work. Kylie had made the run down to Mote's Summerland Key facility during the presentation, a two-hour round-trip drive.

The corals in the bucket were *Acropora cervicornis*, the fast-growing variety that has been disappearing at alarming rates. What makes them "super" is the methods of sexual reproduction that the Mote team uses in the lab when breeding them. They would cross a female that has survived a bleaching event with a male that survived a disease outbreak. They hoped such resilience would be passed along to the resulting genotypes, which are then propagated, fragmented, and grown in sea-based or land-based nurseries like the one under installation at Bud N' Mary's.

Between the morning workshop and the afternoon dive session, the group thrummed with eager energy. Recreational divers are always itchy to get into the water. A dentist from Tampa on a dive holiday with his college-age daughter was giddy. He'd dived all over the Caribbean. Knowing the reefs in Florida had less coral cover than the other sites he'd visited, he figured the outplanting would be an interesting diversion from a typical dive on the beleaguered reefs here. I asked him if he'd ever volunteered for conservation efforts in the past. He hadn't.

Neither had most of the rest of the divers. They just seemed to want to do something cool underwater. And with fewer corals to look at, this was a novel experience with obvious upside. Only a veterinarian named Stacy, who had moved permanently to the Keys specifically to indulge her "dive obsession," had ever been involved in coral restoration.

While the passengers and volunteers prepped for the trip, I spoke with Kylie Smith about the origins of I.CARE. Smith had studied the impacts of bleaching and hurricanes on transplanted corals in the Upper Keys. To get to her sites, she hired a local dive operator named Michael Goldberg, and she soon found him asking lots of deep questions about her work.

Our volunteer team out-
planting staghorn
corals near Islamorada.
The only surviving examples
of this species that I saw in
Florida were the result of
restoration work.

Smith then attended the Reef Futures Symposium in 2018, a forum dedicated to intervention
science. I'd heard a number of researchers talk
about that specific conference and year as a pivotal
moment, coming as it did on the heels of back-to-
back bleaching events around the world. The research
community was also in shock and still mourning the
untimely passing of Ruth Gates, a great champion of
human intervention in corals. That Reef Futures event
was a cathartic moment where many scientists
steeled their resolve and recommitted to making a
difference. Many researchers came away from that
event with renewed energy, including Smith.

Soon after, she met with Goldberg at an Islamorada brewery and hatched a plan with the dive shop
owner. "Michael was already doing cleanup dives. His
customers liked having a purpose underwater," she told
me as we prepped for our restoration dive. "We talked
about restoration and we had an 'aha' moment right
there at the brewery. That's where I.CARE was born."

The pair made a handshake agreement. They
would enlist eager divers as their restoration work-
force, using the latest scientific techniques to outplant
coral fragments that had been bred for resiliency.
Not only would these volunteer divers offer their
time, spending precious vacation hours underwater
doing work, but they'd pay a premium for the
opportunity: the additional fee would be used to
support the program. This higher price tag wasn't
a deterrent: the trip had sold out on the day that
I stopped by. I was only able to join because of a
last-minute cancellation.

As we boarded the boat, we were organized into
teams, each unit headed by an I.CARE volunteer.
My restoration partner was Stacy, the diving veterinarian. Rick, the diving dentist, and his daughter,
Jess, rounded out our quartet. McKenzie, a biology
student, was the young volunteer who would supply
the gear and oversee the quality of our work.

Once we reached the dive site, there was a moment of chaos as twenty people splashed into the water and sorted into groups. Our team found McKenzie and drifted into the murky water after her. She carried a crate filled with the coral fragments, hammers, pliers, zip ties, and wire brushes. We submerged and she showed us a rocky patch of hard bottom covered with dead coral rubble. I saw no other corals in the area. This patch of reef needed our help.

We used the wire brush to scrape away algae and muck from the rock. Then we used the hammers to chip and scrape the substrate clean. Stacy and I took turns. It was difficult to hover in place. The surge tugged us back and forth, and our group of five divers jostled for position around the small work area. Having cleared a ten-inch circle, we pounded nails into the rock. The hammer slipped and glanced and slipped again. Stacy was superior at this task. But then she performs delicate surgery on animals while I clumsily poke a keyboard for a living.

Still, McKenzie was a stern taskmistress. She checked our nail work, and if one wiggled, she pulled it out and we had to start over. But once the nails were firmly set into the limestone, we moved on to the corals. We used the zip ties to fasten the staghorn fragments firmly to the nails. All five fragments in the cluster were of the same genotype. As they grew into a thicket, they would recognize one another and begin to fuse together and form one large colony, taking a sudden leap in maturity. Coral colonies reach sexual maturity not by age but by size, and multiple fragments growing together is one way to jump-start the process of accelerating them toward breeding age.

Tying the fragments snugly to the nails was another delicate procedure, in which Stacy again excelled. But despite her handiwork, we'd only just begun our second cluster of five corals when our hour was up and we had to follow McKenzie back to the surface for air.

We climbed onto the boat to change tanks and take a break between dives. The deck buzzed with conversations about how difficult the task had been. As slowly as our team had worked, I learned that we were ahead of most of the other groups, who were still wrapping up their first clusters. I made a mental note always to partner with a small-animal surgeon when doing restoration work.

Back in the water, I switched from coral husbandry to photography. Stacy, now partnered with volunteer McKenzie, finished quickly. This allowed us some time to explore the rest of the reef. As we finned around, I saw plenty of fish: grunts, some sergeant major fish, and the quick shadow of a nurse shark slipping away. We drifted through a forest of waving sea fans. These large, purple soft corals are beautiful and dynamic, pulsing with the surge of water. But they clung to rock that was clearly dead heads of hard coral, now weedy and overgrown. There were only a few scabby remnants of reef-building corals with patchy tissue cover. I didn't see a single staghorn coral other than those we had planted. In fact, I wouldn't see another *Acropora cervicornis* my entire time in Florida.

This tour of a reef devoid of corals tempered some of the hope I'd been starting to feel through our act of outplanting. Would our little patch of corals survive? The I.CARE volunteers claimed an 80 percent survival rate after one year in the wild. I tried to imagine returning in several years' time to see a thicket of staghorn corals where I'd been working. It was a heartening thought. But the expanse of dead corals around us was so vast. How long would it take to replant a reef of this size?

The divers climbed back into the boat one by one. There was less of a buzz now. Working underwater is taxing. These recreational divers were getting a taste of what it's like to be a research scientist. Even in the warmest of water, a chill eventually sets in after a few hours below the surface, especially if you're just hovering in place working instead of cruising around to gawk at sea life.

The captain, Michael Goldberg, came down from the top deck and addressed the divers as they stowed their gear. He spoke slowly and thoughtfully. "Thank you for coming out. I hope you had fun," he said. "And I hope you have an appreciation for how hard this work is. And I hope I see you again. I believe that together we can make a difference."

The divers pondered the weight of his words.

"I've got great news, volunteers," Smith then said. "We've now planted 1,460 corals through the I.CARE program. That's amazing work!" Amid the cheers and hoots, I followed Goldberg topside as the engines rumbled to life.

On the motor back to the marina, I asked Goldberg why he'd started the program with Smith.

"I had to do something," he said. "For years, I've been watching it go like this..." he held his arm like a down ramp. "I was ready to get out. I told my wife, 'It's time to quit.' But then I met Dr. Smith and the I.CARE project started to come together."

"What will success look like ten years from now?" I asked. He thought for a moment, studying the gauges and dials on the console.

"If this program is self-sustaining. If it's starting to happen around the Caribbean. And if the reefs come back, maybe then I'll step away from all this. I've got other things I've been wanting to do. But I'll stick around until it's continuing on its own."

I considered the little patch of corals we'd left behind. Would they fuse to the rock, merging to form the sort of healthy thickets I'd seen on Laughing Bird Caye in Belize? Or was this just a last stand of our good intentions?

We rode on in silence. Then Goldberg patted the console of his boat. It seemed we were pondering the same questions. "This has given us a good life," he said. "I need to give something back."

12

To the End of America

Lower Keys

"KAREN AND MICHELLE..."

"...are gettin' in the water."

"Today's gonna be..."

"...another super day!"

The scientists traded lines of an impromptu jingle while the small boat bucked on the water at a wavelength that could make even experienced sailors sick. It tugged on its mooring and tanks clanged in the hold while dark clouds massed to the south. But Karen Neely and Michelle Dobler were cheerful as they prepared their gear, loading up giant syringes with a goopy antibiotic paste and checking charts that mapped the underwater ridges of Looe Key down to single corals. It would be another long, hard day on and under the water. And though this duo was the only team on the frontlines between Miami and the Dry Tortugas fighting the relentless killer called SCTLD, the attitude on the boat was buoyant. They wistfully cast themselves as superheroes saving corals from the threat of SCTLD on the stormy

summer seas, and their playful "Super Week" jingle was a part of that energy.

Despite the positive vibe, this was the day I'd been most dreading on my itinerary. For years I'd watched the progress of this disease from afar as it marched steadily down the Keys, the animated map on the NOAA website expanding by the month, the red area of infection chewing its way down the chain of islands. The lone holdout had been the Dry Tortugas, seventy miles past Key West, but just days prior to my visit here, lesions of SCTLD had finally been spotted there. The disease now affected the Florida Reef Tract in its entirety.

Many scientists work in the theoretical. They analyze, observe, study. If they're successful when working on a crisis like this disease, they often make recommendations for government agencies or resource managers to implement. One demoralizing aspect of science is its slow pace. And when the data show us exactly what needs to be done—as in the case of climate change—and society fails to take action, or continues to exacerbate the problem, it can crush your spirit. I'm not the first to observe that science these days tends to be a process of writing a very detailed obituary of the world we love.

But Neely and Dobler were different. They did analysis: measuring the prevalence and progress of disease on individual coral heads, tracking the bug as it burned through one stand of corals after another. But they weren't just watching the disease; they were actually fighting it, one coral head, one bone-white, blighted lesion at a time.

We splashed into the water and I trailed Neely into the twisting canyon of Looe Key. It is one of the seven sites along the Florida Reef Tract identified as "iconic" by a multiagency program that targets these ecological gems for protection and restoration. And it is indeed a beautiful spot. There are mountainous corals, huge boulders covered in live tissue. I even spotted my first thick and graceful branches of the threatened elkhorn corals I'd seen in Florida.

But there was also lots of disease.

Neely drifted from coral to coral, studying each one. Some had a small yellow tag fixed to a nail, indicating it was a coral that had shown signs of disease and been treated. If a new coral showed white, dying tissue of the disease, it would get its own tag and Neely would note it on her clipboard and take photos.

But her work didn't stop with the monitoring. If there were fresh lesions, either on a new coral or one that had been tagged, she pulled her giant syringe, a cross between a needle and a caulking gun, and squeezed out a line of white paste along the edges of the lesions like weather stripping on a windowpane, sealing off the dead and infected tissue from the rest of the live coral head.

The tubes contain a marine ointment developed specifically for use on corals, which is mixed with powdered amoxicillin. Though the cause and mechanism by which SCTLD acts are still unknown, this treatment has proven effective in trials. The good news is that when it's applied to a diseased lesion on a coral colony, it usually works. One study on *Montastraea cavernosa* corals showed a 95 percent effectiveness rate in stopping the spread of diseased legions. The bad news: treating a coral once doesn't necessarily prevent new lesions from appearing.

The treatment was so effective that the Florida Department of Environmental Protection contracted for Neely's team to spend at least a hundred days on the water applying the antibiotics. For a researcher, this was a unique situation: both doing the research and using the results to actually save corals gave them a sense of purpose. By her back-of-the-envelope estimates, the corals they'd saved through this mitigation work were the equivalent of outplanting more than 800,000 new coral fragments, and they'd done it at a fraction of the cost of restoration. She figures they can treat diseased corals for about ten dollars each.

So this is why Neely and Dobler sing superhero jingles amid the seeming impossibility of only two scientists halting the spread of the most relentless and devastating of coral diseases on a two-hundred-mile stretch of the Florida Reef Tract: because what they do is working.

Neely is a researcher with Nova Southeastern University, a colleague of Brian Walker, and she patrols the southern reaches of the Florida Reef Tract while his team works in the north. She figures that they spend more than their contracted number of days on the water, up to 150. "That's the benefit of being based down here," she told me. "If we look out the window and see good weather, we can just go."

As I followed her from coral to coral, I photographed her applying the treatment to a beleaguered brain coral. This round boulder with its deep, meandering grooves had only a narrow, winding patch of healthy brown tissue. The rest was a translucent white. It was almost beautiful in its contrast, like a globe of a strange planet. Neely took out her tube and smeared a line of the amoxicillin paste around the remaining patch of healthy tissue, a thin firewall against a marching front of death and disease. If this treatment was successful, the amoxicillin, designed to release slowly over multiple days, would halt the infection. With luck, the little patch of remaining healthy tissue would reclaim the old skeleton, if algae or soft corals didn't get there first. Or if there wasn't a mass bleaching event. Or if the already weakened coral wasn't infected by another disease. Or if a careless boater didn't drop an anchor on it. Or if a hurricane didn't barrel through and roll the entire colony over.

A little later on that dive, she showed me a reminder that disease is only one of multiple threats. A colony the size of an industrial refrigerator was tipped on its side, with a few patches of tissue remaining. "Hurricane Irma," Neely wrote on her clipboard in explanation.

We circled to another colony. She encouraged me to put down my camera. I took up the syringe and squeezed out a thread of putty, smearing it along the edge of a disease lesion. It was delicate work as I rose and sank with each inhalation and exhalation, and as I was tugged back and forth by the surge. But it was also enormously satisfying. There's an intimacy, running your finger along the sickened edge of this great, ancient community of animals. I felt suddenly responsible for it. I felt committed to its future; I thought that I might like to visit it again someday to check up on how it's doing. I began to understand why Neely and Dobler sing in the mornings.

Running low on air, I returned to the boat bobbing above us. But the world had transformed during the dive. The launch bucked and rocked.

Page 176: Keystone, a decorative material featuring the embedded fossils of Florida corals, was once mined at this quarry on Windley Key.

Above: David Vaughn poses in front of raceways from one of the portable nurseries that he hopes to ship around the world as part of his Plant a Million Corals project.

The seas were boiling, huge waves rolling. Lightning split the sky and thunder cracked. A storm cell had popped up. Snorkel boats moored nearby were packing up and hurrying back to shore. Dobler surfaced and climbed aboard the boat for a new tank. Despite the storm, she was not ready to call it a day. There were more coral colonies to visit. "It's safer underwater anyway," she said with a nod toward the darkened sky as icy rain pelted our faces. So back into the water we went.

Toward the end of the afternoon, I followed Neely to a rare coral. It was one of the last remaining *Dendrogyra cylindrus*, or pillar corals, in Florida waters. Considered functionally extinct, fragments of this species existed mainly in tanks and aquariums at institutions up and down the tract, like what I'd seen at Frost Science. I'd seen fragments in aquariums and dead skeletons in the water, ghosts of this species, but this one was still alive.

She began to circle and treat the lesions. Over the years, she'd watched this species die off. It's especially susceptible to SCTLD. Now, with the success of the amoxicillin paste, she might be able to save this solitary survivor.

She calls the pillars "unicorn" corals because of their shape. They rise like a cluster of columns from a ruined Greek temple. When healthy, they extend their polyps and tentacles, even in the daylight, so they look fluffy and even cuddly.

This coral was one of the last of its kind. I had thought it might be a sort of thrill to see the last of something in the wild. Or maybe there would be a morbid fascination. But I felt neither. Instead, I choked back tears.

"What does success look like ten years from now?" I asked on the way back to port. This had become my stock question.

"If these corals are still alive," Neely said, gesturing over her shoulder at the reef fading behind us,

"then I'd say we were successful." Then she pointed to the goopy syringes lying in a kettle on the floor of the boat. "But if we're still doing this, then I'd say we weren't successful."

She believed that with twenty boats and teams like hers, they'd be able to knock stony coral tissue loss disease into the background, if not eliminate it outright. I turned to Dobler and asked the same question.

"If other people are doing this, like dive shops," she said, "that would go a long way. And if we weren't monitoring, just going out and treating, we could do a lot more corals."

This was to be the last day on Looe Key for the duo for a while. They were being called to the Dry Tortugas to join a disease strike force there. The recent arrival of SCTLD in that iconic national park was an urgent call to action. The team would be camping with other groups on the uninhabited islands. They'd be going out each day for a full week in an effort to curtail the spread of a deadly killer, and at night they'd sleep in the remains of an old fort on an island without power or water. And when they awoke the next morning to reequip their boat and gear for the struggle, I was fairly certain they'd be singing.

My next stop on the Florida Reef Tract was on the far end of Summerland Key. I pulled into a parking lot of vehicles with license plates from Illinois, Texas, and Missouri. This was Florida National High Adventure Sea Base, where Boy Scouts from around the country had assembled to sail, kayak, dive, snorkel—and grow corals.

I joined a presentation to one group of scouts given by a man with a bushy white beard, long gray locks, a safari hat, and a mischievous twinkle in his blue eyes. He was like a coral Gandalf. "First, I'd like to apologize to the young people here," he began. "We've lost 50 percent of the world's corals. And it's happened on our watch."

This was David Vaughn, former head of coral restoration at the nearby Mote Marine Laboratory, who now ran a nonprofit called Plant a Million Corals. He continued to set the grim stage. He explained how Florida corals had dropped to 2 percent of historic coverage. He talked about the difficulties of restoring corals once they're lost; how new colonies can take up to seventy-five years to reach sexual maturity; and how, once they do manage to produce fertilized eggs, only one in a million is likely to settle. With odds like that, the notion of restoring reefs in our lifetimes seemed absurd.

But then his tone changed as he began to tell of an accidental discovery. As he was rearing fragments of coral in tanks and agonizing over the demoralizingly slow pace of their growth, he dropped a small coral that had taken years to grow. It shattered into pieces. In frustration, he put the fragments on a shelf in the tank and forgot about them. The next time he looked, the broken pieces of coral showed invigorated growth. He compared it to a skin graft, how our healing response accelerates our own growth processes.

Through further experimentation, he took a coral, cut it into pieces, and then glued these fragments close to each other. The fragments began growing at an accelerated pace. And once they touched, they recognized they were genetic clones from the same colony and they fused back together. Through this process, he was able to grow a coral the size of a baseball in eleven weeks. This would have taken fifteen years in the wild.

Vaughn dubbed the process "microfragmentation." Next he proved that a sexually mature colony could be produced through this process in about two years, something that would take twenty-five to seventy-five years to happen in the wild.

"I want you to know that there is hope underwater," Vaughn told the scouts. "For ten million dollars, I think we could take elkhorn corals off the endangered species list.

Having concluded the lecture on a high note, Vaughn led the scouts to a coral nursery at the edge of the base. There were a dozen basins the size of billiard tables with hundreds of coral fragments on racks in the shimmering water. Here the camp counselors led the scouts through the process of caring for the fragments and also how to use a band saw and ceramic plugs to create more fragments.

Joey Mandala, who runs this coral program, showed me around. "I want scouts to participate in every aspect of the process, from work in the nursery to outplanting on the reef," he said as we watched scouts sampling water, recording data, and cleaning tanks. "The goal is to outplant 2,000 to 4,000 corals each year," he told me.

"What does success for you look like in ten years?" I asked.

"If a scout can outplant corals, and then come back as a counselor and see how corals they have planted have grown, that would be success," he told me. "Maybe fifteen years after that they could come back with their own kids and see the progress."

I turned to Vaughn, the coral restoration pioneer.

"What do you say to critics who say that putting live corals back into a damaged environment full of stressors is akin to planting trees during a forest fire?"

"If you can tell me what day the stressors will be gone, I'll wait until then," he said.

Vaughn's plan wasn't limited to what was happening here at the sea base. He wanted to replicate this land-based nursery around the world. Through his nonprofit, he'd developed entire nursery systems that fit into standard shipping containers. He planned to ship them to tropical locations across the globe. "We can have them up and running in six hours," he said.

Karen Neely applies a firewall
of amoxicillin paste to the last
remaining patch of tissue on
this large brain coral.

"What about other criticisms—that restoration is slow and expensive and doesn't relieve the problems causing the decline? That it provides false hope?" I asked.

Vaughn snorted. His eyes sparkled. Hope was what kept him going. He wasn't going to entertain the idea that it could somehow be false. His micro-fragmentation work had given him a new outlook. Prior to that, like many scientists, he'd been in mourning. "Coral reef scientists needed a self-help group," he said. "It was like underwater trauma." Action was his antidote to despair. "It's no longer an option to see what Mother Nature does," he said.

After seeing the work happening up and down the Florida Reef Tract, I was beginning to believe that, in a world of 2 percent coral cover, human intervention was our best hope of saving a few last Florida reefs for future generations.

An old friend joined me as I completed my survey down the Florida Reef Tract. Ryan McMinds was a PhD student I'd met years before on Lizard Island at the start of my coral journey. Now a professor at the University of South Florida, McMinds hadn't been diving for more than two years, a hard stop after endlessly crossing the globe sampling corals during his dissertation research. He wanted to get underwater and I wanted his perspective. He'd done some of his early student work in the Keys, and I was interested to learn if he'd noticed changes over the past decade.

We began with a snorkel charter offshore of Marathon in the Middle Keys. The boat chugged to a spot called Alligator Reef, where we could see dark patches of reef separated by yellow-green stretches of sand. "It feels good to be out on the water," he said as we joined the tourists and shuffled toward the platform on the back of the pontoon boat. A skeletal iron lighthouse that had been built in 1873 presided over the patches of reef, and dark clouds hung on the horizon, a precursor to Hurricane Elsa, then roiling at the edge of the Caribbean.

We slipped into the bathtub-warm water, frothed on the surface by a stiff breeze and snorkeling tourists. Immediately I spotted a large, healthy-looking cluster of rust-brown *Acropora palmata*, the iconic and endangered elkhorn coral. I was heartened.

But then as McMinds dove down into the water, a feeling of dread returned. It was hard to find more coral species. We could see the skeletal outlines of ancient corals, and plenty of dead coral in the rubble, but most of the reef was covered with waving purple sea fans. They were beautiful, and they're also threatened. But they weren't hard, reef-building corals. Much of the reef was also covered with white *Palythoa*, a spongy encrusting animal that is related to corals. But they're not true reef builders, and they opportunistically spread to areas where hard corals have died off. They're also toxic.

Ryan dove down time and again to identify corals and I photographed them. We were trying to find as many different species as we could, an informal survey. We saw several nice-sized colonies, but they were isolated and rare.

I suddenly realized what had unsettled me. McMinds was wearing the same black Oregon State rash guard and orange swim trunks as when we'd first met on Lizard Island. He'd worn that same uniform as I followed him to Mo'orea, Hawai'i, and Saudi Arabia. I'd filmed and taken hundreds of photos of him in coral-rich locations. So there was a feeling of familiarity. But the landscape was different this time. Instead of the dense coral cover in the background of the photos there were only one or two colonies visible in the frame. The contrast was striking. Florida waters contained forty-five different species of corals. That afternoon on Alligator Reef, we'd found seven.

My spirits lifted when a shadow on the periphery caught my attention. A massive manta ray, black and graceful, with two remora hitching along for the ride, glided through a cut in the reef. A snorkeling boy squealed, grabbed his mother's arm, and paddled frantically after the gentle monster before it slipped around a bend in the reef canyon. The boy paddled after, delighted by this glimpse of wildness.

Then I heard a whistle and looked to the boat. Our captain was signaling us to climb back aboard. The wind was picking up and the storm was fast approaching.

The next morning we drove down to Key West, the dead end of Highway 1. This is where tourists flock to cut loose, and where drunken bar crawls have been encouraged long before Ernest Hemingway famously staggered home from Sloppy Joe's every night. But our mood was less than celebratory after we spent our last full day diving the Western Dry Rocks, six miles past the southernmost tip of the United States. The coral cover was lower here than anyplace I'd yet seen on the tract. We counted six species of stony corals, some of them tucked into corners and under ledges. I switched to a macro lens on my camera and was able to fill the photo frame with beautiful coral polyps and darting gobies, cropping out the barren wreckage around it. We were paired with a solo diver named Mary who had a knack for pointing out eels and lobsters, so that provided further distraction from the obvious message of reef decline. It was an enjoyable dive and there were plenty of interesting things to see, but after we climbed back aboard, we rode to shore largely silent. At one point McMinds turned to me. "It's a lot less than it used to be...the coral cover," he said.

We didn't end the day on a somber note, though. We joined three young coral researchers for a cookout. All of them worked in coral research at Mote Marine Lab. Grace Klinges was an old friend of McMinds from Oregon, a microbiologist now studying at Mote. Chelsea Petric was a staff biologist working on coral resilience experiments. And Zach Craig, a former student of David Vaughn's, managed the station's coral nurseries and worked as a restoration specialist.

The conversation started as it would at any barbecue: pets and weather. The price of housing in Key West. Where to find the best coffee in town. But then as the night wore on and we sat in the shadow of a banyan tree with its ropy trunk, the topics turned to hard science, as they always do with researchers in the evening and after a beer or two.

McMinds had become intrigued, during our trip, about the mechanism that caused Vaughn's microfragmented corals to grow so quickly. "Do you think it has something to do with the telomeres?" he asked. "They're those nucleotide sequences associated with specialized proteins at the ends of linear chromosomes."

"Interesting. I hadn't thought of that," Klinges said.

As the conversations spun into a level of scientific detail that made me wonder if they'd switched languages, Craig made me feel better: "Don't ask me," he shrugged, looking at me. "I'm just a coral farmer."

Even though I couldn't quite follow the conversation, it brightened my spirits to see McMinds bandying about scientific ideas with other researchers. The pandemic had kept many of us out of the water for too long. But he was back in his element. I heard the stirrings of a new collaboration. He had voiced a novel idea. Would it lead to a new project? A published paper? Would it shed light on how fragmented corals healed? Might it unlock the secret to understanding what supercharged coral growth? It's a thrill to see the spark of science in action.

Still, I was also brooding about our last dive and the paltry coral cover we'd seen. And I didn't want to leave Florida on a down note.

"Are there any reefs here where I can snorkel from shore and see corals?" I asked. I was doubtful. Most of the Florida reefs lay miles offshore.

"Fort Zach is really nice," Petric said.

"Yeah, there's a lot of coral cover on the back side of the jetties just off the beach. We did a whole outplant project there a few years ago, and they're growing," Craig said.

What he described sounded interesting, though it didn't sound like a wild reef. But I needed to get back in the water one last time.

The next morning I awoke before dawn and drove out to Fort Zachary Taylor on the west end of the island and on the very edge of America. The beach was empty. I walked to the waterline with my camera. A pair of riprap jetties, parallel to the beach, lay barely a dozen yards out. They were big, gray lumps of rock, obvious artificial structures placed there to keep this sliver of sand, one of the few nice sand beaches in the Keys, from washing away.

I pulled on my fins and mask for the last time. I gripped my camera and dove forward. The water was murky. I could hear the buzz of fishing boats heading out to the Gulf Stream with dreams of leaping tarpon and sailfish. I heard the water slapping the rocks. As I reached the riprap jetty and rounded the corner to the ocean side, I heard something else, a sort of crackling all around me.

And then I saw it.

There was a dinner-plate-sized coral smeared onto boulder otherwise covered in algae fuzz. The coral was dull green in the murky water, like some strange kind of spreading mushroom. But the tissue looked healthy. I finned on. Then I saw another coral the size of a grapefruit perched on a rock as if on display. On the next rock, another.

As I snorkeled on, there were more corals. Some large boulders were entirely covered with corals, mostly grooved brain corals, but also star corals and

lobed corals. In many places, the colonies smushed up against each other. I saw other life, too: tiny gobies, shrimp, and Christmas tree worms.

I was so surprised by the number of corals that I almost didn't notice the fish. There were many—grunts, angelfish, wrasses. A three-foot barracuda trailed me with suspicion, and I felt almost like a voyeur, like I was invading some private space that wasn't meant to be seen. Next, I came across five growing pucks of starlet corals, a fingerprint of restoration work. These healthy disks were growing closer together. Someday they would fuse to form a coral head that was suddenly decades older than it should be. There was a mystery to how and why this happened, and maybe soon McMinds and Klinges would crack the code, offering new insight.

Most notable was what I didn't see. I didn't see any diseased or dying coral.

I rounded the far edge of the riprap jetty and dove down, swimming through a school of glittering juvenile fish so thick that the visibility dropped to inches. I hovered within this shimmering cloak for as long as I could hold my breath. Then I surfaced and swam reluctantly back toward shore. I had a long day of driving ahead.

On the beach, I paused, turning to face the water one more time. The riprap jetties squatted unassumingly in the shallows, clumsy piles of boulders that offered no hint of what lay below the surface. They were placed there by humans, and they were covered in coral colonies that were also mostly introduced by humans. But it was still a reef, and it was rich with corals. There wasn't the diversity of life found on other reefs—few sponges and soft corals. Fewer invertebrates. No branching corals. But it was teeming with fish and it was the healthiest reef I'd seen in Florida. All this just a short swim off a public beach.

I looked past the jetties. Another seventy miles in the distance, beyond the edge of the horizon, lay the Dry Tortugas. Neely and Dobler would be loading up their boat and stuffing amoxicillin ointment into tubes. They'd be singing their superhero jingle, joyful to have a clear role to play in the global struggle against dying coral. Somewhere over my shoulder to the north, Brian Walker's students would also be loading their boat for another day of tending lonesome old giants. I knew that a ragtag collection of environmentalists, fishers, and scientists were keeping their eyes on Varadero, ready to counter the government's and developers' next move. In a few hours, Jen Vander Veur might be leading another group of volunteers into the highlands of Wahikuli to plant native grasses. Before they begin, they'll listen to a haunting chant sung in the once-forbidden language of a rising people. In Belize, Lisa Carne would be looking for a way to expand her nursery system to more cayes.

I won't say that I felt hope at that moment. Maybe it was something else. Consolation? No—stronger that that. It was a sort of faith, a deep and abiding love for those of my own species who refuse to give up the fight. I thought of all the young and idealistic graduate students I'd met. I thought of the scouts I'd seen at work on Summerland Key and the future we were leaving them. And then I thought of my own teenaged daughter, who had only recently learned to dive and was so enthralled by the 17 percent coral cover she'd seen in Belize that she was already planning her next trip. Her eyes had only just been opened to the world of coral reefs. She might not see what I have. But there was still much left for her to explore.

As I walked back to the car, the final lines of a Jim Harrison poem came to mind:

Her uncertain future,
which by nature she ignores,
so much better to me than none.

Two struggling coral colonies on Looe Key: on the left a mound of an *Orbicella faveolata* with less than half of its live tissue remaining, and on the right the columns of a *Dendrogyra cylindrus* with barely any surviving coral polyps. The tag indicates that it's been treated with amoxicillin paste. Both of these species are susceptible to SCTLD.

Lisa Carne snorkels over a restored
elkhorn and staghorn reef near
Laughing Bird Caye in Belize.

Afterword:
Bracing for the Storm

AS I DROVE NORTHEAST from Key West along the long corridor of alternating strip malls, mangroves, and wide-open waterscapes of Highway 1, I was looking for any excuse to delay my departure from the tropics. You never know these days when a snorkel or dive among live corals might be your last.

Recalling that restoration guru David Vaughn lived across the canal from the Mote Marine Lab, I decided to pay him a visit as I passed the cement slab face of the hurricane-proof research building. Though I've had doubts about restoration as the ultimate solution to the plight of corals, my visit to Fragments of Hope in Belize and my trip down the Florida Reef Tract had begun to swing me around. In July of 2021, the International Coral Reef Symposium issued a report that established three pillars for addressing coral reef decline: reducing global climate change threats, improving local conditions, and engaging in active restoration. This third pillar would have been controversial only a few years earlier.

What other options were there, especially for this region? Like it or not, restoration is a necessary part of the future of reefs. It's expensive, and outplanting corals will not stop climate change. But while critics claim that it offers corporate polluters a fig leaf, drains money from worthier causes, or convinces a malleable public that a solution to the coral crisis is at hand, I had seen no solid evidence to back up such bar-stool aspersions. Here in Florida people were pushing up their sleeves, putting in long days on the water, and doing what they could. They were carving a future for reefs one coral at a time. They grew and outplanted coral, treated disease, and studied the surviving colonies, desperately seeking a way out of this mess.

I'd been inspired by the goal Vaughn had pitched to the Boy Scouts to plant a million corals before he retired. "I'm looking forward to the day when I can raise the target to a billion," he'd said, hinting that retirement was never his true goal.

So I thought I needed to hear more of this before I left. I'd been heartened by the Fort Zachary Taylor snorkel trail and its riprap reef and coral cover comparatively superior to the offshore reefs. While I would pose as a journalist, asking Vaughn some questions about his project, what I was really after was another dash of hope to carry with me onto the plane.

He was loading anchors and chains into a truck emblazoned with the "Plant a Million Corals" logo when I drove up to the yard. A sailboat bobbed in the canal beside his house. He waved, unfazed by this stranger who showed up at random to talk about corals.

I asked him questions as he made preparations for Hurricane Elsa, which was then massing south of Cuba. Vaughn's house is on pilings, and the workshop where he develops prototype equipment for his portable container nurseries is underneath. He was lifting his coral tanks an additional two feet off the ground so that they were above the high-water mark left by Hurricane Irma a few years earlier. You might expect panic at the prospect of another storm, but he was sanguine and philosophical. He grew more excited about what I told him I'd seen that morning at Fort Zach in Key West. He had been head of the Mote project that created the snorkel trail, for which they'd outplanted some 12,000 corals.

"Isn't that amazing?" he asked. "The last time I was there, I could literally hear the reef, all the fish and the snapping shrimp. The fish are drawn there because they can smell all that live, healthy coral tissue."

Vaughn's blue eyes sparkled. He has an elfin quality, and with his bushy white beard he's got the allure of a sort of coral St. Nick. I asked him about his program to send shipping-container labs to island nations around the world, and if he had any examples nearby. I wanted a glimpse into Santa's coral workshop.

"You've got good timing. I was just about to head over to the farm to tie down the containers. You can ask me questions while I work. I might ask you to carry an anchor."

I followed him down the road to an open patch of ground surrounded by cyclone fencing. It had once been a shrimp farm, and Vaughn now leased a corner of it for his project. Two new shipping containers awaited customization, and a third, with hand-painted graphics, was surrounded by prototype raceways, each of them a largish, shallow bathtub that could hold hundreds of coral fragments.

"We can ship these anywhere in the world," he told me, "and each container has everything you need. We even added solar power for sustainability. I can fly out and help have it set up and running in six hours."

"How many corals will one of these systems produce?"

"Ten thousand a year. That's a restoration project the size of Fort Zach. Just imagine a small island country doing that year after year in different locations. It could be transformational," he said, his eyes animated with sea sparkle again. This wasn't a sales pitch; Vaughn had faith. He believed that transformation was possible. As if to ward off any doubts he went back to his truck and pulled out a seven-hundred page book he'd edited called *Active Coral Restoration*. He flipped through pages filled with research and case studies, pointing out evidence for how his system would work. He flipped to a page in the front. The book was dedicated to the life of his old friend Ruth Gates. He held up the cover: it was a photo of Laughing Bird Caye. The wide world of corals was small indeed.

After a tour of the project, Vaughn enlisted my help in securing the site. He wove a nylon cord through the series of raceways, binding them together and then fixing them to the edge of a container. If the winds picked up, the basins would be tethered instead of scattering into the mangroves. Then we dragged chains out of his truck and shackled the containers to anchors dug into the ground. A direct hit from Elsa would mean that the whole low-lying area would be covered by water, and while the anchors might not prevent the wind and waves from tossing the containers about, they might keep them from moving too far or drifting out to sea.

Again I was struck by how calm he was in the face of the approaching storm. Not only might it upend all this work on his fledgling nonprofit, blowing away the container labs that were awaiting customers, but a direct hit on one of the many coral nurseries in the shallow flats up and down the Florida Reef Tract would be a devastating setback for the region as a whole.

But he'd been through storms before. During Hurricane Irma, he hunkered down in Mote Lab. While others had evacuated, he opted to stay close so as to keep an eye on his projects. He snuck out of the hurricane-proof structure as the storm's eye settled over the facility. The rising waters threatened to spill over the top, so he started grabbing fragments and tossing them into taller, deeper tanks. He'd managed to relocate most of the corals before the back wall of the eye slammed into Summerland Key. Through this effort, he'd managed to save thousands of fledgling corals for future outplanting.

As I drove back north toward Miami, I realized I'd found in that afternoon some of the hope I'd been seeking. And I'd also found a metaphor. Those of us who follow the story of the beleaguered coral reefs all need to brace for the storm we know is coming. Even if the world's governments decide on and implement an aggressive, proactive program to eliminate fossil fuels and end carbon emissions in accordance with the Paris Agreements, the temperatures will still continue to rise. The carbon our society has produced since the industrial revolution will remain in our atmosphere and oceans for millennia to come. The corals that survive in such a future will need to continue to adapt. It may be hubris to think that people can help speed up biology or evolution or replant entire complex ecosystems. We like to think ourselves cleverer than nature. We are nothing if not an audacious species. Our outsized brains and egos are what got us into this mess. But maybe they can help us get out of it, too.

So the storm will come. The devastation will continue. Laughing Bird Caye could someday be hit by another of the more frequent and intense hurricanes prowling the Caribbean, and in moments all of Lisa Carne's work there could be obliterated. The Colombian government might give the dredging process a green light and the magic of Varadero could be wiped out for the sake of someone's idea of progress. I already knew that the Lizard Island I'd visited in 2014 has transformed: reefs hit by unprecedented bleaching and some species of corals eliminated entirely. From Hawai'i to Polynesia and the Red Sea, I understood that it was all perched on the edge of survival. A budget crunch could pull the University of Arizona's support for Biosphere 2 and developers might realize their dreams to transform it into a shopping mall. Even my little tank hung in a delicate balance. One lengthy power failure could stress most of the corals beyond saving.

How will we face the threats that are coming? Like David Vaughn, will we risk our own survival to rush out during the eye of the hurricane to save a few fragments from destruction? Can the addition of one more chain and anchor keep our hope from blowing away in the storm?

It's hard to say. But you only know if you try.

We all need anchors—emotional, physical, ecological, political—in order to brace for what's coming in this era of habitat destruction and anthropogenic change. When it comes to corals, we can anchor our hearts and souls to this big blue and green rock hurtling through the heavens in any number of ways.

We can anchor ourselves with the knowledge that what remains, little though it may be throughout much of its historic range, can still be beautiful. Dead coral rock structure can still swarm with fish until it eventually erodes away. Waving sea fans and soft corals will recruit to this rock formerly covered with stony corals. They're lovely and they flow with the pulse of the surge. For centuries the leftover structure of reefs may remain, slowly eroding and covered in sponges and soft corals and the occasional tiny little holdout scleractinian. Seeking the last stony corals can be a game, like a scavenger hunt. And when you find these lonely little creatures you can look close, zoom in until the viewfinder of your camera or the whole of your scuba mask is filled with a pattern of tiny polyps, a macro view of a vanishing universe of coral. You might marvel. You may weep.

You can anchor yourself with political action. By fighting the obstinate unwillingness of politicians to do anything about climate change. By fighting the trolls who would watch the world burn out with sheer, gleeful mendacity merely to score political points. You could harangue them, campaign against them, run against them. You can herald the coming Armageddon from street corners to all who will listen and even those who won't. You can call out the hypocrites with righteous data. You can console yourself with the fact that the scientists have been right, the proofs coming in waves of devastating weather.

You can anchor yourself by personal action. By restoring a watershed or signing up for a coral restoration project. You can donate to foundations and you can become an ecotourist instead of a regular tourist. You could build solar panels on your home and electrify your car and pay your power

company a premium for clean energy. You can lower your carbon footprint, divest from fossil fuels, invest in green funds, cycle to work, walk to public transportation, or eat lower on the food chain. A likely side effect might even be that you also live better and longer as a result.

You can anchor yourself by looking deep into time, assured that millions of years after we're gone, should we take corals down with us, they will curl up again out of the marine muck to start building reefs just as they did in the early Jurassic. They will attract and sustain marine life as they embark once more on their magnificent construction projects, and hundreds of millions of years after that, long after any sign of human civilization has vanished from the planet, the leavings of these future corals will form strata in the mountaintops to mark their existence. "Mt. Everest is marine limestone," John McPhee reminded us. Someday, corals will rise again to the greatest of heights. Long after the blip of our species has been written and forgotten, in a future so distant it's beyond comprehension.

So these are the ways we can brace for the coming storm, steel our emotions, stiffen our spines, open our hearts. We humans, like coral reefs, are also wonders of nature. With our creativity, drive, cleverness, and ingenuity, we too are evidence of the boundless genius of evolution. We build our civilization on land while corals build their complex cities just below the surface of the sea. We stare at one another through the surface pane of water that separates us. We will continue to explore these intersections of our two worlds until one or the other of us vanishes from the planet for the balance of history.

Hope is a human trait that exists in a place where it can't be rotted by disease or smothered by the sediments of despair and cynicism. I have seen plenty of evidence of this in my journeys. Maybe it is an unlikely hope or a false hope, but it exists and it blossoms and it can burn bright in the gloaming. As close as I've come to giving in to cynicism, I haven't quite been able to bring myself to descend entirely. Every trip into the water, every new discovery, every solitary coral recruit on an otherwise blighted reef, every conversation with a starry-eyed idealist or weary fighter provides a glimmer of faith in my own species. I cast my anchor chains into loose sands of hope and desperation, a final Hail Mary in preparation for the storm, praying it will be enough to keep my heart from being washed away in the tsunami brewed in the furious storm of our own making.

And in the light of the morning after that storm has blown through, we'll emerge blinking from our shelters to sift through the wreckage. And then we'll pick up and continue, as we always have, to move forward on the grand human project to protect, understand, and maybe salvage corals from our own greed and curiosity. And then, too, we might begin to save ourselves in the process.

Bibliography

Albins, Mark A. "Effects of invasive pacific red lionfish *Pterois volitans* versus a native predator on Bahamian coral-reef fish communities." *Biological Invasions*, 15(1), June 23, 2012, 29–43. https://link.springer.com/article/10.1007/s10530-012-0266-1.

Allam, Lorena, and Nick Evershed. "The Killing Times: The Massacres of Aboriginal People Australia Must Confront." *Guardian*, March 3, 2019. https://www.theguardian.com/australia-news/2019/mar/04/the-killing-times-the-massacres-of-aboriginal-people-australia-must-confront.

Alling, Abigail, Mark Nelson, and Sally Silverstone. *Life Under Glass: Crucial Lessons in Planetary Stewardship from Two Years in Biosphere* 2. Synergetic Press: New York and London, 2020.

Al-Shobakky, Waleed. "The University the King Built." *New Atlantis*, Winter 2018. https://www.thenewatlantis.com/publications/the-university-the-king-built.

Bahr, Keisha D., Paul L. Jokiel, Robert Toonen. "The unnatural history of Kāne'ohe Bay: coral reef resilience in the face of centuries of anthropogenic impacts." *PeerJ*, May 12, 2015. https://peerj.com/articles/950/.

Barrington, Kate. "Keeping lionfish in the home aquarium." *ratemyfishtank.com*, June 26, 2021. https://www.ratemyfishtank.com/blog/keeping-lionfish-in-the-home-aquarium.

Beckwith, Martha Warren. *Hawaiian Mythology.* United States: University of Hawaii Press, 1976.

Bindoff, N. L., et al. "Changing Ocean, Marine Ecosystems, and Dependent Communities." In *IPCC Special Report on the Ocean and Cryosphere in a Changing Climate*, edited by H.-O. Pörtner, DC, et al. UN Intergovernmental Panel on Climate Change, 2019. https://www.ipcc.ch/srocc/chapter/chapter-5/.

Bowen, James. *The Coral Reef Era: From Discovery to Decline*. Springer: New York, 2015.

Brodie, Jon, et al. "Are increased nutrient inputs responsible for more outbreaks of crown-of-thorns starfish? An appraisal of the evidence." *Marine Pollution Bulletin* 51, 2005, 266–278.

Brymer, Eric, and Anne-Marie Lacaze. "The benefits of ecotourism for visitor wellness," in *International Handbook on Ecotourism*, ed. Ballantyne, R., and J. Packer (Cheltenham, Gloucestershire: Edward Elgar Publishing Limited, 2013), 217–229.

Casey, Nicholas. "Colombia Signs Peace Agreement with FARC After 5 Decades of War." *New York Times*, September 26, 2016. https://www.nytimes.com/2016/09/27/world/americas/colombia-farc-peace-agreement.html.

Casey, Nicholas. "Colombia's Peace Deal Promised a New Era. So Why Are These Rebels Rearming?" *New York Times*, May 17, 2019. https://www.nytimes.com/2019/05/17/world/americas/colombia-farc-peace-deal.html.

Chapman, Jennifer K., "Working up an appetite for lionfish: A market-based approach to manage the invasion of *Pterois volitans* in Belize," *Marine Policy* 73 (2016) 256–262.

Chapman, Jennifer K, et al. *Belize National Lionfish Management Strategy*, 2019–2023. Blue Ventures Conservation, London, UK. 102 pages.

Cook, James, J. C. Beaglehole, and R. A. Skelton. *The Journals of Captain James Cook on His Voyages of Discovery*. Cambridge University Press, Cambridge: 1955, 279.

Cornwall, Christopher E., et al. "Global declines in coral reef calcium carbonate production under ocean acidification and warming." *Proceedings of the National Academy of the Sciences of the United States of America* 21 (May 25, 2021). https://doi.org/10.1073/pnas.2015265118.

Cornwall, Warren. "Researchers embrace a radical idea: engineering coral to cope with climate change." *Science*, March 21, 2019. https://www.sciencemag.org/news/2019/03/researchers-embrace-radical-idea-engineering-coral-cope-climate-change.

Cousteau, Captain J. Y., with Frédéric Dumas. *The Silent World: A Story of Undersea Discovery and Adventure Unfolding Wonders Never Before Seen by Man*. Pocket Books: New York, 1955.

Darwin, Charles. *The Structure and Distribution of Coral Reefs*, 3rd Edition. D. Appleton and Company: New York, 1897.

Dobbs, David. *Reef Madness: Charles Darwin, Alexander Agassiz and the Meaning of Coral*. Pantheon: New York, 2005.

Dowling, Ross. "The history of ecotourism," in *International Handbook on Ecotourism*, ed. Ballantyne, R., and J. Packer (Cheltenham, Gloucestershire: Edward Elgar Publishing Limited, 2013), 15.

Dybas, Cheryl, and Zachary Boehm. "When coral reefs change, researchers and local fishing communities see different results." *National Science Foundation Research News*, March 7, 2019. https://www.NSF.gov/discoveries/disc_summ.jsp?cntn_id=297840&org=NSF.

Earle, Sylvia A. *Sea Change*. G. P. Putnam's Sons: New York, 1995. *Economist*. "Where corals lie; Ruth Gates." November 17, 2018.

Edmunds, Peter J., and Virginia M. Weis. "Ruth D. Gates (1962–2018)."*Nature Ecology & Evolution*, December 10, 2018.

Eichenseher, Tasha. "A Culture Written in Stone and Soil: Archaeologists and farmers tell the gritty story of French Polynesia." *National Geographic News*, February 23, 2011. https://www.nationalgeographic.com/adventure/article/110223-biodiversity-cultural-tradition-moorea-archaeology-marae.

Fenner, Robert M. *The Conscientious Marine Aquarist: A Commonsense Handbook for Successful Saltwater Hobbyists*. Microcosm: Vermont, 1998.

Fitzgerald, Sunny. "The super-corals of the Red Sea." *BBC*, April 8, 2020. https://www.bbc.com/future/article/20200408-the-middle-eastern-corals-that-could-survive-climate-change.

Florida Atlantic University, "What's killing coral reefs in Florida is also killing them in Belize: Study of Belize Barrier Reef Shows Nitrogen Enrichment from Land-based Sources Doubled in Four Decades," *ScienceDaily*, August 3, 2021. www.sciencedaily.com/releases/2021/08/210803105534.htm.

Gates, Ruth. "Assisted Evolution: Can 'Super Corals' Help Save Reefs?" *WWF Fuller Fund Lecture*, November 30, 2016. https://vimeo.com/193751472.

Gates, Ruth. "Seawater temperature and sublet coral bleaching in Jamaica." *International Society for Reef Studies, Springer-Verlag*, August 30, 1989.

Gillespie, Alexandra. "Coral Restoration Nursery and Dives to Launch in Islamorada." *Scuba Diving*, June 16, 2020. https://www.scubadiving.com/coral-restoration-nursery-and-dives-to-launch-in-islamorada.

Hall, C. Michael. "Ecotourism and global environmental change," in *International Handbook on Ecotourism*, ed. Ballantyne, R., and J. Packer. (Cheltenham, Gloucestershire: Edward Elgar Publishing Limited, 2013), 54.

Hauck, Brian. "The Super Sucker Project: An Update on the Battle Against Alien Algae in Hawai'i." *Lawai'a Magazine*, Issue 5, 2010.

Havergal, Chris. "Staying Away from Politics." *Inside Higher Education*, March 12, 2015. https://www.insidehighered.com/news/2015/03/12/president-kaust-says-he-wont-criticize-saudi-policies.

Hodges, Montana S., George D. Stanley Jr. "North American coral recovery after the end-Triassic mass extinction, New York Canyon, Nevada." *GSA Today*, October 2015, 25:10, 4–9.

Hodges, Montana S., George D. Stanley Jr., Christopher L. Hodges. "Reevaluating Reefal Recovery: Evidence for Robust Early Jurassic Coral Populations in North America." *GSA Annual Meeting, Indianapolis, IN*, January 2018.

Hoegh-Guldberg, O., et al. "Coral Reefs under Rapid Climate Change and Ocean Acidification." *Science*, December 14, 2007, 318:5857, 1737–1742.

Hoegh-Guldberg, O., et al. "Len Muscatine (1932–2007) and his contributions to the understanding of algal-invertebrate endosymbiosis." *Coral Reefs* 26, no. 4 (December 2007): 731–739.

Houtmann, Michael. "Effect of end-Triassic CO_2 maximum on carbonate sedimentation and marine mass extinction." *Facies*, 2004, 50, 257–261.

Hughes, Terry. "Back-to-back bleaching has now hit two-thirds of the Great Barrier Reef." *The Conversation*, April 11, 2017. https://theconversation.com/back-to-back-bleaching-has-now-hit-two-thirds-of-the-great-barrier-reef-76092.

Hughes, Terry. "Yes We Can Save the World's Coral Reefs." *TEDx Talks*.TEDxJCU Cairns, November 2016. https://www.youtube.com/watch?v=x5LshSZn5RA&t=28s.

Hurley, Timothy. "1st detailed map of Hawaii reefs shows coral decline." *Honolulu Star Advertiser,* December 14,2020. https://www.staradvertiser.com/2020/12/14/breaking-news/1st-detailed-map-of-hawaii-reefs-shows-coral-decline/#story-section.

Iovenko, Chris. "Reef Restored: How Belize Saved Its Beloved Coral." *Christian Science Monitor*, May 15, 2019. https://www.csmonitor.com/Environment/2019/0515/Reef-restored-How-Belize-saved-its-beloved-coral.

Jury, Chris. "When Corals Spill Their Guts." *Reefs.com*, July 23, 2011. https://reefs.com/2011/07/23/when-corals-spill-their-guts/.

Kirch, Patrick Vinton. *A Shark Going Inland Is My Chief: The Island Civilization of Ancient Hawai'i*. University of California Press: Berkeley, 2012.

Kittinger, John H., et al. "Historical Reconstruction Reveals Recovery in Hawaiian Coral Reefs." *PLOS ONE*, October 3, 2011. https://journals.plos.org/plosone/article?id=10.1371/journal.pone.0025460.

Kleinhaus, Karine, et al. "Science, Diplomacy, and the Red Sea's Unique Coral Reef: It's Time for Action." *Frontiers in Marine Science* 26, February 16, 2020. https://doi.org/10.3389/fmars.2020.00090.

Klesius, Michael. "The Big Bloom—How Flowering Plants Changed the World." *National Geographic*. July 2002. https://www.nationalgeographic.com/science/article/big-bloom (accessed May 31, 2021).

Knowlton, Nancy, et al. "Rebuilding Coral Reefs: A Decade of Grand Challenge." *International Coral Reef Society and Future Earth Coasts*. http://coralreefs.org/wp-content/uploads/2021/07/ICRS_2021_Policy_Brief_low_resol.pdf.

Kolbert, Elizabeth. "The Darkening Sea." *New Yorker*, November 20, 2006, 82:38, 66–75.

Lapointe, Brian E., Alexander Tewfik, and Myles Phillips. "Macroalgae reveal nitrogen enrichment and elevated N:P ratios on the Belize Barrier Reef." *Marine Pollution Bulletin*, 2021; 171: 112686 DOI: 10.1016/j.marpolbul.2021.112686.

Layt, Stuart. "Global satellite network now monitoring the health of coral reefs." *Brisbane Times*. May 21, 2021.https://www.brisbanetimes.com.au/national/queensland/global-satellite-network-now-monitoring-the-health-of-coral-reefs-20210521-p57tzs.html.

López-Victoria, M. "A paradoxical reef from Varadero, Cartagena Bay, Colombia." *Coral Reefs* (2015) 34:231, https://www.researchgate.net/publication/272566166_A_paradoxical_reef_from_Varadero_Cartagena_Bay_Colombia.

Maclean, Frances. "The Lost Fort of Columbus." *Smithsonian Magazine*, January 2008.

Marhaver, Kristen. "A Day in the Life of a Baby Coral." *TED.com*, March 16, 2016. https://ideas.ted.com/a-day-in-the-life-of-baby-coral/.

Marley, David. *Historic Cities of the Americas: An Illustrated Encyclopedia*. United Kingdom: ABC-CLIO, 2005.

Martindale, Rowan C., David J. Bottjer, and Frank A. Corsetti. "Platy coral patch reefs from eastern Panthalassa (Nevada, USA): Unique reef construction in the Late Triassic." *Palaeogeography, Palaeoclimatology, Palaeoecology*, October 20, 2011, 41–58.

McCalman, Iain. *The Reef: A Passionate History*. Scientific American/Farrar, Straus & Giroux: New York, 2014.

McPhee, John. *Annals of the Former World*. Farrar, Straus & Giroux: New York, 1998.

National Oceanographic and Atmospheric Administration. *Coral Reef Condition: A Status Report for Florida's Coral Reefs*. https://marinesanctuary.org/wp-content/uploads/2019/07/FKNMS-Report-Final-072819.pdf (accessed August 14, 2021).

National Science Foundation. *Fact Sheet: NSF by the Numbers*. https://NSF.gov/news/factsheets/Factsheet_By%20the%20Numbers_05_21_V02.pdf (accessed June 1, 2021).

Neely K. L., K. A. Macaulay, E. K. Hower, and M. A. Dobler. "Effectiveness of topical antibiotics in treating corals affected by Stony Coral Tissue Loss Disease." *PeerJ*, April 21, 2020. https://doi.org/10.7717/peerj.9289.

Nelson, Mark. "Biosphere 2: What Really Happened?" *Dartmouth Alumni Magazine*, May-June 2018. https://dartmouthalumnimagazine.com/articles/biosphere-2-what-really-happened.

Nunn, Patrick, and Nicholas J. Reid. "Aboriginal Memories of Inundation of the Australian Coast Dating from More than 7000 Years Ago." *Australian Geographer*. 47 no. 1, September 2015: 11–47.

Parletta, Natalie. "More insights into the complexities of corals." *Cosmos*, August 29, 2020. https://cosmosmagazine.com/nature/marine-life/more-insights-into-the-complexity-of-coral/.

Price, Jonathan G. "Geology of Nevada." *Nevada Bureau of Mines and Geology Special Publication* 33, 2004.

Queensland Government, Parks and Forests. "Nature, Culture and History." *Lizard Island National Park*. Updated April 16, 2020. https://parks.des.qld.gov.au/parks/lizard-island/about/culture.

Rafferty, John P. "Just How Old Is *Homo sapiens*?" *Brittanica.com*. N.d. https://www.britannica.com/story/just-how-old-is-homo-sapiens (accessed May 31, 2021).

Reardon, Sara. "FARC and the forest: Peace is destroying Colombia's jungle—and opening it to science." *Nature*, June 12, 2018. https://www.nature.com/articles/d41586-018-05397-2.

Reid, Craig, Justin Marshall, Dave Logan, and Diana Keline. *Coral Reefs and Climate Change: The Guide for Education and Awareness*. 2nd ed. (ed. Angela Dean). Brisbane: CoralWatch, the University of Queensland, 2012.

Reuters. "Saudi fires cleric who criticized mixed university." October 4, 2009. https://www.reuters.com/article/us-saudi-education-idUSTRE5932RQ20091004.

Rhyne, Andrew, Michael F. Trusty, and Les Kaufman. "Long-term trends of coral imports into the United States indicate future opportunities for ecosystem and societal benefits." *Conservation Letters* 5, June 12, 2012, 478–485.

Richards, Zoe. "Almost 60 coral species around Lizard Island are 'missing'—and a Great Barrier Reef extinction crisis could be next." *The Conversation*, July 1, 2021. https://theconversation.com/almost-60-coral-species-around-lizard-island-are-missing-and-a-great-barrier-reef-extinction-crisis-could-be-next-163714.

Riley, Alex. "The Women with a Controversial Plan to Save Corals," *BBC Earth*, March 22, 2016. http://www.bbc.com/earth/story/20160322-the-women-with-a-controversial-plan-to-save-corals.

Roche, Ronan C. "Recreational Diving Impacts on Coral Reefs and the Adoption of Environmentally Responsible Practices within the SCUBA Diving Industry." *Environmental Management* 2016; 58: 107–116. https://link.springer.com/article/10.1007%2Fs00267-016-0696-0.

Rohwer, Forest, and Merry Youle. *Coral Reefs in the Microbial Seas: The Influence of Fishing, Nutrients, Bacteria, Viruses, and Climate Change on Nature's Most Wondrous Constructs*. United States: Plaid Press, 2010.

Rosen, Rebecca J. "How Much Are the World's Ecosystems Worth?" *Atlantic*, June 16, 2014. https://www.theatlantic.com/business/archive/2014/06/how-much-are-the-worlds-ecosystems-worth/372862/.

Rubin, Ewelina T., et al. "Molecular Mechanisms of Coral Persistence within Highly Urbanized Locations in the Port of Miami, Florida." *Frontiers in Marine Science*, July 20, 2021. https://doi.org/10.3389/fmars.2021.695236.

Saudi G20 Presidency. "G20 Riyadh Summit Week: Securing a Future for the World's Coral Reefs." *Cision PR Newswire*, November 19, 2020. https://www.prnewswire.com/in/news-releases/g20-riyadh-summit-week-securing-a-future-for-the-world-s-coral-reefs-872965377.html.

Schiermeier, Quirin. "Great Barrier Reef saw huge losses from 2016 heatwave." *Nature*, April 18, 2018. https://www.nature.com/articles/d41586-018-04660-w.

Seelye, Katherine Q. "Ruth Gates, Who Made Saving Coral Reefs Her Mission, Is Dead at 56." *New York Times*, November 5, 2018.

Setter, Renee. "Warming, Acidic Oceans May Nearly Eliminate Coral Reef Habitats by 2100." Research presented at the Ocean Sciences Meeting of the American Geophysical Union, San Diego, CA, February 2020. https://news.agu.org/press-release/warming-acidic-oceans-may-nearly-eliminate-coral-reef-habitats-by-2100/.

Sherriff, Lucky. "Jam-packed Colombian island preserves quiet way of life." *CNN*. August 27, 2018. https://www.cnn.com/travel/article/santa-cruz-del-islote/index.html.

Shick, J. Malcom. *Where Corals Lie*. Reaction Books Ltd: London, 2018.

Shilling, E. N., I. R. Combs, and J. D. Voss. "Assessing the effectiveness of two intervention methods for stony coral tissue loss disease on *Montastraea cavernosa*." *Scientific Reports* 11, 8566 (2021). https://doi.org/10.1038/s41598-021-86926-4.

Spadaro, Jason Angelo, and Mark J. Butler IV. "Herbivorous Crabs Reverse the Seaweed Dilemma on Coral Reefs." *Current Biology* 31, no. 4, February 22, 2021: 853–859.

Stephens, Lester D., and Dale R. Calder. *Seafaring Scientist: Alfred Goldsborough Mayor, Pioneer in Marine Biology*. University of South Carolina Press: Columbia, 2006.

Stimson, J. Frank. "Tahitian Names for the Nights of the Moon." *Journal of Polynesian Society*, 37-3, September, 1928: 326–337.

Stolarski, Jarosław, et al. "The ancient evolutionary origins of Scleractinia revealed by azooxanthellate corals," *BMC Evolutionary Biology*, 11, October 28, 2011. https://bmcecolevol.biomedcentral.com/articles/10.1186/1471-2148-11-316.

Talbot, Ret. "Quantifying the aquarium trade to help it become more sustainable." *Mongabay.com*, January 26, 2016. https://news.mongabay.com/2016/01/quantifying-the-aquarium-trade-to-help-it-become-more-sustainable/.

Theroux, Paul. *Happy Isles of Oceania*. Mariner Books: New York, 2006.

United Nations Environment Programme. "Projections of Future Coral Bleaching Using IPCC CMIP6 Models: Climate Policy Implications, Management Applications, and Regional Seas Summaries," Nairobi, Kenya: 2020. https://wedocs.unep.org/20.500.11822/34219.

University of California Museum of Paleontology. "Understanding Evolution." August 22, 2008. http://evolution.berkeley.edu.

University of Hawai'i Foundation. "World without Coral—Ruth Gates Series." YouTube, March 5, 2018. https://www.youtube.com/watch?v=wcSv3pkpfQQ.

University of Miami Rosenstiel School of Marine & Atmospheric Science. "New report projects severe coral bleaching globally in this century." *ScienceDaily*. www.sciencedaily.com/releases/2020/11/201120132615.htm (accessed August 10, 2021).

Vail, Lyle, and Ann Hoggett. "Australia Museum Lizard Island Research Station Report 2014." *Australia Museum*. March 2014. https://media.australian.museum/media/dd/Uploads/Documents/32982/lizard-island-report-2014.952584b.pdf.

Vandermissen, Jan. "Experiments and Evolving Frameworks of Scientific Exploration: Jean André Peyssonnel's Work on Coral." In *Expeditions as Experiments: Practising Observation and Documentation*, edited by Mariann Klemun and Ulrike Spring, 51–72. Palgrave Macmillan: London, 2016.

Vaughn, David E., ed. *Active Coral Restoration: Techniques for a Changing Planet*. Plantation Key, Florida: J. Ross Publishing, 2021.

Veron, J. E. N. *A Reef in Time; The Great Barrier Reef from Beginning to End*. Cambridge, Massachusetts: Harvard University Press, 2008.

Veron, J. E. N. *Corals in Space & Time: The Biogeography and Evolution of the Scleractinia*. Ithaca and London: Comstock/Cornell, 1995.

Walker, Barbara L. E. "Mapping Moorea's Lagoon: Conflicts over Marine Protected Areas in French Polynesia." *Institute for Social, Behavioral, and Economic Research*, University of California at Santa Barbara, September 2, 2001.

Walker, Barbara L. E., et al. "Perceptions of environmental change in Moorea, French Polynesia: the importance of temporal, spatial, and scalar contexts." *GeoJournal*, 2014, 79: 705–719.

Walsworth, Timothy E., Daniel E. Schindler, Madhavi A. Colton, et al. "Management for network diversity speeds evolutionary adaptation to climate change," *Nature Climate Change*, July 1, 2019. https://doi.org/10.1038/s41558-019-0518-5.

Wetzel, Corryn. "The Planet Has Lost Half of Its Coral Reefs Since 1950." *Smithsonian Magazine*, September 17, 2021. https://www.smithsonianmag.com/science-nature/the-planet-has-lost-half-of-coral-reefs-since-1950-180978701/.

Wheeling, Kate. "How Modern Emissions Compare to Ancient, Extinction-Level Events." *EOS*, April 7, 2020. https://eos.org/articles/how-modern-emissions-compare-to-ancient-extinction-level-events.

Wilcox, Christie. "Ruth Gates, renowned coral scientist and conservation advocate, dies at 56." *Washington Post*, October 31, 2018.

Yarrabah Aboriginal Shire Council. *Council History*. https://www.yarrabah.qld.gov.au/council/council-history (accessed June 1, 2021).

Yeung, Jesse. "Climate Change Could Kill All of Earth's Coral Reefs by 2100, Scientists Warn," *CNN*, February 20, 2020. https://www.cnn.com/2020/02/20/world/coral-reefs-2100-intl-hnk-scli-scn/index.html.

Yong, Ed. "The Fight for Corals Loses Its Great Champion." *Atlantic*, October 29, 2018. https://www.theatlantic.com/science/archive/2018/10/optimist-who-believed-saving-corals/574240/.

Yong, Ed. "Mysterious Rings around Reefs Have No Simple Explanation." *Atlantic*, April 26, 2019. https://www.theatlantic.com/science/archive/2019/04/mysterious-halos-surround-coral-reefs/588097/.\

Acknowledgments

I'M GRATEFUL TO those who spoke with me at length about corals over the past seven years, sometimes on camera, often by phone or video chat, and sometimes across a cafe table or from either side of a boat. I've tried my best to do justice to their insight and knowledge. There are myriad specialties in coral science and conservation, as there are in the practices of fishing or growing corals in tanks or the fascinating study of paleontology. I've touched on many of these and tried my best to represent the work and ideas of the experts faithfully. Any mistakes are my own. Scientists do detailed needlework, and from it writers seize bits to produce messy quilts that we hope to be somewhat serviceable.

My traveling companions, on various points of this journey, were invaluable in finding the story and getting the shot. These included Justin Smith, Darryl Lai, Daniel Cespedes, Rebecca Vega Thurber, Ryan McMinds, Jesse Zaneveld, Mateo Lopez Victoria, Monica Medina, Valeria Pizarro, Worm, Nicholas Son, Mohammad Bin Sarhab, Cali, the Ocho Hermanos, and my daughter, Bailey. I've had the pleasure of speaking with dozens of the brightest and most committed resource managers, researchers, and conservationists in the world of corals. Many of them are named in the text. Some who are not include Virginia Weis, Billy Causey, Jane Lubchenco, Alan White, Jorge Angulo, Dan Whittle, Scott Atkinson, George Stanley, Sam Teicher, G. P. Schmahl, Emma Hickerson, Michelle Johnston, Tom Goreau, Judith Lang, and Michael Timm.

I must also thank editor Nick Houtman, who published several stories that evolved into chapters in this book in *Terra Magazine*. The editors of *Narrative.ly* also ran a variation of a chapter in their exceptional publication.

Kevin Buch taught me to dive safely and went above and beyond to arrange for permits and reciprocity. Annie Athon Heck gave me freedom to chase the story while remaining gainfully employed. My wife, Nancy, provided patience and understanding and kept the corals in our tank alive while I roamed the shallow seas. My dauntless agent, Kimberley Cameron, found the perfect home for this story, and my editor, Kevin Stevens, and the team at Imagine Books have been ideal partners, making this book much better than it would have otherwise been.

Index

About the Author

David Baker is a writer, photographer, and filmmaker. His feature documentaries include *Saving Atlantis*, *American Wine Story*, and *Three Days of Glory*. He is the author of the critically acclaimed novel *Vintage*, and his fiction and nonfiction have appeared in a range of publications. He leads a media production team at Oregon State University, where he has covered research projects around the world. He lives in Oregon on the rainy side of the mountains with his wife, daughter, two dogs, and a host of other critters, including a tank full of corals. When he's not surfing, hiking, fishing, or doing something outdoors, he is usually reading and occasionally writing books.

LEAF PLATE CORAL
Montipora capricornis

BIRDSNEST CORAL
Stylophora pistillata

LETTUCE CORAL
Agaricia agaricites

LETTUCE CORAL
Agaricia agaricites

STAGHORN CORAL
Acropora cervicornis

LEAF PLATE CORAL
Montipora capricornis

BIRDSNEST CORAL
Stylophora pistillata

STAGHORN CORAL
Acropora cervicornis

CAULIFLOWER CORAL
Pacillopora meandrina

CAULIFLOWER CORAL
Pacillopora meandrina

LETTUCE CORAL
Agaricia agaricites

LEAF PLATE CORAL
Montipora capricornis

STAGHORN CORAL
Acropora cervicornis

BRAIN CORAL
Colpophyllia natans

BIRDSNEST CORAL
Stylophora pistillata

LEAF PLATE CORAL
Montipora capricornis

BIRDSNEST CORAL
Stylophora pistillata

LETTUCE CORAL
Agaricia agaricites

LETTUCE CORAL
Agaricia agaricites

STAGHORN CORAL
Acropora cervicornis

LEAF PLATE CORAL
Montipora capricornis

BIRDSNEST CORAL
Stylophora pistillata

STAGHORN CORAL
Acropora cervicornis

CAULIFLOWER CORAL
Pocillopora meandrina

CAULIFLOWER CORAL
Pocillopora meandrina

LETTUCE CORAL
Agaricia agaricites

LEAF PLATE CORAL
Montipora capricornis

STAGHORN CORAL
Acropora cervicornis

BRAIN CORAL
Calpophyllia natans

BIRDSNEST CORAL
Stylophora pistillata

LEAF PLATE CORAL
Montipora capricornis

BIRDSNEST CORAL
Stylophora pistillata

LETTUCE CORAL
Agaricia agaricites

LETTUCE CORAL
Agaricia agaricites

LEAF PLATE CORAL
Montipora capricornis

STAGHORN CORAL
Acropora cervicornis

BIRDSNEST CORAL
Stylophora pistillata

STAGHORN CORAL
Acropora cervicornis

CAULIFLOWER CORAL
Pocillopora meandrina

CAULIFLOWER CORAL
Pocillopora meandrina

LETTUCE CORAL
Agaricia agaricites

LEAF PLATE CORAL
Montipora capricornis

STAGHORN CORAL
Acropora cervicornis

BRAIN CORAL
Colpophyllia natans

BIRDSNEST CORAL
Stylophora pistillata

LEAF PLATE CORAL
Montipora capricornis

BIRDSNEST CORAL
Stylophora pistillata

LETTUCE CORAL
Agaricia agaricites

LETTUCE CORAL
Agaricia agaricites

LEAF PLATE CORAL
Montipora capricornis

STAGHORN CORAL
Acropora cervicornis

BIRDSNEST CORAL
Stylophora pistillata

STAGHORN CORAL
Acropora cervicornis

CAULIFLOWER CORAL
Pacillopora meandrina

CAULIFLOWER CORAL
Pacillopora meandrina

LETTUCE CORAL
Agaricia agaricites

LEAF PLATE CORAL
Montipora capricornis

STAGHORN CORAL
Acropora cervicornis

BRAIN CORAL
Colpophyllia natans

BIRDSNEST CORAL
Stylophora pistillata